A DUTY TO RESIST

A DUTY TO RESIST

When Disobedience Should Be Uncivil

Candice Delmas

OXFORD
UNIVERSITY PRESS

OXFORD
UNIVERSITY PRESS

Oxford University Press is a department of the University of Oxford. It furthers
the University's objective of excellence in research, scholarship, and education
by publishing worldwide. Oxford is a registered trade mark of Oxford University
Press in the UK and certain other countries.

Published in the United States of America by Oxford University Press
198 Madison Avenue, New York, NY 10016, United States of America.

Library of Congress Cataloging-in-Publication Data
Names: Delmas, Candice, author.
Title: A duty to resist : when disobedience should be uncivil /
Candice Delmas.
Description: New York : Oxford University Press, 2018. |
Includes bibliographical references and index.
Identifiers: LCCN 2018000829 (print) | LCCN 2018016706 (ebook) |
ISBN 9780190872229 (online course) | ISBN 9780190872205 (updf) |
ISBN 9780190872212 (epub) | ISBN 9780190872199 (alk. paper)
Subjects: LCSH: Direct action. | Civil disobedience. |
Government, Resistance to.
Classification: LCC JC328.3 (ebook) | LCC JC328.3.D436 2018 (print) |
DDC 303.6/1—dc23
LC record available at https://lccn.loc.gov/2018000829

5 7 9 8 6

Printed by Sheridan Books, Inc., United States of America

CONTENTS

ACKNOWLEDGMENTS

This book would not have seen the light of day without David Lyons, my graduate advisor and friend. In a little-read article on Henry David Thoreau, "Political Responsibility and Resistance to Civil Government," David deplored philosophers' neglect of "the idea that political responsibility can include a duty to disobey" and defended this duty on the basis of two common arguments for political obligation. His engagement with the subject was brief, just two pages, but they influenced my own intellectual focus. I cherish the time I spent studying with David. His generosity and passion for social justice inspire me.

I thank my colleagues at Northeastern University for their feedback, support, and congeniality. I have the pleasure of working there with members of the Philosophy and Religion and Political Science Departments, and gained much from these interdisciplinary interactions. I wrote large portions of the book while a Dworkin-Balzan Fellow at the New York University (NYU) School of Law's Center for Law and Philosophy in 2016–2017. I am grateful to NYU Law and the Balzan Prize Foundation for their generous support. I thank Liam Murphy, Samuel Scheffler, Jeremy Waldron, Moshe

Halbertal, and Katharina Stevens for their kindness and stimulating conversations. I am most indebted to Daniel Viehoff for his constructive feedback.

The book revisits material initially published elsewhere: "Disobedience, Civil and Otherwise," *Criminal Law and Philosophy* 11, 1 (2017): 195–211; "Civil Disobedience," *Philosophy Compass* 11, 1 (2016): 681–691; "Political Resistance for Hedgehogs," in *The Legacy of Ronald Dworkin*, ed. Will Waluchow and Stefan Sciaraffa (Oxford: Oxford University Press, 2016), 25–48; "False Convictions and True Conscience," *Oxford Journal of Legal Studies* 35, 2 (2015): 403–425; "Samaritanism and Civil Disobedience," *Res Publica* 20, 3 (2014): 295–313 (Springer); and "Political Resistance: A Matter of Fairness," *Law and Philosophy* 33, 4 (2014): 465–488. I am grateful to Wiley, Springer, and Oxford University Press for permission to use parts of this material.

I thank the organizers and attendants of NYU Law's Global Fellows Forum, the University of Richmond's Political Philosophy Learning Community, and the American Society for Political and Legal Philosophy Conference at the APSA meeting in San Fransisco, for their constructive critical engagement with my arguments. For comments on individual chapters and sections, I thank Sean Aas, Guy Aitchison, Amna Akbar, Juliet Hooker, Robert Jubb, David Lyons, Gabriel O'Malley, Avia Pasternak, and Amélie Rorty. I am most indebted to William Smith and Robin Celikates for their helpful reviews of the book and support for my project. I also wish to thank the third, anonymous reviewer for detailed feedback. I am grateful to Kimberley Brownlee, whose work I have long admired, for her mentorship. Thanks to Samantha Hirshland for her research assistance and to Isaac Shur for indexing the book. To Simon Waxman I owe sharper arguments and better flow. I am grateful to Lucy Randall at Oxford University Press for her editorial work.

Thanks to my family in France—my parents, Stéphane and Chantal Delmas, and my brother Gregory—and my friends in Boston (especially Helena de Bres) for their love and support. Thanks to Rose Mwobobia for giving me the peace of mind I needed to write the book. I dedicate it to the loves of my life: Gabriel, Marcel, and Augustin.

A DUTY TO RESIST

Political Obligation(s)

RIDING FOR FREEDOM

The attacks started when the riders reached the bus depot in Rock Hill, South Carolina. There were thirteen of them, seven Black men and six White. They had set out from Washington, DC, a few days earlier—May 4, 1961—on their way to New Orleans. There was no special reason for their visit to Rock Hill. They had just stopped to stretch their legs, use the restroom, and get off the road for a few minutes.

But at the Greyhound station, twenty White men, some of them members of the Ku Klux Klan (KKK), were waiting for the group. The bus riders were not some anonymous thirteen. They were Freedom Riders, dispatched by the Congress of Racial Equality (CORE) to break the laws of the American South. CORE had organized its first freedom ride, known as the Journey of Reconciliation, fourteen years earlier, after the U.S. Supreme Court ruled in *Irene Morgan v. Commonwealth of Virginia* (1946) that racial segregation was prohibited in commercial interstate travel. But southern authorities ignored the Court and continued to uphold decades-old Jim Crow ordinances denying Blacks equal rights on the highways.

That meant integrated buses themselves could be banned from the roads, and bus stations could bar Blacks from their waiting rooms. When the Freedom Riders arrived in Rock Hill, they found a mob with enforcement on its mind. It was there that a young KKK member, Elwin Wilson, famously and savagely beat John Lewis, a Black man who, like the other Freedom Riders, was thoroughly trained in and committed to nonviolence. Many years later, Wilson would publicly repudiate his actions and apologize to Lewis, who had become a senior member of the U.S. Congress and a highly respected elder statesman of the civil rights movement. But that was a long way off. In 1961, the air was so thick with anti-Black violence that Martin Luther King Jr., who had drawn national attention by leading the 1955–1956 Montgomery bus boycott, refused to support the Freedom Rides. The activists would "not make it to Alabama," he warned.

In spite of King's well-earned pessimism, the Freedom Riders and their two buses, one Greyhound and one Trailways, did make it to Alabama. Just outside Anniston, a small city in the northeast of the state, a group of Klansmen pelted the arriving Greyhound with rocks and slashed its tires. After forcing the driver to stop, the Klansmen firebombed the bus. As it burned, they held the doors shut to ensure that no one could get out. For reasons that are not clear, the mob eventually retreated, and the gasping riders escaped—only to be assaulted on the side of the road. In town, another group of Klansmen boarded the Trailways bus and beat the Freedom Riders nearly to the point of unconsciousness.

Bloodied but undaunted, the Freedom Riders continued to Birmingham, where a large crowd waited with baseball bats, iron pipes, and bicycle chains. Police Commissioner Bull Connor and his men participated in the assault. Jim Peck, White and a veteran of the

Journey of Reconciliation, was beaten so badly that his head wounds alone required fifty-three stitches. The first hospital Peck was taken to refused to provide him with treatment. He nearly died on his way to another.

Hearing of the violence, U.S. Attorney General Robert Kennedy dispatched the National Guard to escort the Freedom Riders safely to Montgomery. But by then, the bus drivers refused to go on. Determined to make it to New Orleans for a planned rally, the Freedom Riders decided to continue by air. Their first flight was canceled due to a bomb threat. Meanwhile, sensing the momentum of the movement, the Student Nonviolent Coordinating Committee (SNCC) organized a new set of riders to travel from Nashville to Birmingham. Connor arrested the activists as soon as they arrived and placed them in jail under "protective custody."

On May 20, all of the Freedom Riders headed to Montgomery, where they were met by yet another mob. Journalists, too, were waiting, and the attack was nationally televised, shocking the public. The journey continued to Jackson, Mississippi, where police arrested nearly a hundred protesters for violating a recently passed breach-of-the-peace statute. After the protesters refused to pay fines of two hundred dollars each, a judge sentenced them to ninety days in jail, where they were beaten and half-starved. By the end of the summer, over three hundred activists were incarcerated in the state penitentiary.

Though the Freedom Riders never reached their stated goal of New Orleans, their movement attracted national and international attention. Attorney General Kennedy petitioned the Interstate Commerce Commission to enforce the Supreme Court's ruling. The commission did so, effectively integrating interstate travel on November 1, 1961. By engaging in peaceful, nonviolent, public disobedience (disobedience of local law anyway), the Freedom Riders helped to persuade the government, and at least some portions of the public, of the Jim Crow system's brutality and injustice. They demonstrated the need for change and to enforce federal law. They and likeminded activists inspired many more people to join the struggle for civil rights.

The Freedom Rides, like the iconic lunch counter sit-ins before them, depended on the courage of citizens engaged in civil disobedience. Those who flouted the law risked life and liberty. They met police and civilian terrorism with nonviolence. They stood before vindictive courts with peaceful resolve. But too much bravery can be hazardous. The example of the Freedom Riders also suggests that civil disobedience and other forms of principled lawbreaking are superogatory, the work of heroes rather than ordinary people and therefore beyond moral requirement. Who among us is willing to confront armed Klansmen, let alone refuse to defend ourselves from their blows? Thus a journalist grappled with these questions when he asked one of the White Freedom Riders why he felt it was his responsibility to take part. "I don't think it's just *my* responsibility," the young man answered. "I think it's *every American's* responsibility. I just think that some people are more conscious of their responsibilities than others."[1]

But is there any such responsibility? For the most part, philosophers have not entertained such responsibility. Those concerned with the rights and duties of citizens generally believe that there is a moral duty to obey the law because it is the law, although they tend to doubt that a satisfying account of this duty can be offered and often attach a string of qualifications to their defense.[2] Those who criticize the duty to obey the law—chiefly among them philosophical anarchists—have not discussed alternative duties that might bind citizens. Even proponents of civil disobedience generally hold that breaking the law is presumptively wrong and only conceive of it in terms of permission, not duty. Finally, feminist philosophers, who have extensively studied the responsibility to resist oppression, have not systematically addressed principled disobedience.

In this book, I defend the existence of moral duties to resist injustice, including through principled—civil and even uncivil—disobedience. Resistance to injustice is, I will argue, our political obligation. Traditionally, theorists hold that political obligation is a matter of obedience: our duty is to follow the law, especially in democratic states, assumed to be nearly just and legitimate. Breaches are accepted only when injustice is intolerable or disobedience is very narrowly constrained, or both. But I will show that the opposite is true—that principled lawbreaking, civil or uncivil, is not only acceptable under most real-world conditions, including those of democratic, nearly just, legitimate states, but that it can also be morally required for people living under these conditions. Hence, this book aims to: (1) think beyond civil disobedience to uncivil forms of principled disobedience, (2) apply defenses of civil disobedience to justify uncivil disobedience, (3) use arguments for the duty to obey to defend duties to disobey, and (4) extend the concept of political obligation to include these duties.

A DUTY TO RESIST

Faced with injustice, activists have long recognized resistance to injustice, including through disobedience, as more-than-optional.

Henry David Thoreau considered resistance to illegitimate governments a moral duty. His 1848 essay "Resistance to Civil Government," posthumously titled "On the Duty of Civil Disobedience" and now widely known as "Civil Disobedience" (Thoreau himself did not speak of "civil disobedience," although he is commonly credited with coining the term), urged citizens to withdraw their support from the government of the United States, given its support of slavery, the war against Mexico, and the atrocious treatment of Native Americans. Thoreau advocated conscientious refusal to pay the Massachusetts poll tax as one practical means of noncooperation.[3]

Inspired by Thoreau, Mohandas K. Gandhi, too, considered non-cooperation with unjust governments a citizen's moral duty. "Every citizen silently but nevertheless surely sustains the government of the day in ways of which he has no knowledge," Gandhi wrote. "And it is quite proper to support it so long as the actions of the government are bearable. But when they hurt him or his nation, it becomes his duty to withdraw his support."[4]

King, indebted to both Thoreau and Gandhi, argued in his "Letter from Birmingham City Jail" that "one has not only a legal but a moral responsibility to obey just laws. Conversely, one has a moral responsibility to disobey unjust laws."[5] In a lesser-known speech at the eve of the 1955–1956 Montgomery bus boycott, King told his audience: "Not only do we have a right to be free, we have a duty to be free. So when you sit down on a bus, when you sit down in the front, or you sit down by a White person, you are sitting down because you have a duty to sit down not merely because you have a right."[6]

Contemporary activists embrace this duty-centered discourse, too. In *Indignez-vous!*, former member of French Resistance and concentration camp survivor Stéphane Hessel calls for peaceful insurrection against growing socioeconomic inequalities, the corruption of democracy under financial capitalism, the treatment of *sans-papiers* (undocumented migrants), and Israel's occupation of Palestine.[7] The book became the manifesto for Occupy and Indignados, the anti-austerity social movements that agitated the United States, Spain, and other Western states after the 2008 financial crisis and especially in the early 2010s. Belgian and French human rights organizations, including Ligue des droits de l'Homme and Collectif contre les expulsions, have defended a moral "duty of solidarity," urging people to disobey laws that prohibit the provision of shelter and assistance to undocumented immigrants.[8] Eric Herrou, a French farmer who is accused of helping undocumented migrants cross the border from Italy in the Roya Valley, "think[s] it's [his] duty" to help them.[9]

Masih Alinejad, founder of the My Stealthy Freedom campaign, which encourages Iranian women to post pictures of themselves without headscarf, in violation of the law, called on non-Muslim women visiting the country to join the fight: "When compulsory hijab affects all women, then all women should raise their voice."[10] Saudi women have filmed themselves driving, in open defiance of the law, and posted the videos on YouTube.[11] In June of 2011, one of the drivers, Maha al-Qahtani, told the *New York Times*, "I woke up today believing with every part of me that this is my right, I woke up believing this is my duty, and I was no longer afraid."[12] In September 2017, Saudi Arabia announced it was ending the ban on women driving; the previously stigmatized, defiant women drivers are now publicly celebrated.

Edward Snowden, who leaked to the press millions of documents exposing the U.S. National Security Agency (NSA)'s massive and invasive surveillance programs, appealed to his duty to blow the whistle, and affirmed that "every citizen has a duty to resist" unethical and immoral law and "to try to build a better, more fair society."[13]

A sense of responsibility to contest injustice permeates the Black Lives Matter (BLM) movement. As BLM cofounder Opal Tometi put it, "We think that everybody, no matter where you are, no matter what your socioeconomic status is, whatever your job is—you have a duty in this moment in history to take action and stand on the side of people who have been oppressed for generations."[14]

Thoreau, Gandhi, and King form a kind of holy trinity of civil disobedience—names uttered endlessly and in admiring tones whenever debates over principled lawbreaking arise. As we will see, though, neither their ideas nor their actions fit the standard conception of civil disobedience that philosophers—John Rawls chief among them—began to articulate in response to the civil rights movement.

According to that conception, civil disobedience is a conscientious, public, nonviolent breach of law, undertaken in a near-just state, by agents who demonstrate their sincere endorsement of the system's legitimacy by accepting punishment, and who seek to persuade the majority to change a law or policy by appealing to widely accepted principles of political morality. Few disobedient actions, today and historically, meet these requirements. And some activists openly flout these for reasons that may nonetheless be worth defending.

Take the English suffragist leader Emmeline Pankhurst, who called for "deeds, not words." What she had in mind were spectacular, oft illegal actions to force the public to pay attention to the injustice of women's oppression. "To be militant in some way or other is . . . a moral obligation," she asserted when supporting women who smashed shop windows, burned golf course grass with acid, and put their bodies on the line through hunger strikes and suicides in pursuit of a more just society. "It is a duty which every woman will owe to her own conscience and self-respect, to other women who are less fortunate than she is herself, and to all those who are to come after her."[15]

More recently, the French syndicalist activist and politician José Bové, who articulates a "duty to disobey" environmental and global labor injustice, has taken up decidedly uncivil disobedience.[16] After he was convicted of vandalizing a McDonald's restaurant in Millau in 1999, Bové became a symbol of the alter-globalization and farmers-union movements. He is also the leader of *Les Faucheurs Volontaires d'OGM* (which could be translated as "The Resolute GMO Reapers"), a group of over six thousand militants who have vowed to destroy genetically modified crops.[17]

In this book, I take seriously activists' appeals to moral duties in the face of injustice. I do so by also taking seriously the traditional notion of political obligation—the duty to obey the law in legitimate, nearly just states. On its face, it may seem that I am forcing the proverbial square peg into a round hole, but I shall argue that the very grounds supporting a duty to obey also impose duties to disobey under conditions of injustice. My argument is based on four grounds: the natural duty of justice (chapter 3), the principle of fairness (chapter 4), the Samaritan duty (chapter 5), and political association (chapter 6).

I have chosen these four grounds because they are well established in ordinary and critical morality. Many philosophers—from Socrates to Rawls—believe one's sole or main political obligation is to obey the law of basically just, legitimate societies. And while philosophers disagree about what grounds this duty, the four principles upon which I rely represent the main competitors. Because philosophers typically view the duty to obey the law as liable to be outweighed by stronger, countervailing reasons (it is "defeasible"), they agree that civil disobedience may be justified. But they merely show that disobedience is sometimes permissible, not that it is ever obligatory, and they do not devote any attention to the circumstances under which uncivil disobedience might be acceptable.[18]

For the most part, theorists do not address what citizens may and ought to do in less-than-nearly-just societies, which fail the test of legitimacy, because they generally believe that disobedience in illegitimate states is not particularly problematic and does not need special justification. Thus, much hinges on the diagnosis of political legitimacy: If the state is legitimate, subjects ought to comply with its law and may sometimes disobey it civilly. And if it isn't, they neither owe the state anything—they have no "political obligation"—nor are they bound to only disobey its law civilly; they may well resort to radical forms of resistance, including, at the extreme, revolution. While this binary view is broadly accepted, accounts of legitimacy (including of how injustice affects it) and diagnoses of particular societies are not. There are deep and intractable disagreements about whether nonideal societies "like ours" (viz., large, industrialized, liberal democratic Western nation-states) qualify as legitimate or not.

Readers will not find an answer to whether such societies are legitimate in this book—I will leave that for others to explore. What they will find is a unified account of political obligation that focuses on duties of resistance under conditions of injustice and applies to all societies, legitimate and illegitimate. This book conceives of resistance as a multidimensional continuum of dissenting acts and practices, which includes lawful and unlawful acts (or "principled disobedience"), and expresses, broadly, an opposition and refusal to conform to the established institutions and norms, including cultural values, social practices, and laws. It shows that resistance to injustice, including through principled disobedience, is sometimes a better avenue to meet the demands of justice, fairness, Samaritanism, and political membership than legal compliance is, and that uncivil acts of disobedience may preserve justice and democracy just as well as civil disobedience. It thus proposes to extend the concept of political obligation to encompass citizens' political responsibilities, including their moral duties to resist injustice and to engage in principled disobedience under certain circumstances.

My account of political obligations engages with champions of the moral duty to obey the law and philosophical anarchists alike. Whichever of the four grounds one endorses either as the basis of the duty to obey the law or more basically as a valid source of obligations, one is also, wittingly or not, committed to the existence of a duty to resist injustice and disobey unjust laws. Anarchists are right to be suspicious of states' demand for unquestioning obedience on the part of their subjects and of theorists' efforts to show that actual societies trigger general duties of compliance. But whereas anarchists reject nonvoluntarily incurred duties, I show that citizens of nonideal societies have numerous, stringent political obligations. Anarchists rarely discuss disobedience, except to say that the absence of political obligation does not have any radical practical implications (this is how John Simmons, for instance, distinguishes philosophical anarchism from its "bomb-throwing" relative).[19] Because of this status-quo embracing tendency, philosophical anarchism strikes me as not only "toothless," to use Chaim Gans's epithet, but also condescending in its insistence that what is right is not necessarily what it is right for "the masses" to believe.[20] In articulating instead a defense of political obligations to resist injustice, including by way of principled lawbreaking, my account purports to be a radical alternative to philosophical anarchism.

In addition, my account could be seen as either an alternative to or an extension of defenses of the duty to obey the law. On most established accounts (certainly all current ones), the duty to obey is pro tanto—ordinarily decisive yet defeasible—and does not arise in the face of serious injustice. Here, my account answers the question: What happens when the moral duty to obey the law fails to obtain, locally or overall? From this perspective, all champions of political obligation could in principle endorse my account of political obligations as a friendly extension of theirs, as some in fact do.[21] However, the duties to resist injustice and disobey the law that I identify may come into conflict with the putative moral duty to obey the law (at least in cases where it is not clear whether the injustice is so severe as to cancel the duty to obey), and champions of the duty to obey and I might disagree over whether the duty to obey should take precedence.

Although my account of political obligations relies on principles commonly used to support the duty to obey the law, I do not argue that all or only such principles ground citizens' obligations in the face of injustice. Thus I do not see how, say, gratitude and deference, which have been invoked in defense of traditional notions of political obligation, could trigger obligations of resistance under unjust conditions.[22] But one might defend political obligations of resistance on the ground of respect for law, which Joseph Raz uses to support a semi-voluntary and particular obligation to obey the law. (William

Scheuerman's defense of Snowden's whistleblowing through the lens of respect for the rule of law is a possible illustration of such argument.[23]) And Carole Pateman and Nancy Hirschmann, who advance forceful feminist critiques of liberal contractual theories of political obligation, entertain the possibility that the demands of democratic consent, well understood, counsel resistance against, instead of acquiescence to, patriarchal government.[24] Still other normative principles that philosophers have not used to support the duty to obey the law, such as freedom-as-nondomination (the unifying theme of civic republicanism) and care (the centerpiece of feminist virtue ethics) may well provoke additional responsibilities.

The sources of political obligation on which I focus are not just widely accepted but also have radical and broad-ranging implications under defective sociopolitical conditions. By putting common liberal principles to radical use in this way, I pursue a strategy associated with Carole Pateman, Iris Marion Young, Lisa Schwartzman, Rae Langton, and other feminists and critical race theorists, who show that liberals, by their own lights, should advocate sweeping political change to combat oppression.[25]

KEY CONCEPTS

I use the term *injustice* broadly, to encompass the overlapping categories of unjust *law* and *agent* and *structural* injustice. Law, the set of authoritative norms and decisions that form a legal system, is unjust, in whole or in part, when it violates substantive or procedural norms of political morality such as due process and respect for everyone as equal. The distinction between agent and structural injustice is useful: agent injustice consists in the direct and deliberate imposition of harms by individuals on other individuals, while structural injustice designates the unintended but unjust outcome of social processes or structures that are based on morally unacceptable values or belief systems. The unjust outcomes may range from unfair distribution of the burdens and benefits of social cooperation (the focus of chapter 4) to mass human rights violations.

Iris Marion Young uses the concept of *structure* to denote, broadly, "the rules and resources brought to actions and interactions," that is, what governs, enables, and constrains social interactions, and, in particular, "the relation of social positions that condition the opportunities and life prospects of the persons located in those positions" or the ways in which different social positions determine individual lives.[26] She explains:

> Structural injustice exists when social processes put large categories of persons under a systematic threat of domination or deprivation of the means to develop and exercise their capacities, at the same time as these processes enable others to dominate or have a wide range of opportunities for developing and exercising their capacities.[27]

That is, structural injustice occurs where a problematic system of norms and entitlements hinder the development of some people's capacities while benefiting others.

The related concept of *oppression*, which I will use interchangeably with "injustice" in the book, describes the inhibition of human abilities as a result of structural injustice. Marilyn Frye defines oppression as "a network of forces and barriers which are systematically related and which conspire to the immobilization, reduction and molding" of people and people's lives, on the basis of their membership in a social group.[28] The harms of oppression are inflicted though disabling structural constraints, including, as Young argues, exploitation, marginalization, powerlessness, cultural imperialism, and violence.[29] These phenomena—and the structures that produce structural injustice—involve the interplay of law, social institutions, cultural understandings, and practices.

Although my concern with principled disobedience will lead me to pay special attention to law, I also examine *ideology*. Following Tommie Shelby, I understand ideology as "a widely held set of associated beliefs and implicit judgments that misrepresent significant social realities and that function, through this distortion, to bring about or perpetuate unjust social relations."[30] Ideology works to conceal structural injustice, making its harms look necessary (natural, inevitable) or justified. Sally Haslanger has also recently illuminated the broad cultural factors—the set of "social meanings that shapes and filters how we think and act"—that need to be tackled in the fight against ideology and to achieve social justice.[31]

Oppression and injustice can be found in societies deemed "legitimate." As I mentioned above, theorists have offered myriad accounts of state *legitimacy*. Many, starting with Thomas Hobbes, conceive of legitimacy as a necessary and sufficient condition for political obligation, so that if the sovereign has a right to govern, its subjects have a correlative duty to obey. Others, like Leslie Green and Christopher H. Wellman (whose account I examine in chapter 5), hold that political legitimacy, understood as justified coercion, is necessary but not sufficient for political obligation.[32] On most contemporary accounts, political legitimacy requires just, effective, and democratic institutions, as we'll see in chapter 3. Yet some theorists, like Simmons, keep justification, legitimacy, and justice distinct. Simmons argues that while subjects' consent (and not society's justice) is a necessary and sufficient condition for state legitimacy, a state may justifiably exercise coercion even without consent from its subjects (i.e., without legitimacy).[33] So different accounts allow for different degrees of injustice to be present in a legitimate society. My account of political obligations in the face of injustice does not assume a particular conception of legitimacy.

As Amartya Sen argues, it is easier to identify injustice than to say what justice consists in: "We can have a strong sense of injustice on many different grounds, and yet not agree on one particular ground as being *the* dominant reason for the diagnosis of injustice."[34] In this spirit, my account works from notions of injustice that many (but by no means all) would recognize as such. Different injustices inflict different harms, from eroding victims' sense of self-worth through small but repeated humiliations, to physically annihilating them through genocide. Slavery, colonialism, and women's disenfranchisement are all deemed seriously unjust, usually because they violate individuals' (or people's) right to self-determination. Racism, religious intolerance, sexism, ableism, anti-LGBTQ+ discrimination, and other cases of unequal group treatment are unjust, on most theories of justice, because they manifest society's unequal respect for some of its members on the basis of morally irrelevant categories. On most accounts, failure to recognize and respect people's dignity, violations of fundamental rights, violent and abusive treatment, and unequal access to political representation are sufficient conditions for diagnosing serious injustice. Most existing societies, including liberal democracies—the best real-world candidates for legitimate societies—are guilty of at least some of these abuses.

Along with justice and injustice, a core term in this study is *resistance*. To resist is to withstand, strive against, or oppose. The concept is ambiguous: for centuries it referred to revolution or rebellion, a sense it still maintains today. Thus about a fifth of the world's constitutions, including those of Germany, the Czech Republic, Thailand, and Rwanda, recognize a right to resist oppression (where oppression designates nondemocratic power and resistance insurrection).[35] The French Revolution's Declaration of the Rights of Man and of the Citizen even affirms citizens' duty to resist in this sense: "When the government violates the rights of the people, insurrection is for the people and for each portion of the people the most sacred of rights and the most indispensable of duties." In turn, political theorists and social scientists generally define resistance as a form of sustained collective action involving "widespread activities that challenge a particular power, regime or policy."[36]

The concept of resistance I have in mind is more capacious, aligned with feminist understandings. Resisting injustice involves refusing to cooperate with the mechanisms that produce and sustain it. (And I am mainly interested in resistance against injustice, although resistance can of course target just law that is wrongly perceived as unjust as well: witness civilians' and officials' active resistance against federally mandated racial integration in Jim Crow states.) Fighting against injustice requires at least making a stand against it, by vocalizing or silently signifying protest. So one-off individual dissent can be an act of resistance, although, at best, resisting means organizing collectively to dismantle systemic injustice and working to set right particular harms caused by agent injustice.

Resistance can designate a broad range of dissident activities, which all express an opposition and/or refusal to conform to a dominant system of values, norms, rules (including law), and practices. To be clear, the "system" that is the target of resistance is not limited to society's basic institutions, but encompasses social structures in Young's sense, culture and ideology, and individuals' actions and attitudes (the latter being problematic in part in virtue of representing common, problematic norms). Acts of resistance may be legal or illegal; visible or covert; violent or nonviolent; injurious or harmless; undertaken by officials, citizens, or noncitizens (e.g., visitors, migrants, or citizens from other countries acting from abroad); and addressed to the public (government, citizenry) or to a private agent (e.g., university, corporation). They may be undertaken to pursue a variety of more or less radical goals, from legal reform to revolution, as we shall see in chapter 1.

I describe illegal acts of resistance that are politically or morally motivated as instances of *principled disobedience*. One subset of principled disobedience is *civil disobedience*: a principled and deliberate breach of law intended to protest unjust laws, policies, institutions, or practices, and undertaken by agents broadly committed to basic norms of civility. This means the action is public, non-evasive, nonviolent, and broadly respectful or civil (in accordance with decorum). This definition of civil disobedience tracks the ordinary understanding of civil disobedience but jettisons its oft-associated subjective elements (regarding the agent's attitudes and dispositions). It is broader than Rawls's definition but much narrower than recent, inclusive accounts of civil disobedience.

Another subset of principled disobedience is *uncivil disobedience*. This category, which theorists so far have neglected, helps us think about acts of principled disobedience that neither appear nor try to be civil, as well as controversial cases of civil disobedience.[37] Acts of principled disobedience that are covert, evasive, anonymous, violent, or deliberately offensive are generally (though not necessarily) uncivil. Examples include guerrilla theater (illegal public performances often designed to shock, in pursuit of revolutionary goals), antifascist tactics such as "black bloc" (which often involves destruction of property), riots, leaks, distributed-denial-of-service (DDoS) attacks, and vigilantism. (Whether some of these acts are criminal or qualify as principled disobedience depends in part on the agents' motivations as well as on the context.)

I defend a *duty* to resist injustice as a core part of our political *obligations* (and I use the terms "duty" and "obligation" interchangeably in this book). To say that something is a duty or obligation is to say that it ought to be discharged: it is a moral requirement. One might object that what we ought to do is circumscribed by what we can do, or, as philosophers are fond of saying, that "ought implies can."[38] Resistance against injustice requires sacrifices too great to be reasonably expected of most people: Freedom Riders were viciously beaten by White supremacist mobs; Manal al-Sharif, who filmed herself driving, in violation of Saudi law, was arrested and jailed. And if resistance comes at too high a price, it cannot be a moral requirement. This is why we admire resisters' courage and sacrifices—because they go well beyond the call of duty.[39]

In response, it is important to clarify the nature of the duty to resist that I defend in this book. It is not legally enforceable, although its violation may be socially sanctioned, for instance, through blame.[40] Like other duties, it is defeasible, that is, it may come into conflict with, and be outweighed by, countervailing considerations. It is a general and imperfect duty, meaning that one has discretion as to when and how to discharge it. It does not demand heroic self-sacrifice, although it prohibits doing nothing (insofar as doing nothing amounts to supporting the unjust status quo). What one ought to do in a particular situation, then, depends on the particulars of that situation—especially the nature of the injustice and one's position relative to it. But the fact that we admire courageous resisters does not mean that resistance can only be supererogatory, that is, only the province of moral saints that we feel we can never measure up to. Rather it means that resisting injustice is difficult and that many of us fall short of fulfilling our basic political obligations.

OUR POLITICAL OBLIGATIONS

The book often takes a historical and theoretical approach to thinking about our political duties. I will turn again in chapter 4 to the conditions the young Freedom Rider felt obligated to resist, and I will argue that his instinct was correct. In 1961, under Jim Crow, one of citizens' central political obligations was to fight racial segregation, and one effective way of doing so was to engage in civil disobedience: one wasn't simply permitted but, depending on one's circumstances, may also have been morally bound to join protest marches, boycotts, lunch counter sit-ins, and other racial-integration campaigns. In later chapters, I discuss those circumstances—aggravating and mitigating—in detail.

But while history informs the analysis, my goals have more to do with the moral obligations citizens face today. I contend that these obligations demand solidarity with protests against racial injustice, labor injustice, gender inequality, and sexual violence. They demand that we educate ourselves about the workings of structural racism and implicit bias; listen to the testimonies of victims of oppression; cultivate moral understanding of and resistance to our own and our children's self-deception; demand accountability for extrajudicial killings by police and others operating under cover of law; draw attention to, and work to dismantle, mass incarceration; directly disobey laws that require reporting or prohibit assisting undocumented migrants; engage in principled disobedience to highlight and eradicate discrimination against women, LGBTQ+ people, ethnic minorities, and people with disabilities; and force our governments to reform unjust trade, labor, environmental, and energy regimes globally. We should challenge and refuse to comply with sexist; racist; Islamophobic; homo-, trans-, and cis-phobic, and ableist cultural and social norms. We should boycott morally tainted products and "buycott" in order to support high-road producers; donate to organizations devoted to social justice and democracy; document and report wrongdoing when we witness it, sometimes even when we are legally prohibited from doing so; partake, as necessary, in workplace strikes; and use our positions, resources, and talents—whether as officials with access to levers of power, celebrities in the public eye, or everyday people with our particular skills and endowments—to relieve suffering and promote justice everywhere we can.

This is a tall moral order, but we needn't let this frighten us into despair or denial. That morality may impose lofty demands is nothing new. What is new is this book's systematic account of citizens' duty to meet those demands by resisting injustice, including through principled—civil and uncivil—disobedience. What is also new is that this account relies on the same grounds commonly used to support the duty to obey the law. Finally, what is new is the proposal to revisit and radically expand our understanding of political obligations, but only by asking us to make good on the commitments we already claim to accept.

Chapter 1

Principled Disobedience

What do suffragists' window-smashing, the Catonsville Nine's na-
palm-soaked draft registries, Snowden's leaks, and Femen's topless
heckling have in common? What does Pussy Riot's "Punk Prayer," their
guerrilla performance in Moscow's Cathedral of Christ the Savior,
share with covert aid to unauthorized migrants, Sea Shepherd's anti-
whaling efforts, and Anonymous's DDoS attacks? Not much at first
glance: these activities involved different targets, sites, methods, and
goals. Some were covert, others public; some violent, others nonviolent; some coercive, others not. Yet all have been severely condemned,
criminally charged, or prosecuted. And all have been described, by
those who approve of them, as instances of civil disobedience.[1] And,
in response, opponents have marshaled an idealized understanding of
civil rights–style disobedience to deny that these acts qualify as civil.

This debate might appear to be one of mere semantics. Why
should we care whether leaks or topless heckling qualify as civil disobedience? On this thinking, one may define "civil disobedience" however one wants, in a manner that includes or excludes some or all of
the disobedient acts listed above. What matters is whether and how
the disobedient acts in question can be justified. This is the central
issue, to be sure—and the object of the next chapter. But first, I want
to think about what is at stake in the conceptual question, why the
main approaches to understanding civil disobedience are defective

and limited, and how we should instead conceive of *principled disobedience* beyond the narrow confines of civil disobedience.[2]

The term "civil disobedience" is used not only to describe but also to evaluate. To call a disobedient act civil is to highlight the agent's principled motivations and communicative intentions, to make a disruptive breach of law intelligible as a speech-act—an address to the community—and, thus, to begin the work of its justification. Especially in the United States, civil disobedience evokes a venerable tradition associated with the likes of Rosa Parks and Martin Luther King Jr. The label is coveted, in a way, sought out to legitimize illegal actions. For instance, social conservatives compared Kentucky county clerk Kim Davis's refusal to issue marriage licenses to same-sex couples to Rosa Parks's refusal to give up her seat on the segregated city bus.[3] It is in part because civil disobedience is exalted that so much is at stake in its meaning, that public discourse and the philosophical literature are hard to revise.

The historical connotations and established meaning of civil disobedience hint at the difficulty of redefining the concept, while its normative significance and appeal explain the reluctance to steer away from civil disobedience and the temptation to expand its scope to encompass any activity with which one is politically aligned. To be sure, there is something special about civil disobedience. But I will argue in the next chapter that there is something special about uncivil disobedience, too, and that we should stop associating incivility with wrongfulness and look to its aptness and potential value under certain oppressive circumstances.

The acts of principled disobedience listed above may be acceptable, but they are not civil, and there should be no need to modify our concept of civil disobedience to incorporate them. Instead, I propose to articulate a basically sympathetic approach to principled disobedience, open to the possibility that these acts are justified. Indeed the next chapter will show that uncivil acts of disobedience can be justified, in part on the basis of the grounds commonly used to justify civil disobedience; and chapters 3–6 will argue that they can even be required in some circumstances, on the basis of the grounds commonly used to support the moral duty to obey the law. A sympathetic approach should be phenomenologically accurate—that is, faithful to practitioners' self-understanding—and politically useful, which is to say able to contribute to public debates. This project is broadly "ameliorative," to use Haslanger's terminology, insofar as it puts forward a framework to assess disobedience that supports emancipatory struggles such as those pursued by the agents mentioned above.[4]

The ordinary conception of civil disobedience associated with Rawls tends to undermine emancipatory struggles (despite the emancipatory potential of an attentive reading of his theory). Shaped by an idealized theory and an unrealistic reading of the African American civil rights struggle, civil disobedience as ordinarily understood by the public and by philosophers deters noncompliance and reinforces the status quo. Kimberley Brownlee and Robin Celikates have instead offered "inclusive" accounts of civil disobedience. These are capacious enough to encompass all the acts of principled disobedience mentioned at the outset, and they offer worthwhile counternarratives to public censure and states' punishment. However, they stretch the concept of civil disobedience beyond recognition and fail to account for activists' deliberate departures from the standard template of civil disobedience. The most promising ameliorative route is not maximal inclusion, I will argue, but a richer repertoire of political resistance that includes uncivil disobedience.

DISOBEDIENCE IN THE CIVIL RIGHTS STYLE

Public understanding of civil disobedience is the product of two different strands: the broadly Rawlsian philosophical conception of civil disobedience and the official narrative of the civil rights movement in the United States. The two have combined into a commonly held conception of what civil disobedience meant in the civil rights movement of the 1950s–1970s—a conception that functions as a counter-resistance ideology, as I shall argue. Although the discussion is centered on the American context, it applies across publics, given the global resonance of the civil rights movement and its associations with figures from Gandhi to Nelson Mandela, the Dalai Lama, Liu Xiaobo, and Malala Yousafzai, and movements from the Palestinian Intifada to the Arab Spring and Spain's Indignados, among others. I am not aware of any comparative research on peoples' understandings of civil disobedience, but one might reasonably expect many similarities with the American conception, itself inspired in important ways by experiences abroad.

Theory and History

Legal, moral, and political theorists in the Anglo-American tradition began reflecting on civil disobedience in the 1960s, in the midst of civil rights and anti–Vietnam War protests in the United States, anti-nuclear protests throughout the West, and decolonization struggles in the global South. Carl Cohen, Michael Walzer, Ronald Dworkin, Richard Wasserstrom, and, most prominently, John Rawls, conceptualized and defended civil disobedience against official and widespread public accusations that disobedience, even if principled, sowed lawlessness and invited violence.

Theorists were successful in carving out a space for civil disobedience in liberal democracy. Erin Pineda highlights the significant impact that theorists had in the U.S. context:

> What emerged out of this effort has been a remarkably stable set
> of ideas about civil disobedience—the forms of action and sets

of attitudes entailed by it—that have remained central to the way that political theory, and the American political public at large, reasons about the definition, role, and justification of disobedient protest.[5]

This stable set of ideas is Rawls's. In his view, civil disobedience is a conscientious, public, nonviolent breach of law undertaken to persuade the majority to change a law or policy in a nearly just society.[6] Rawls understood publicity to require that agents give authorities fair notice of their planned disobedient activity, act in public, and appeal to the community's shared conception of justice. He thought that nonviolence excluded the use of force (or coercion, in Rawls's usage) and actual or likely infliction of harm against persons. In addition, agents of civil disobedience are supposed to accept, and even seek out, the legal consequences of their actions. In doing so they demonstrate their general "fidelity to law," endorsement of the system's legitimacy, and belief that the latter generates a moral duty to obey the law.

Thus, in Rawls's vision, civil disobedience contrasts with armed resistance, rebellion, and revolution, which use violence and covert tactics, and whose agents reject the system's legitimacy, lack respect for established law, seek to evade punishment, and pursue radical goals. Rawls further sets forth three necessary justificatory conditions, which purport to minimize the disruptive effects of civil disobedience: the act must (1) target a serious violation of the first principle of justice in Rawls's theory ("the principle of equal basic liberties"), (2) be undertaken as a last resort, and (3) be coordinated with other groups with similar grievances.

Rawls did not devise his account out of thin air. It came from, and refined, some of the ideas articulated by activists themselves. We might say, though, that he brought these ideas together in a way that "stuck" and that his concerns about the threat of principled disobedience to law and order were shared by the dominant majority—that is, people who viewed their society as democratic and basically just.

What inspired this account was not the radical activism of Thoreau and Gandhi. Though icons of civil disobedience, their actions do not fit inside Rawls's boundaries. Thoreau's tax refusal lacked the publicity now associated with civil disobedience; it became public only because he later wrote and lectured about it.[7] Tellingly, his essay was originally titled "Resistance to Civil Government" and posthumously retitled "On Civil Disobedience." Gandhi had revolutionary goals. As David Lyons has argued, neither man deemed, or had any reason to deem, his state—antebellum United States or British Raj—legitimate.[8]

It was the style of King and others involved in the Black civil rights struggle that most clearly shaped the standard account. Campaigns such as the Good Friday march in Birmingham (which violated a court order), lunch counter sit-ins, and Freedom Rides satisfied many of Rawls's demanding criteria.[9] They appealed to constitutional principles of political morality and pursued modest goals of reform, not revolution. Activists thoroughly trained in and committed to nonviolence disobeyed the law publicly, often giving authorities advance notice of their plans. They responded to state and mob violence peacefully and willingly submitted to arrest and jail for their lawbreaking. They displayed the essential marks of civility.

By praising activists' respect for law and emphasizing their endorsement of the system's legitimacy, philosophers reassured law-and-order opponents. But this strategy distorted political reality.[10] For activists' outward submission to law did not in fact reflect their endorsement of the system's legitimacy or their acceptance of a moral duty to obey the law. The standard account wrongly—that is, implausibly and objectionably—ascribed these attitudes and beliefs to civil disobedients whose choices in fact were mainly driven by strategic rather than moral considerations. For example, the Montgomery bus

boycott demanded the end of segregated seating in public buses—
not the end of racial segregation—because social and legal change
are known to occur in a piecemeal fashion. Indeed, its organizers initially demanded only courtesy and the hiring of Black drivers. But
King's objective went far beyond buses. "The thing to do," he wrote,
"is get rid of the system."[11] And Southern authorities' unyielding response reflected a shared understanding of what was at stake in apparently limited reform.

King denied that the United States of Jim Crow deserved respect and called the caste system "unjust" and "evil."[12] His famous
insistence, in the "Letter from Birmingham City Jail," that civil disobedience expresses the "highest respect for law," has been widely
misunderstood. It appears in the context of his discussion of natural
law's tenet that "an unjust law is no law at all" and can only be properly
understood to enjoin respect for just law, as opposed to deference to
any law at all by virtue of its being a law. In turn, the commitment
to nonviolence was a strategic choice, not a reflection of absolutist
moral principle or fidelity to law. King acknowledged the aptness of
anger, and the legitimacy of violence in self-defense, but argued that
the civil rights movement ought to be steadfastly nonviolent so as
not to risk frightening the White majority (he deemed fear a central
affective component of anti-Black racism).[13] He denied the standard
equation between nonviolence and non-coercion, observing that
nonviolent civil disobedience can "create such a crisis and establish
such creative tension that a community that has constantly refused
to negotiate is forced to confront the issue."[14] King also conceived of
submission to arrest and punishment in symbolic terms, as a "powerful and just weapon," and as a matter of prudence, given that civil
rights activists were outnumbered and outgunned.[15]

In short, civil rights groups adopted their particular style of civil
disobedience for context-dependent, tactical purposes. Yet theorists
and pundits turned these tactics into deep moral commitments on the

part of agents supposedly eager to demonstrate their endorsement of the state's legitimacy, and placed these subjective requirements at the core of their defense of real-world civil disobedience.

Rawls's Theory

Let me pause and consider an objection on behalf of Rawls before turning to the ideological work that the standard conception of civil rights style civil disobedience does. Rawls's followers stress his explicit restriction of the account of civil disobedience to the special context of the nearly just society. Nearly just societies publicly endorse, and are ordered by, principles of justice such as the ones Rawls defends in *A Theory of Justice*. They are democratic. They generate a moral duty to obey the law that is grounded in the duty of justice, which demands supporting just institutions (chapter 3 examines this account). Civil disobedients are to accept the political system as nearly just only when *it is*, and the United States of his time could obviously not be deemed nearly just, according to Rawls's own standards of near justice.[16]

I agree that an attentive reading of Rawls's theory yields the conclusion that it shouldn't be applied to Thoreau's, Gandhi's, and King's civil disobedience. Nevertheless, it has been so applied, and it has clearly inspired the standard account of civil disobedience I just critiqued. Rawls invites the application of his theory to the activism of his day when he characterizes his account of civil disobedience as an incursion into "partial compliance theory," defined as the study of "the principles that govern how we are to deal with injustice." He highlights the importance of such inquiry: "Obviously, the problems of partial compliance theory are the pressing and urgent matters. These are the things that we are faced with in everyday life."[17] So one might reasonably find it strange if Rawls's discussion about this "pressing and urgent" issue of civil disobedience didn't apply to real-world civil disobedience. He also appears to believe that U.S. society was nearly just. In 1964, before the end of de jure racial segregation, he writes, "I shall assume, as requiring no argument, that there is, at least in society such as ours, a moral obligation to obey the law," a condition that could only hold in a nearly just society.[18]

In any case, *Theory of Justice* does have emancipatory potential. In it Rawls is open to the possible justification of forms of principled disobedience beyond civil disobedience in unjust as well as nearly just societies. He argues that sometimes, when political systems are ordered by defective conceptions of justice, "one may have no recourse but to oppose the prevailing conception and the institutions it justifies in such ways as promise some success."[19] He also writes that "sometimes," if the civil disobedient's appeal to the majority "fails in its purpose, forceful resistance may later be entertained."[20] And in *Justice as Fairness: A Restatement*, Rawls notes the risk that, even in an apparently well-ordered, nearly just society, "when the strains of commitment seem to us excessive . . . we become sullen and resentful, and we are ready as the occasion arises to take violent action in protest against our condition."[21] However, Rawls does not discuss the acceptable escalation path from civil to uncivil disobedience, or the potential justification of the latter. Thus we need fuller exploration of partial compliance theory.

History and Ideology

The official reading of the civil rights movement is not just inaccurate in its presentation of agents' attitudes and ideals. It also functions, thanks in part to this inaccuracy, as a counter-resistance ideology.

First, the official narrative undercuts political radicals by falsely equating the civil rights movement with the campaigns led by King and the Southern Christian Leadership Conference, thereby ignoring the contributions of ideologies, groups, and campaigns such as Black nationalism, the Black Panther Party, the Nation of Islam, pan-Africanism, Black workers' movements, prisoners' rights movements, Black feminism, third-worldism, and assorted Marxist liberation movements. Adherents of some of these less-recognized groups resorted to violence and called for an overthrow of the racist, imperialist system. But official history brushes these activists aside. It may be that some of them threatened the civil rights movement's success, but without these radical movements as foil, King's movement would not have looked so moderate, and therefore may not have gained support from White liberals.[22] In his "Letter from Birmingham City Jail," King poses his movement of nonviolent direct action as the only alternative to Black violence. He stressed that "the streets of the South would be flowing with floods of blood," but for his movement.

> And I am further convinced that if our white brothers dismiss as "rabble rousers" and "outside agitators"—those of us working through the channels of nonviolent direct action . . . millions of Negroes, out of frustration and despair, will seek solace and security in black ideologies, a development that will lead inevitably to a frightening racial nightmare.[23]

And so the history we tell is one in which a nonviolent, state-legitimizing civil disobedience movement single-handedly wins the struggle for civil rights. The larger, longer, and more pugnacious process of political resistance is ignored, lest anyone get the wrong idea about how to protect themselves or vindicate their rights.

Second, the accepted narrative overstates the victory of the civil rights movement, as crystallized in the 1964 Civil Rights Act, the 1965 Voting Rights Act, and the Federal Housing Act of 1968, thereby discouraging further activism. Fifty years on, many of the social ills that inspired the movement remain unaddressed: residential and school segregation continue to divide Americans by race; many states have counteracted Black voters' access to representation and the political franchise through electoral redistricting, voter ID laws, and felon disenfranchisement; Blacks still suffer disproportionately from poverty and unequal opportunities in education, work, and healthcare; racism is pervasive, openly so in a White-supremacist, nationalist movement rebranded "alt-right"; courts and the public oppose race-conscious antidiscrimination policies as outdated and unnecessary; and police profile, abuse, and even kill Blacks with near impunity. The civil rights movement accomplished important gains, but in overstating these, we portray American society as having realized the demands of justice and therefore successfully generated a moral duty to obey the law.

Third, the emphasis on civil rights activists' nonviolence counsels compliance in the face of Black victimization. In *Between the World and Me*, Ta-Nehisi Coates writes of Black History Month,

> Every February my classmates and I were herded into assemblies for a ritual review of the civil-rights movement. Our teachers urged us toward the example of freedom marchers, Freedom Riders, and Freedom Summers, and it seemed that the month could not pass without a series of films dedicated to the glories of being beaten on camera. *Why are they showing this to us?* Why were only our heroes nonviolent? Back then all I could do was measure these freedom-lovers by what I knew. Which is to say, I measured them against children pulling out [guns] in the 7-Eleven parking lot, against parents wielding extension cords, and the threatening intonations of armed Black gangs saying, "Yeah, nigger, what's up now?" I judged them against the country I knew, which had acquired the land through murder and tamed it under slavery, against the country whose armies fanned out across the world to extend their dominion. The world, the real

one, was civilization secured and ruled by savage means. How could the schools valorize men and women whose values society actively scorned? How could they send us out into the streets of Baltimore, knowing all that they were, and then speak of nonviolence?[24]

Coates highlights the hypocrisy and even absurdity of urging nonviolence upon children whose daily lives are dominated by violence, in a country founded upon, and continually engaged in, the same. Here and elsewhere in his writings, he shows how the official narrative valorizes docility and deters the population—especially Blacks— from unruly kinds of resistance. As he puts it elsewhere, "When nonviolence is preached by the representatives of the state, while the state doles out heaps of violence to its citizens, it reveals itself to be a con."[25]

Fourth, the official narrative's categorical condemnation of violent resistance obscures state-authored and state-condoned violence. Angela Davis stressed this in a 1972 interview with Swedish reporters who asked whether she approved of the use of guns and violence. In response, she problematizes the assumptions underlying the question, describing "the violence that exists on the surface everywhere" for Blacks, which she experienced firsthand in Los Angeles: being eyed with suspicion, constantly stopped and frisked by police, treated as criminals or agitators. She goes on:

And then you ask me whether I approve of violence... That just doesn't make any sense at all. Whether I approve of guns? I grew up in Birmingham, Alabama. Some very, very good friends of mine were killed by bombs—bombs that were planted by racists. From the time I was very small I remember the sound of bombs exploding across the street, our house shaking. I remember my father having to have guns at his disposal at all times because of the fact that at any moment we might expect to be attacked. The man who was at that time in complete control of the city government—his name was Bull Connor—would often get on the radio and make statements like "Niggers have moved into a White neighborhood. We'd better expect some bloodshed tonight!" And sure enough there would be bloodshed.[26]

In the face of a regime of terror, some Blacks responded by arming themselves for protection. Davis's analysis suggests that those who condemn Black (mostly self-defensive) violence tend to do so in a vacuum, without regard to, and in ways that obfuscate, the state's own encouragement and commitment of violence against Blacks.

Fifth, and related, ubiquitous calls for civility conceal and distract from what Bernard Harcourt calls "incivility of politics"—the harms it regularly inflicts on citizens. All too often these demands, implicit in the official history of civil rights, are wielded disingenuously by those in power to deter noncompliance and even law-abiding dissent.[27] Austin Sarat finds in *Walker vs. Birmingham*, the 1963 Supreme Court ruling that upheld the city of Birmingham's injunction against civil rights activists, "an instance in which the demand for civility was taken to a frightening extreme," to the point of "pathology."[28] The ruling described activists as "impatient," and, Sarat finds, implied that they were "uncivil, disrespectful, and dangerous."[29] The Court put "respect for judicial process" above all else: it upheld the arrests of activists, including King and Ralph Abernathy, on the grounds that they ought not have disobeyed the injunction, even though it would not have withstood constitutional scrutiny. Civility is equated with law-abidance and deference—abidance by an unjust and unlawful court order, and deference to a racist city itself openly noncompliant with federal law.

Walker vs. Birmingham is not an isolated sickness of the body politic; it is symptomatic of widespread social ills. Recall that the White clergy called King's civil rights movement "rabble rousers." Harcourt notes in his analysis of the political uses of civility and incivility,

> The faculty to define certain speech as uncivil, to castigate a speaker, to call for, urge, or demand civil discourse—and to get away with it—is intimately connected to one's place in the political realm. It is also, unquestionably, a political stratagem. . . . Calling out incivilities and urging greater civility in political discourse are arrows in the quiver of the political arts. Although they are presented as neutral, they are not. They represent, instead, a way to seize the political high-ground. As such, they often redound to the benefit of those who are in stronger political positions. Often, they serve the interests of the more dominant or mainstream political voices.[30]

The powerful often use calls for civility to control and silence activists, to cast a negative light on their activities and prejudice the public against them. Calls for civility ignore and obscure the differentials of power—the fact that it is easy for those in power, and harder for entrenched minorities, to speak and be listened to and therefore to be civil. The former have ready access to the public sphere, while the latter not only lack such access but are also vulnerable to discrimination, prejudice, and epistemic injustice (which consists in doing wrong to people in their capacity as knowers, for instance by failing to really listen to them or by deflating the credibility or sincerity of their testimony).[31]

By misrepresenting the historical realities of social change, and articulating a set of associated beliefs and judgments about civil disobedience, the history and theory of civil disobedience warp public understanding of liberation struggles. To be clear, what is at stake in the official narrative of the Black freedom movement is not simply historical accuracy: this narrative and the theory of civil disobedience it rationalizes provide the benchmark against which other social and political movements are judged. Usually they are judged harshly—for what can live up to an ideal?—and therefore branded uncivil and dangerous.

In the official narrative of civil rights and the standard theory of civil disobedience, we thus have something like an ideology, which includes a defense of the status quo through a series of conformist moves: affirmation that our society is a nearly just one, erasure of state-authored violence, and celebration of submission and docility. Such implicit counter-resistance ideology demands in response an accurate history of the struggle for civil rights, to replace the sanitized and distorted official picture, and an ameliorative account of political resistance.

INCLUSIVE ACCOUNTS OF CIVIL DISOBEDIENCE

Theorists dissatisfied with the standard, Rawlsian account have articulated "minimalist" or "inclusive" concepts of civil disobedience that extend to all sorts of principled lawbreaking.

Brownlee's is one such account. She problematizes the conceptual distinctions standardly drawn between civil disobedience and other types of dissent, noting that civil disobedients may intend a revolution and that conscientious objectors often seek broad reform and not simply personal exemption. For Brownlee, civil disobedience "must include a deliberate breach of law taken on the basis of steadfast personal commitment in order to communicate our condemnation of a law or policy to a relevantly placed audience."[32] This kind of civil disobedience need not be public or nonviolent. What sets it apart from ordinary crime, radical protests, and private conscientious objection (or "personal disobedience" in her terminology) are its constrained, communicative, and non-evasive properties, which mark the agent's efforts to engage an intended public in dialogue. Thus Brownlee conceives of the suffragist tactics as civil disobedience and she has argued that Snowden's actions were civilly disobedient on her account but not on Rawls's.[33]

For his part, Celikates, who spearheads the radical democratic approach, has also been a vocal critique of the standard liberal account of civil disobedience. He challenges the narrowness and ideological underpinnings of the criteria of publicity, nonviolence, willingness to accept punishment, appeal to shared principles of justice, and even conscientiousness. As counterexample to the latter criterion, he points to cases of self-interested civil disobedience, for instance to protest a new highway slated to pass through one's neighborhood.[34] Celikates understands civil disobedience as

> an intentionally unlawful and principled collective act of protest (in contrast to both legal protest and "ordinary" criminal offenses or "unmotivated" rioting), with which citizens—in the broad sense that goes beyond those recognized as citizens by a particular state—pursue the political aim of changing specific laws, policies, or institutions (in contrast to conscientious objection, which is protected in some states as a fundamental right and does not seek such change) in ways that can be seen as civil (as opposed to military).[35]

This broad conception imposes no requirement on the agent's attitude toward the system, her target, or the principles she appeals to. The civilly disobedient act need not be done publicly. Celikates also rejects the nonviolence proviso, on the grounds that it reduces civil disobedience to a merely symbolic protest (a speech-act) and thereby ignores the confrontation it unavoidably creates.[36] Both Celikates's and Brownlee's inclusive conceptions maintain Rawls's core insight that civil disobedience is essentially a communicative act aimed at political change, but they leave much else up for grabs.

Celikates's and Brownlee's accounts of civil disobedience are ameliorative in the sense I explained earlier: they are, and present themselves as, efforts to justify emancipatory resistance to injustice. Both include in the category of civil disobedience controversial acts of resistance performed by suffragists, sanctuary workers, and others. The thrust of Brownlee's argument in *Conscience and Conviction: The Case for Civil Disobedience* is that civil disobedients have stronger claims to legal protection than do conscientious objectors—protections that, in liberal societies, are considerable. She also defends a moral right of civil disobedients to evade legal punishment. Celikates, meanwhile, offers a radically democratic understanding of disobedience as a dynamic contribution to political processes, contra what he sees as the "overly constrained, domesticated and sanitized" understanding of civil disobedience offered by mainstream liberal accounts.[37]

I am sympathetic to both accounts, but principled disobedience as I shall articulate it is, I think, more politically useful and phenomenologically accurate than these ameliorative versions of civil disobedience.

First, Brownlee and Celikates stretch the concept of civil disobedience beyond recognition, encompassing in it some features previously deemed to be incompatible. For instance, sabotage and violence can be civilly disobedient on Brownlee's view.[38] And Celikates, in a co-authored article, dubs Anonymous civilly disobedient even when the group members conceal their identity, use coerced botnets to launch DDoS attacks, and admit mixed motivations including just a zeal for pranks.[39] These features, the authors recognize, are usually seen as "other" to, or even "opposites" of, civil disobedience. Because of this, inclusive accounts of civil disobedience stand little chance of convincing the public and therefore score low on the political-usefulness quotient.

A second problem with inclusive accounts is that they miss the point of many disobedient actions, which is to *refuse* to follow the standard script of civil disobedience. Emmeline Pankhurst defended suffragists' use of "militant methods" (including heckling, window-smashing, sabotage, and hunger strikes) and characterized herself as a "soldier" in a "civil war" waged against the state. Ukrainian-French radical feminist collective Femen brands its disobedience as radical and provocative, not civil, by calling its tactics—which include "sex attacks, sex diversions and sex sabotage"—*sextremism*.[40] Cultural critic Mark Dery conceives of "culture jammers"—such as billboard bandits, hacktivists, and media hoaxers—as "artistic terrorists" and "communication guerrilla" fighters.[41] And Black Lives Matter activists hint at the rupture between their work and understandings of civil disobedience with the slogan "Not Your Grandfather's Civil Rights Movement." In short, agents may see themselves, and seek to be perceived, as radical and provocative rather than civil.[42]

There may be other good reasons for activists to openly reject civility: incivility can be used as a strategy to publicize a group's cause. Or, again, agents may not be in a position to claim civility. In his discussion of poor urban Blacks' acts of spontaneous defiance, Tommie Shelby notes,

> Spontaneous rebellion reaches its apotheosis in the urban riot, where looting, mass destruction of property, and brutal violence are on public display. When legitimate avenues for political action fail to produce results or are closed off, such public unrest can seem to be the only power the ghetto poor can wield collectively that has a chance of garnering concessions from the state.[43]

And Avia Pasternak writes that, in the absence of the political capital needed to organize lawful protests and even civil disobedience campaigns, "political rioting could be the only accessible form of political participation for the seriously marginalized members of society, at least in the very initial stages of protest."[44] Recourse to civil disobedience may be closed off to other marginalized populations. Prisoners, who are often stripped of their civil and political rights (disenfranchisement is known as "civic death") and barred from effective communicative action, cannot take part in civil disobedience even if they wish to. And some activists may explicitly reject civility in order to expose the falseness of the presumption of equal standing within the standard conception of civil disobedience.

As things stand, we are not equipped to analyze and justify these departures from the template of civil disobedience: the public understanding of civil disobedience excludes uncivil disobedience from the realm of justifiable disobedient protest, Rawls only discusses civil disobedience and restricts it to the nearly just society, and inclusive accounts such as Brownlee's and Celikates's erase the distinctiveness and underlying intentions of uncivil means by encompassing them within civil disobedience. In my view, most of the ameliorative action takes place outside civil disobedience: we should expand our repertoire of potentially acceptable modes of principled disobedience beyond civil disobedience, readily granting the incivility of certain disobedient acts and opening ourselves to the possibility that some types of uncivil disobedience can be justified.

A MATRIX OF RESISTANCE

So, how we understand civil disobedience, how we distinguish it from other forms of resistance, matters. How *should* we understand it? The way forward and out of the deadlocked debates in which sympathizers affirm, and opponents deny, that a given act of resistance qualifies as civil disobedience, consists in expanding our repertoire of potentially acceptable modes of unlawful resistance beyond civil disobedience. We should readily grant the incivility of certain disobedient acts and open up to the possibility that some acts of uncivil disobedience are justified. A matrix of resistance seeks to lead this way forward. This matrix will not offer necessary and sufficient conditions for its central concepts—resistance, principled disobedience, civil and uncivil disobedience—but simply highlight some features of the concepts, like constellations on the matrix rather than sharply outlined categories.

I use "resistance" to designate a broad range of dissident activities, of varying scope and impact, which express opposition, and perhaps refusal to conform, to a dominant system of values, norms, rules, and practices. Such rules and practices may be codified in law. Resistance is, by definition, principled—that is, morally or politically motivated. Resistors basically share an urge to respond to (if not also to change) perceived injustice. They may or may not recognize the system's legitimacy. The principles that ground resistance may or may not be worthy of public recognition (resistance in pursuit of White nationalism, for instance, is unjustifiable).

Resistors may address private or public actors, at home, abroad, or at the global level. They may pursue a variety of goals including, but not limited to, communicating condemnation of an accepted norm, law, court sentence, police order, or practice; denouncing wrongs and democratic deficits; alerting the public to a wrong; asserting rights; protecting oneself and others; protecting animals and the environment; promoting important values such as freedom and transparency; seeking legal reform; seeking cultural changes; asserting dignity; gaining collective self-determination; expressing solidarity; frustrating a wrong; calling for secession; refusing to participate in wrongful activities; protesting historical wrongs; and retaliating against wrongdoers. This versatile list shatters the traditional dichotomy between civil disobedience and resistance-as-rebellion, outlining instead a capacious concept of resistance encompassing lawful dissent, principled disobedience and, at the limit, revolution. As should be clear, resistors may be wrong in their assessment of wrongs and injustices, and the goals they pursue may or may not be justified: the matrix of resistance sketched here does not prejudge the assessment of particular acts.

Elements of this concept of resistance exist in other theories, but none are so comprehensive. On the one hand, feminist philosophers have long advanced a fluid notion of resistance, understanding its role in denouncing unjust conditions, changing cultural norms (e.g., through consciousness-raising and everyday resistance), and asserting self-respect.[45] However, they have largely been concerned with lawful acts and social movements. Theorists of civil disobedience, on the other hand, focus on a particular, narrowly constrained style of unlawful protest.

I am not aware of any account of resistors seeking revenge for perceived wrongs. Yet many acts of slave resistance could fall in this category, from work slowdowns to cheating on the weight of a daily crop by adding stones or soaking cotton in water.[46] Instances of jury nullification may also fit the bill. For example, some of the jurors in O. J. Simpson's murder trial have admitted voting to acquit him as "payback" for police brutality.[47] And "Operation: Avenge Assange" saw Anonymous conduct a series of DDoS actions in retaliation against a dozen corporate websites, including Visa and PayPal, for their decision to freeze donations to WikiLeaks (under government pressure) after it published classified state documents leaked by Chelsea Manning.[48] In short, there are numerous gaps in current discussions of resistance, which this matrix of resistance aims to fill.

Resisting injustice involves refusing to cooperate with, and trying to undermine, the mechanisms that produce and sustain it. One may do so through lawful acts such as marches, denunciations of wrongs, verbal or symbolic expressions of solidarity, advocacy, human rights lawyering, silent protests, and online activism. Lawful resistance may be uncivil: think of the Westboro Baptist Church's hateful protests at gay soldiers' funerals, internet trolls, or politically conscious yet offensive hip-hop like N.W.A.'s 1988 "Fuck Tha Police," which Shelby conceives as a kind of "impure political dissent."[49] Jessica Bulman-Pozen and David Pozen have recently theorized another kind of lawful resistance under the banner "uncivil obedience," which they define as hyperbolic, literalistic, or otherwise unanticipated adherence to a legal system's formal rules.[50] Examples include motorcyclists strictly adhering to the speed limit in order to protest it and the creation of a political action committee by the TV host Stephen Colbert in order to ridicule Federal Election Commission rules.

Among unlawful acts of resistance I am interested in "principled disobedience," a category that encompasses civil and uncivil disobedience, and other kinds of lawbreaking that may be aptly characterized as neither (such as terrorism).[51] Principled disobedience refers to politically or morally motivated resorts to illegality in the opposition or refusal to conform to the system's dominant norms. Illegality raises special issues given states' claims to subjects' obedience, agents' liability to legal sanction, and the common view that lawbreaking is presumptively wrong. In order to unpack these issues, I have determined to focus on principled—especially civil and uncivil—disobedience.

Civil disobedience is one subset of principled disobedience. It designates deliberate breach of law intended to protest unjust laws, policies, institutions, or practices and undertaken by agents broadly committed to basic norms of civility. There are four such norms associated with civil disobedience: publicity, non-evasiveness, nonviolence, and decorum.

On the standard account, recall, publicity (the agent's performance of the act in the open), non-evasiveness (her acceptance of legal sanctions), and nonviolence (which rules out the use of force and infliction of harm) are necessary to the disobedient act's communicativeness—its nature as a speech-act—and civility. But there is more to it. Consider Pussy Riot's "Punk Prayer": public, non-evasive, and nonviolent, this guerrilla-style protest song in a Russian Cathedral was nonetheless denied the label of civil disobedience because, detractors argued, it desecrated a religious place and defiled the state. Members of the group were convicted of "premeditated hooliganism," which is defined as "the flagrant violation of public order expressed by a clear disrespect for society." Campus protests in the United States, whether or not they involve illegality, are regularly deemed "uncivil" even when they meet the three norms of civility. Many journalists and other members of the public do not view student protests as the nonviolent speech-acts that, for the most part, they are, focusing instead on what are seen as rude, even "hysterical" shouting-down tactics. Or again, acts of principled lawbreaking that are public, non-evasive, and nonviolent, such as road blocks, may be so disruptive that they are not seen as civil. According to critics, religious sacrilege, refusal to listen to one's adversary, and grave disruptiveness constitute failures to treat the audience respectfully, and are therefore incompatible with the civil disobedient's civility.

These critiques point to a fourth norm of civility, which I conceive as decorum. For liberals, civility-as-decorum is what we need to get along with people with whom we disagree. It concerns the ways citizens ought to interact with each other in the public sphere, when debating political questions. Specifically, citizens ought to set aside comprehensive (religious and moral) values, appeal to the values of public reason, and listen to others' views with respect and fair-mindedness.[52] On the standard liberal picture, citizens who want to enter the public sphere ought to behave in a dignified and polite manner and avoid causing offense. Civil disobedients, in particular, ought to treat their audience respectfully, as people they seek to persuade. Pussy Riot's attack on religion caused outrage; shouting down runs afoul of the demand that we listen respectfully to others with whom we disagree; and even peaceful roadblocks may cause such an inconvenience to the public that they are seen as reckless and disrespectful. All three may be deemed to be offensive and disrespectful (though in different ways) and thus to fall short of civility-as-decorum.

This is not to say, however, that any denial of civility should always be taken at face value, as Sarat's analysis of *Walker* evinces. San Francisco 49ers' quarterback Colin Kaepernick's silent protest in 2016, as he sat during the national anthem to protest racial oppression, provoked widespread outrage. Kaepernick was condemned as a "traitor," disrespectful to the flag.[53] But his protest, and the "take-a-knee" campaign that followed the next year, has been lawful and respectful. Construing it as a breach of civility-as-decorum seems exaggerated and disingenuous. Those in power often unjustly wield accusations of incivility to silence and stigmatize protesters—especially when these are Black.

The definition of civil disobedience as a public, nonviolent, nonevasive, respectful principled breach of law intended to persuade the majority captures well the public's rather narrow understanding of the boundaries of acceptable political protest. It constitutes a pared-down version of the standard Rawlsian account, as it does not include any subjective requirements such as the agent's endorsement of the system's legitimacy and acceptance of the moral duty to obey the law.

The basic norms of civility at the core of civil disobedience suggest the following features of uncivil disobedience: covertness, evasiveness, violence, and offensiveness. We might conceive of uncivil disobedience as a cluster concept, for whose application we treat any one of the four features—covertness, evasiveness, violence, and offensiveness—as sufficient. But, in recognition of the complexities of political action and difficulties of drawing clear definitional lines, I prefer to simply say that acts of principled disobedience that are covert, evasive, anonymous, more than minimally destructive, or deliberately offensive are *generally* uncivil, especially if they display more than one of these traits. Some acts of uncivil disobedience are primarily communicative, but many do not aim to persuade an audience—seeking instead to prevent or redress wrongs—though they may still include communicative elements. Examples include coercive strikes, riots, guerilla street art, DDoS actions, hunger strikes, covert assistance to undocumented immigrants, unauthorized whistleblowing, vigilantism, and the strategies commonly labeled as direct action, such as ecosabotage and animal rescue operations.

Strikes are coercive and violent when participants deploy force against employees who choose to work during the strike ("scabs") and those hired by the company to keep production running ("strikebreakers"). Riots involve collective public violence such as looting, property destruction, and harm against persons. Guerilla street art is covert and evasive, typically done under cover of night. DDoS actions are usually anonymous and evasive, and often coercive insofar as they enroll involuntary computer botnets through malware. Hunger strikes are evasive and coercive, involving threat of suicide and the deliberate and repeated defiance of official orders, and imposing serious burdens on the targeted authorities. Unauthorized whistleblowing poses serious risks of harms to persons, such as undercover agents and informants, and to national security. Vigilantism usually includes violence against persons. Ecosabotage involves deliberate and more than minimal destruction of property (e.g., monkey-wrenching) and sometimes the endangerment of persons (e.g., tree spiking).

Acts of conscientious objection, which fall in the category of principled disobedience when they are illegal (much conscientious objection is legally protected in liberal societies), may be civil or uncivil depending on the form they take. For instance, U.S. draftees could conscientiously object to the Vietnam War through public protests and civil disobedience or covertly and evasively—uncivilly—through draft dodging (e.g., escaping to Canada)—or both.

This concludes our conceptual investigation of resistance and disobedience. As we saw, the standard understanding of civil disobedience combines the philosophical, broadly Rawlsian conception of civil disobedience and the official narrative of the civil rights movement in the United States into an unrealistic and problematic conception of civil rights–style civil disobedience that serves to deter dissent and resistance. Minimalist accounts of civil disobedience, for their part, fail to be politically useful or phenomenologically accurate. I proposed instead a broad, multidimensional matrix of political resistance that includes principled disobedience, both civil and uncivil.

Chapter 2

In Defense of Uncivil Disobedience

A night like others in the Parisian banlieue (suburb) of Aulnay-sous-Bois: police stop youths and ask to check their ID, suspecting drug dealing. Théo L., a twenty-two-year-old Black social worker with no criminal record is arrested. An onlooker films the arrest, showing the young man tear-gassed, forced to the ground, and beaten by four policemen. Later Théo would tell TV interviewers that police hit him repeatedly, spitting racist insults. At some point, one of the officers took his telescopic baton and "he drove it into my buttocks . . . I had no strength left. It was as if my body had left myself. I thought I was going to die," Théo said from the hospital where he was treated for a "deep anal tear." The officers handcuffed him and took him to a police car, where he was again insulted, spat at, and beaten "in the private parts."

Théo's brutal arrest and rape in February 2017—which the French police called "an accident"—triggered protests against pervasive and systemic police brutality in several Parisian banlieues. In Bobigny, Argenteuil, and Saint-Denis, protesters and the anti-riot police clashed: police tear-gassed protesters, who in turn hurled bottles and stones at police. One resident described "young people with their faces hidden behind scarves carrying iron bars. There were bins filled with smoke overturned on the ground." Youths burned cars and buses, ransacked stores, and attacked police patrols. A public bus driver and a journalist covering the demonstration were injured. The police arrested dozens of protesters, including minors.

Even when their participants claim to be reacting to social injustice, riots—and the acts of looting, vandalism, property damage, and violence they comprise—are typically seen as politically counterproductive and morally impermissible. Political riots such as the French banlieues riots of 2017 and the ones that shook France in 2005 after the death of two teenagers during a police chase are an archetype of uncivil principled disobedience. I aim to show that some types of uncivil disobedience, including political riots, vigilante self-defense, whistleblowing, sanctuary assistance, and graffiti street art, can be justified—not in exceptional circumstances but systematically, and even in supposedly legitimate, liberal democratic states.

CONSTRAINTS

There is, we are told, a moral duty to obey the law in legitimate states—a duty grounded in widely accepted normative principles. It is my claim that these same principles can justify and even require resistance in the face of injustice, including resistance through principled disobedience. In later chapters, I will examine how these four grounds—the duty of justice, the duty of fairness, the Samaritan duty, and associative duties—justify and constrain the use of principled disobedience to resist injustice. For the moment, though, I wish to address some basic constraints on principled lawbreaking that apply especially to uncivil disobedience. These constraints allow us to distinguish between, say, the Ku Klux Klan's vigilante terrorism and the self-defensive vigilantism of the Deacons for Defense and Justice under Jim Crow, or between British feminist street artist Bambi's politically conscious graffiti and swastika vandalism.

Resistors must act with respect for other people's interests, including, but not limited to, their basic interests in life and bodily integrity; their interests in non-domination and in choosing the values that shape their lives; and their interest in protection by a stable, secure system of rights. That is, these basic human interests constrain both the legitimate goals and the appropriate means of resistance, and one should accept and seek to protect these basic interests when engaging in principled disobedience.

Of course resistors always act for the sake of some interests—the question is what kind of interests they pursue (Are they basic human interests or special interests of privileged groups?), and how to weigh these against other important interests when they come into conflict. Thus disobedience may affect the majority's interest in a stable legal system, but principled lawbreaking may sometimes be necessary to protect people's basic interests in life and bodily integrity. One may have to use force to defend oneself or others. And some violence, such as well-targeted destruction of property or the forceful removal of scabs during a strike, may be justified on balance to secure people's fundamental interest in non-domination—say, in having some control over the decisions that affect them.[1]

Resistors should generally seek the least harmful course of action feasible to achieve their (legitimate) goal, that is, from among those courses of action that have a reasonable chance of success. This constraint does not rise to the level of necessary condition for the justification of principled disobedience, in part because agents may sometimes justifiably settle for second or third best if, say, *the* least harmful course of action demands too much sacrifice on their part. That the course of action should have a reasonable chance of achieving the goal of resistance should not be misunderstood: it does not require that every act lead directly to reform or directly lessen oppression. Recall the variety of goals that may motivate resistance. A small act of everyday resistance, such as confronting a man's catcall or misogynist tweet, may only get one harassed; it certainly will not, in itself, change sexist mores. Yet its aim may simply be to force this man to reflect on his treatment of women. And it may be that an aggressive confrontation, likely to further antagonize the man, would not have a reasonable chance of succeeding at making him think, but that it would be successful if the goal is simply for the woman to assert her dignity and express anger at being objectified. In short, the success of resistance should not be measured solely in terms of the (good) social consequences it brings about (through direct action or policy reform): it may instead be measured by whether and how well it gets its message across to its intended audience (including, at the limit, oneself).

Note what respect for people's basic interests does *not* necessarily entail: it does not require that disobedients express themselves in a respectful tone, demonstrate moral seriousness, and exemplify self-restraint. The latter are demands of civility (they may also be a matter of political efficiency). One may respect people's basic interests un-civilly, in an offensive tone, using vulgarity and humor, expressing anger and even rage. Incivility does not necessarily violate people's basic interests.

IN DEFENSE OF (UN)CIVIL DISOBEDIENCE

Disobedience—even principled and civil—is generally conceived as wrongful for at least four reasons. First, disobedients violate the moral duty to obey the law, which binds citizens in legitimate states; second, disobedience undermines law and order and thereby destabilizes society; third, disobedients flout democratic processes; fourth, disobedients threaten "civic friendship," the social glue and ethos that binds people together. Champions of civil disobedience have responded to each objection successfully: today, few deny that civil disobedience can be justified and has a role to play in liberal democracy. But their justifications apply beyond the boundaries of civility, to justify some types of uncivil disobedience.

The Duty to Obey the Law

Many theorists believe that disobedience violates our political obligation, the moral duty to obey the law. In their view, it is essential that citizens of pluralist societies, in which people disagree about matters of justice, recognize this duty. Yet philosophers agree that the duty to obey the law (if it exists) is defeasible. In particular, it does not arise where injustice is severe and persistent. Civil disobedience can thus be justified at least where the moral duty to obey is nonbinding.

But this is not all: many theorists argue that civil disobedience is compatible with the moral duty to obey. For instance, David Lefkowitz has articulated a disjunctive account of political obligation according to which citizens of legitimate liberal democracies have a moral duty either to obey the law or to disobey it civilly.[2] The moral right to civil disobedience embedded in this account rests on citizens' basic right to political participation.

Importantly, in some cases, citizens might better respond to the normative principles that support the duty to obey the law by engaging in principled disobedience—civil or otherwise—rather than by complying with the law. This is what I show in chapters 3–6: that we should expand the concept of political obligation to include duties to resist injustice and disobey the law, even in liberal democracies, and that these duties rest on some of the same grounds commonly used to support the moral duty to obey the law.

Free-Riding

A second objection to disobedience is that it is a form of moral self-indulgence akin to free-riding: by according oneself a larger say in public matters, the agent objectionably allows a personal exception to prevailing rules.[3] The agent claims, in effect, to better understand what the public good requires than do fellow citizens. Asserting such privilege amounts to a violation of fairness or mutual reciprocity.

But civil disobedience has been adequately defended against such claims, and the same defense might be applied to uncivil disobedience: the disobedient agent does not profit from lawbreaking and indeed bears significant burdens and risks, including social sanctions, arrest, and punishment.[4] Let me add a caveat: the requirement that the agent not personally gain from disobedience is in fact problematic. People, especially those oppressed, have a lot to gain from the establishment of justice, including better life prospects, improved material conditions, and heightened self-respect. There is obviously nothing problematic with such personal investments in anti-oppression struggles.

In any case, the objection that unlawful resistance involves making oneself an exception or free-riding on others' compliance and thereby failing to treat others as equals does not withstand scrutiny. Agents often resort to disobedience because they, or those on whose behalf they act, or with whom they stand in solidarity, are marginalized and excluded, deprived of a say in the decisions that affect them. The oppressed are the ones treated as less than equals, and therefore disobedience intended to protest this inferior treatment cannot reasonably be thought of as violating mutual reciprocity.

Noncommunicative uncivil disobedience, such as direct action, however, calls for a different kind of response to the free-riding objection, since it does not necessarily seek to denounce the marginalization of some members of the community. For instance, agents providing covert assistance to migrants or engaged in vigilante self-defense aim first and foremost to prevent harms. Their apparent disregard for laws and the outcomes of democratic processes may seem like an assertion of moral superiority, a way to say, "I know better than everyone else what is right and wrong."

But this objection conceals the targets' own responsibility for the harms agents seek to prevent. When disobedients are justified, it is typically because the state endangers or harms some people or unjustly fails to protect them from harm. Thus the Lavender Panthers existed only because—and so long as—the San Francisco police did not intervene to protect gays from homophobic violence. The first sanctuary movement grew in the 1980s to help refugees from Central America who, although they were fleeing civil conflicts partly caused and sustained by the United States, were refused asylum in the country. Judging them as presumptuous and self-righteous seems misguided and unfounded.

If this is right, then cases of justified uncivil disobedience do not involve agents' making exceptions of themselves or free-riding on citizens' compliance with the law. Indeed, I will argue in chapter 4 that, under unjust sociopolitical conditions, citizens' compliance with the law, not disobedience, is akin to free-riding.

The Rule of Law

Another objection is that any disobedience—be it criminal or principled, civil or uncivil—sows anarchy and invites violence. A society where everyone disobeys all laws they find unjust would be no better than the state of nature, where everyone individually decides what is right and wrong.[5] States cannot tolerate such exercise of discretionary judgment. If one violates the law each time one thinks it is unjust, one destabilizes society and undermines law and order. Doing so is wrong because it prevents the legal system from performing its essential function of protecting rights.

In response, republican and liberal theorists have argued that, far from undermining the stable system of rights, civil disobedience can instead strengthen it. For Hannah Arendt, mass civil disobedience always occurs under unstable political circumstances and ultimately stabilizes society by reenacting the horizontal social contract (whereby the multitude becomes a people) and strengthening civic bonds.[6] Ronald Dworkin conceives of civil disobedients as engaged in constitutional disputes over the law and contributing in that way to law's integrity.[7] And Scheuerman argues that, far from undermining it, "civil disobedience buttresses the rule of law," as "fidelity to the law" demands "of conscientious political actors that they push for dramatic change that might deepen both law's legitimacy and its efficacy."[8] Beyond the particulars of these arguments, the potential of civil disobedience to protect rather than undermine the rule of law is now widely accepted in the literature, and to a lesser extent in public discourse.

What about uncivil disobedience, though? Can it also exemplify respect for the rule of law and serve to bolster law's integrity? I believe it can. Consider one type of uncivil principled disobedience purporting to preserve the rule of law: government whistleblowing, defined as unauthorized seizure and disclosure of state-classified information.

There are many plausible candidates for unauthorized whistleblowing that strengthened the rule of law: Daniel Ellsberg's leaks of the Pentagon Papers, which uncovered the state's commission of war crimes in Vietnam, Cambodia, and Laos, as well as deception at home; Deep Throat's leaks about the Watergate scandal, which resulted in punishment for others' lawbreaking; and Snowden's whistleblowing on the NSA's massive, unconstitutional domestic surveillance program.

Leaks of this nature, which expose serious wrongdoing and abuses, promote the rule of law. While many people describe instances of government whistleblowing they approve of as civil disobedience, in part because of their common potential to support the rule of law, it is important not to confuse the two. Government whistleblowing usually fails to adhere to norms of civility (especially publicity and non-evasiveness) and poses threats to national security by irreversibly undoing the secrecy the state had determined appropriate or necessary. Through their disclosure, government whistleblowers thus usurp the power of the state to determine, and to have exclusive authority over, the boundaries around state secrets. Government whistleblowing is thus typically uncivil in some ways, but it can be justified, like civil disobedience, on the grounds that it strengthens the rule of law. (In chapter 3, I will base the justification of whistleblowing more broadly on the duty of justice.)

Democracy

A fourth objection to disobedience is that it erodes democratic authority. By flouting democratic lawmaking processes, and refusing to comply with their outcomes, disobedients make themselves enemies of democratic ideals and undermine the conditions for democratic concord.

Liberal philosophers such as Rawls generally concede this objection: they view civil disobedience as essentially antidemocratic but highlight its potential to enhance justice, against flawed majoritarian decisions. These theorists stress that, by disobeying civilly, the agent communicates that she is neither disobeying lightly nor taking advantage of others' compliance with the law.

Republican and democratic theorists have articulated their alternative accounts of disobedience largely in response to this objection concerning democracy. They have shown that, far from threatening democracy, much civil disobedience purports to invigorate democratic institutions, for instance by combatting the rigidifying tendencies of state institutions and highlighting democratic deficits.[9] These theorists often use alter-globalization, anti-nuclear, and Occupy activism to illustrate this potential of civil disobedience. They make two important points. First, civil disobedients often protest precisely a lack of democracy, such as their exclusion from collective decision-making processes, and can thus advance democratic causes. Second, civil disobedience should be conceived as an exercise in political participation, not as an extra-institutional form of action that is only appropriate when normal political processes fail.

I reflect later in the chapter on the question of whether some communicative acts of uncivil disobedience should be conceived as a form of political participation. But for now, I simply want to show that the first point about the democratic potential of civil disobedience can apply to uncivil disobedience, too. To this end, Cornell Clayton persuasively argues that incivility is a "symptom of division," not the source of it. To dismiss incivility as a threat to an otherwise-stable democracy is most likely to assert stability (the kind that stems from a shared commitment to mutual reciprocity) where it has already been lost. Clayton further notes that "uncivil behavior has often advanced democratic causes" in contexts of division.[10]

A look at historical and current practices of resistance indeed suggests that agents may choose uncivil forms of disobedience to the same democratic effects that theorists attribute to civil disobedience. The suffragists escalated from words to deeds—first civil then uncivil disobedience—to demand the democratic franchise. Some of their uncivil acts, such as storming legislative assemblies and electoral precincts, as well as burning with acid the golf course and bowling greens frequented by Members of Parliament, were clearly intended to assert political agency and protest exclusion. More recently, hacktivists such as the late Aaron Swartz have used digital disobedient tactics—mostly uncivil—to protest the illegitimacy of online governance and invite fellow citizens to understand, care about, and participate in the effort to democratize the internet. Some guerrilla communication tactics, such as those of ACT UP (the AIDS Coalition to Unleash Power), may also be framed as uncivil protests against government apathy in the face of the AIDS crisis and against the public's wrongful indifference to the fate of the LGBTQ population (a violation of the democratic imperative to treat everyone with full concern and as equals). For instance, a 1989 ACT UP protest against pharmaceutical price-gouging on the floor of the New York Stock Exchange stopped trading for the first time in history. Later that year, nearly five thousand protesters stood outside New York's St. Patrick's Cathedral to denounce the Catholic Church's opposition to safe sex education, while a few dozen ACT UP and WHAM! (Women's Health Action and Mobilization) activists went inside to interrupt mass, chant slogans, lay down in the aisles, and even desecrate communion wafers. As these examples suggest, there may be uncivil pursuits of democratic inclusiveness, agenda-setting, and other measures to improve democratic legitimacy.

To recap, none of the four objections—from the duty to obey, free-riding, the rule of law, and democracy—sets a viable moral prohibition against principled disobedience. Meanwhile, the arguments offered in response by champions of civil disobedience can be extended to justify some uncivil forms of principled lawbreaking. However, one might object that this extension of the instrumental value of civil disobedience to uncivil disobedience ignores the moral significance of civility. In the next section, I respond to arguments for preferring civil over uncivil disobedience and identify some valuable uses of incivility.

WHO'S AFRAID OF INCIVILITY?

Effectiveness

It is almost an article of faith that incivility is counterproductive. This is clearest in the ordinary (and near-universal) approval of nonviolent resistance and disapproval of violent resistance. Some empirical evidence backs up the point. Analyzing 323 twentieth-century violent and nonviolent civil resistance campaigns, Erica Chenoweth and Maria Stephan find that nonviolent campaigns that have reached a significant size are twice as likely to succeed as violent campaigns. (It is worth noting, however, that most of the civil resistance movements they classify as nonviolent, from the anti-apartheid struggle in South Africa to the First Palestinian Intifada, often in fact include violent flanks. A movement is violent, in their view, if it rests primarily on armed insurrection.) While many violent decolonization movements were successful in the 1970s and 1980s, the success of violent resistance campaigns has since declined. For their part, nonviolent campaigns have become increasingly successful since the 1950s, and especially since the end of the Cold War.[11]

While this statistical argument for nonviolence holds across sociopolitical contexts, political scientists argue that violence is especially counterproductive in liberal societies. Chenoweth has recently warned against anti-Trump resistance by means of uncivil, "black block" tactics such as Nazi punching, street fighting, and rioting.[12] The main rationale is that the public is turned off by violent protests, which therefore risk undermining the objectives of an otherwise-nonviolent movement. She and Stephan estimate that available social scientific and historical evidence supports the "negative radical flank effect" better than the "positive radical flank effect": that violence decreases rather than increases the leverage of challengers, by threatening mass mobilization.[13]

These are important findings. But note that the argument asserts equivalence between civility and nonviolence. When we keep the two features distinct, we realize that nonviolent acts of uncivil principled disobedience—such as leaks, which proliferate in Trump's White House, and guerrilla communication—are not singled out as problematic and may be useful to civil protests. In addition, not all principled disobedience is communicative, and that which is nonviolent and covert is unlikely to be detected by the public and to have the negative effects supposedly associated with failures of civility.

More generally, effectiveness may not be measured solely in terms of contribution to a mass civil resistance campaign. Individual actions may be socially beneficial ("effective") whether or not they lead to reform. Thus the Lavender Panthers' organized use of self-defensive violence against homophobic aggressors in San Francisco in the 1970s can be justified, even if violence shouldn't be used in the larger political struggle for gay rights. Covert (uncivil) disobedience—such as that undertaken by sanctuary workers as they provide food, shelter, and legal aid to unauthorized migrants—can directly frustrate injustice and benefit people in dire need in ways that are not available to civil disobedients.

So the empirical argument for the superior effectiveness of nonviolent resistance and civil disobedience in the context of large movements does not suffice to establish uncivil disobedience's ineffectiveness or counterproductivity. In fact, uncivil disobedience may be effective for other purposes.

Forward-Looking Concerns

Why prefer civil over uncivil disobedience? Another instrumental or pragmatic rationale points to the socially beneficial consequences of civil disobedience as compared with uncivil disobedience. It comes in two versions, which are both grounded in forward-looking concerns, and boil down to the notion that resistors should choose courses of action that enact and foster the just society they aspire to.

One version of this pragmatic argument is encapsulated in the principle "the means should prefigure the end." According to this principle, which is generally attributed to political anarchists, the values guiding resistance in liberation struggles should be those animating the ideal world. The "should" here is pragmatic or prudential: one simply cannot achieve a just, egalitarian society free from oppression and state violence through a movement that is hierarchically organized and that uses violence to dominate others. In the words of James Guillaume, a friend and collaborator of Mikhail Bakunin, "How could one want an equalitarian and free society to issue from an authoritarian organization? It is impossible."[14] From this perspective, prefiguration is a necessary condition for liberation movements' success (at least where ideals of justice, freedom, and equality are concerned). More basically, a struggle whose participants routinely violate its expressed ideals falls prey to charges of inconsistency and hypocrisy, which are likely to diminish public support and to affect the movement's legitimacy. This prefiguration argument can thus support the superiority of civil over uncivil disobedience, presuming that one seeks a civil future characterized by democratic concord.

On the other version of the pragmatic argument, even if the ruling group's mistreatment of a subordinated group warrants revolutionary activity, and even if revolution could succeed (contrary to the prefiguration argument), there are still good forward-looking reasons for resistors to exercise restraint and disobey civilly. Andrew Sabl develops this argument for civil disobedience in the context of the "piecewise-just society," which involves "fair treatment, mutual cooperation, and a sense of justice by a ruling group with respect to its own members, simultaneous with a cruel and near-absolute tyranny towards people outside its own membership."[15] Powerful members of society, by dominating and brutalizing other groups in society, may well have made themselves liable to violent resistance. But the fact that they have shown themselves capable of governing on fair terms of cooperation within their own group offers reasons to believe in their capacity "to extend this habit to their relations to other groups," and thus to disobey civilly, in a way that treats current oppressors as future equals.[16] According to Sabl, "a regard for future possibilities," especially "the desire not to foreclose future coopera- tion," underpinned King's civil rights movement, for instance.[17] In short, civil disobedience offers the best (perhaps the only) chance of fostering the prospects for post-struggle democratic concord, by displaying equal concern for all and a commitment to fair coopera- tion in the struggle. I address this second point in the next section, where I contend that sometimes powerful members have shown themselves capable of governing fairly among equals, but not willing to extend this capacity beyond their own group.

One strategy to respond to the prefiguration argument for civil disobedience consists in denying that resistance need be guided by the values it aims to promote. History casts doubt on the anar- chist argument that freedom from oppression is not possible unless resistors abide by the ideals that motivate their struggle in the first place, as many successful decolonization movements involved vio- lence (and there is no reason to attribute the extent to which some of these movements historically failed to establish stable democratic regimes to their use of violence in the struggle). Norman Geras defends revolutionary violence on the grounds that the means "re- flect their own beginnings"—that is, the oppression and tyranny that revolutionaries seek to overcome.[18] Lisa Tessman has argued that re- sistance to oppressive circumstances may need to be guided by values that we would normally condemn—such as rage and hatred—in order to successfully lead to a just, hate-free society.[19] Angela Davis's vindication of African Americans' armed self-defense against racist violence and Ta-Nehisi Coates's skepticism toward ubiquitous calls for nonviolence in a society founded upon and engaged in violence illustrate this strategy at work.

It is also not clear that activists disposed to use some uncivil, including violent, methods in the struggle for emancipation are thereby exhibiting inconsistency or betraying their ends. For instance, did female suffragists who burned golf course turfs with acid and engaged in other acts of sabotage and destruction reveal their unfitness to cooperate with men in the gender-just society they envisioned? Opponents thought so, calling the suffragists "unladylike" and "unnatural" and successfully committing some of them to insane asylums. These opponents claimed that women's uncivil disobedience was a living refutation of their feminist ideal of gender equality. Yet nothing supported these judgments. Uncivil disobedience neither necessarily reflects problematic ideals and goals nor necessarily thwarts the possibility for future cooperation with fellow citizens.

(In)civility and Civic Friendship

Civil disobedience is supposed to be better than uncivil disobedience not just because, as we have seen, it leads to superior outcomes, but also because civility is a moral duty in liberal democracy. Citizens of liberal democracies have a special duty to comport themselves in ways that nurture and preserve civic bonds. Aristotle talked about "civic friendship" to describe citizens' bonds in just polities, their concern for each other's flourishing (they "wish their fellow citizens well"), and their shared values and sense of justice.[20] The modern, liberal version of civic friendship is thinner but still important: it consists in citizens' willingness to live together despite their differences and their common endorsement of mutual reciprocity.[21]

Law-abidance and civil interpersonal relations cement the ties of civic friendship in large modern states, while refusal to abide by the law and incivility dissolve these bonds. In Rawls's words, "[r]esistance cuts the ties of community."[22] But liberal theorists showed that, by acting civilly, disobedients still demonstrate their commitment to mutual reciprocity. The civility of civil disobedience, in short, defuses its tendency to erode civic bonds and destabilize society. Theorists thus carved a special niche for civil disobedience as the only form of unlawful resistance compatible with the demands of life in a liberal democracy. (Conscientious objection might be viewed as another form, but to the extent that it is to be not simply tolerated but also legally protected in liberal societies, it should not count as unlawful resistance.)

Uncivil disobedience, by definition, violates civility, and so could potentially damage civic friendship. One might respond by examining contexts and types of uncivil disobedience that are unlikely to undermine civic friendship, such as covert assistance to undocumented migrants. But let us instead agree that some types of communicative uncivil disobedience—urban riots and anti-police rallies, for instance—are in fact likely to undermine civic friendship. My contention is that this may be a virtue rather than a problem: in some circumstances, uncivil disobedience may appropriately highlight—and, yes, undermine—all-too-flimsy or illusory ties of civic friendship. It may do so in ways that advance the cause of justice and democracy. But even where there is no hope of sociopolitical reform or moral suasion, uncivil disobedience may still have intrinsic value insofar as it constitutes a meaningful expression of political solidarity and assertion of agency in the face of injustice.

There is a place for uncivil disobedience in liberal democratic societies when the following conditions apply: the public is assured of the state's commitment to respecting everyone's full and equal status, a commitment typically embedded in a constitution or other basic law that guides institutional design and lawmaking; some citizens are effectively (de facto but not de jure) denied full and equal status;

and the injustice of this denial is not publicly recognized, perhaps because that injustice is not deliberate but results from the interplay of
social practices and institutional structures, as in cases of structural
injustice. Under these circumstances, the majority may be bound by
civic friendship, but for oppressed minorities, it is an illusion.

In this case, the oppressed minority might fruitfully resort to
civil disobedience, and no doubt observers will counsel that doing
so provides the best chance of winning over the majority, based on
the forward-looking concerns previously articulated. But uncivil disobedience might be more effective because of its ability to radically
disrupt the status quo. Uncivil disobedients force the community to
confront the disconnect between its reality and its professed ideals.
Put another way, by appearing to question civic friendship, they
question the authenticity of the community's commitment to that
friendship. Incivility calls civility's bluff.

Uncivil disobedience also questions the rules of public engagement, the standards and boundaries of civility and public reason: who
gets to speak, as well as where, when, and how. In doing so, uncivil
disobedience helps to isolate the deceptions of civic friendship. Pussy
Riot and Femen model this powerfully. Their sensational "sextremist"
acts reveal the patriarchy that actual civic friendship accommodates
and present that evil as an adversary to confront and offend. By not
playing by the rules, uncivil disobedients point to the exclusionary
effects of established rules and invite their rethinking. They contest
and disrupt the moral and political consensus.

Some democratic theorists like Celikates insist that civil disobedience, broadly conceived to include what is on my view uncivil
disobedience, can achieve this sort of disruption. But I think it is important to distinguish civil from uncivil disobedience, in order to denounce disingenuous brandings of incivility and explore the distinct
potential of acts of uncivil disobedience. BLM protesters marching
with their hands raised in surrender and chanting "Hands up, don't

shoot!" have been called "troublemakers" and deemed uncivil. The lie of civic friendship is clear in the refusal to grant civility to opponents of the status quo. What ties of community are there if the majority cannot bring itself to hear oppressed minorities even when they follow all of the strictures of civility?

Compare these civil protests to uncivil events loosely associated with, but not organized by, the Movement for Black Lives: rock-throwing, looting, and rioting, as in Ferguson, Baltimore, Charlotte, and Milwaukee in the aftermath of fatal instances of police violence against Blacks. Avia Pasternak refers to the unrest in these US cities, as well as the uprisings in the Paris banlieues in 2005, as "political rioting," defined as "a form of political protest against injustice, which involves the public and illegal use of collective violence, and which aims to express outrage, frustration and defiance of the law."[23] Pasternak argues that political riots can be partially justified in the face of serious and persistent injustice, in light of the valuable goals they can serve: democratic inclusion, expression of collective defiance and disrespect, and legal reform. The riots in Ferguson, Baltimore, and the French banlieues may be seen as aiming at all three goals: inclusion of poor Black and Brown urban youth in the public sphere, popular expression of frustration at and distrust of the state, and direct democratic community control of law enforcement agencies.

The rioters issued their demand to end police brutality by putting into question the society's professed commitment to mutual reciprocity and forcing the wider population to examine who exactly is tied together by the bonds of civic friendship. The only honest response, these riots suggest, is not everyone. Those left outside the bonds must use means that civic friendship abhors because they are not allowed to participate on civil terms. The civil protests of BLM may well have articulated the same claim, but political riots were more successful in projecting the seriousness of the problem, in part by threatening further disruption. Civil disobedients cannot vex the status quo in the same way. As Susan Bickford has argued, civility (or "niceness") "can make people less likely to perceive actual injustice and oppression"[24]—and, I shall add, less likely to perceive the urgency of certain rights claims.

That society took notice of the riots does not mean they achieved their goals. The frustration expressed in rioting has not induced any recognition and shame in White Americans' (or Frenchmen's) consciousness. In fact the public now views protests against police violence even more negatively than in 2014, at the start of the BLM movement. According to a Harvard-Harris survey conducted in July 2017, a majority of Americans (57 percent) "feels unfavorable towards Black Lives Matter protests." Only 35 percent of Whites feel favorably toward the movement.[25] The problem is not simply that most people remain unmoved; it is that they don't hear the rioters' speech—don't take the riots to be conveying anything but violence. This lack of reception—often the result of moral and epistemic deafness to Black suffering, which Charles Mills calls "White ignorance"—helps to clarify why we should not prioritize civic friendship: the inability to recognize struggle even when it is declared straightforwardly is symptomatic of the divisions within the polity.[26] Civic friendship is dead long before rioters come to bury it.

Hence my defense of uncivil disobedience—including of some political riots—does not rest on the larger community's successful uptake of, let alone political or moral conversion in response to, messages conveyed uncivilly. Uncivil disobedients may have no hope of bringing about any changes anyway. They may have no reason to believe in the dominant group's willingness to include marginalized and powerless groups into the social cooperative venture. Recall that the forward-looking argument for civil disobedience is based on the oppressors' demonstrated capacity to govern as full and equals among themselves, and expected capacity to extend this kind of government to everyone. But this capacity to govern fairly, without the *willingness* to do so, hinders rather than hints at future concord. Yet it is worthwhile for uncivil disobedients to express their indignation at the inauthenticity of the public commitment to mutual reciprocity, even if it turns out to be counterproductive to the goal of persuading the public.

Protesters' central goal is often to grow the movement's base rather than to garner public support. "The most likely audience to join the cause," Amna A. Akbar notes about the protests associated with the Movement for Black Lives, "is not White people, but other Black folks."[27] It is easy to overlook this "internal audience" of protests while focusing on messages to the larger public. Political riots too have an internal audience: fellow oppressed people. It is to the latter that rioters address themselves, when they highlight illusory ties of civic friendship and repudiate society's unfair treatment of certain groups. By pointing to a shared landscape of oppression, uncivil disobedients further express solidarity with fellow oppressed people. Finally, their expressions of disrespect and anger may be seen as assertions of agency and dignity in the face of threats to both. Certain kinds of uncivil disobedience are thus non-instrumentally valuable—as warranted judgments about society's failures, as expressions of solidarity, and as affirmations of agency.

To recap, acts of uncivil disobedience do not necessarily erode civic friendship, but even when they do, they may be justified on the (broadly liberal and democratic) grounds that they contribute to advancing justice and democracy, by jolting the public into recognizing pressing claims of oppression. And even if acts of uncivil disobedience are counterproductive to the broader goal of affecting sociopolitical change, they may still constitute intrinsically valuable expressions of dissent, solidarity, and agency. Acts of uncivil disobedience that threaten a concord that wrongly excludes some people can thus be justified, under certain circumstances.

Traditional liberal theorists are not wrong to understand civility as a good thing. We should not underestimate the importance of respect for others as equals or of a commitment to mutual reciprocity. The trouble is that we, even those of us in democratic societies, do not live in a world of equals. The constraints civility imposes on subjects of pluralist modern societies are reasonable under conditions of basic equality, such as among privileged and powerful populations (although the latter sometimes may elect, and even ought, to join uncivil protests in solidarity with those oppressed). Indeed civility reasonably constrains the behavior of members of society who are secure in their position of privilege or power, especially as they relate to disadvantaged members of society. But those who shoulder the burdens of oppression cannot reasonably be expected to satisfy the demands of civility, since these demands aim to preserve civic bonds that do not extend to them and even serve to maintain their oppression (recall the ideological function of the widespread calls for civility which I described in chapter 1). Incivility may therefore be appropriate—and uncivil disobedience may be justified—where agents are oppressed, silenced, and otherwise marginalized.

IMPLICATIONS

What follows from this defense of uncivil disobedience? Agents engaged in justified acts of uncivil disobedience are doing the right thing. They may be doing something presumptively wrongful (breaking the law, offending, resorting to force or coercion), but they are not doing wrong on balance, under the circumstances. One might be tempted to say that they have an excuse for what they did. But excuses are inseparable from admissions of wrongdoing. To excuse someone is to explain why they had reason to believe they were doing the right thing even though they didn't. Justifications are different: they point to the reasons for acting the way the agent in fact acted. The next four chapters are devoted to identifying these reasons: they show that the duty of justice, the duty of fair play, the Samaritan duty, and political associative duties, which are commonly used to ground obedience, provide weighty, binding reasons for resisting injustice, including through principled—civil and uncivil—disobedience.

Agents who engage in justified acts of uncivil disobedience deserve praise in recognition of the difficulties of fulfilling one's political obligations under unjust conditions (chapter 7 is devoted to these difficulties). What does this imply for how the state should treat them? I will not say much about this important question, mainly because I think we need to change hearts and minds about uncivil disobedience before having any chance of changing the law. That is why the book is devoted to political ethics, not legal issues.

But, to speak to the matter only briefly, I believe the state should treat uncivil disobedience differently from civil disobedience. Recent theorists defend a moral right to engage in civil disobedience, on the basis of which civil disobedients deserve special treatment from the state. Lefkowitz, who derives the moral right to civil disobedience from the more general right of political participation, contends that civil disobedients have a moral claim against punishment (i.e., condemnation) but not penalty, which states impose for the purpose of deterring conduct.[28] William Smith likewise conceives of the moral right to civil disobedience as an "important component of the bundle of rights to political participation that would be affirmed by a reasonable conception of justice," and argues that it protects citizens from the imposition of punishment but is compatible with moderate penalties.[29] For Brownlee, who bases the moral right to civil disobedience on a humanistic principle of respect for agency and dignity, this right implies a claim right against both punishment and penalty. She defends two criminal defenses for principled disobedience, one exculpatory—the "demands-of-conviction defense"—and one justificatory—the "necessity defense."[30]

The moral right to civil disobedience, whatever its basis, implies the permissibility of civil disobedient acts, independently of their justification. I do not defend such right to uncivil disobedience, since when uncivil disobedience is not justified, it is often also morally impermissible. But when uncivil disobedience is morally justified, in my view, agents ought not to be punished by the state. This does not mean that agents should have a legal right to disobey. What it does mean is that law enforcement officers should choose not to arrest agents, prosecutors should decide to drop criminal charges against defendants, judges should exercise leniency in sentencing, and juries should choose not to convict defendants (jury nullification).

This is unlikely to happen as a matter of course, especially in regimes regulated by defective principles of political morality. But at the very least, liberal democratic societies must provide all principled disobedients with the opportunity to defend their actions in trial. They do not always have this opportunity. For instance, should Snowden return to the United States to face justice for his leaks of classified information, the terms of the Espionage Act would bar him from attempting to justify his actions. Even where disobedients have the opportunity to defend their actions, the chances of succeeding are slim given that the injustice agents were responding to in the first place probably infect the courtroom, too, typically in the form of prejudice and its attending testimonial injustice.[31]

In any case, the reasons for action identified in the following chapters could ground justificatory defenses for principled disobedients of all kinds, whether civil or uncivil: a public-interest defense on the basis of the duty of justice, a necessity defense similar to Brownlee's on the basis of the Samaritan duty, a fairness-based defense invoking the duty of fair play, and a dignitary defense on the basis of political association. Although I shall not further discuss these, they are all possible legal implications of this account of political duties to resist.

Chapter 3

Justice and Democracy

In 2016 and 2017, two huge troves of documents threw light on the shady world of offshore finance. The first, known as the Panama Papers, exposed the Panama-based law firm Mossack Fonseca's creation of secret offshore havens to facilitate tax evasion for "politicians, fraudsters and drug traffickers as well as billionaires, celebrities and sports stars."[1] The second, known as the Paradise Papers—its name evokes both the French term for offshore haven, *paradis fiscal*, and the beautiful islands where offshore finance firms tend to be located—leaked from Bermuda-based Appleby, the world's most prestigious offshore law firm. The Paradise Papers confirmed how widespread and easy tax evasion is for the super wealthy.

These leaked documents show that billionaires, corporations, universities, oligarchs, criminals, artists, top officials, and at least one head of state conceal their assets behind offshore shell companies, evade taxes and scrutiny, and invest in industries that the public finds objectionable. For instance, Britain's Queen Elizabeth's private estate invests millions of pounds offshore, including in Brighthouse, a financial lender accused of irresponsible practices. Northeastern University, which ranks fourth in the GreenMetric Ranking of World Universities for its sustainable campus (and first in the United States), invests part of its endowment in fossil fuels. And some of the politicians who set the laws governing offshore funds were identified as major clients of offshore firms.

Appleby argues that it does nothing illegal in providing banking and tax services to its clients. But offshore financial secrecy is nonetheless a threat to justice and democracy. Systematic tax evasion by the rich flouts the spirit of the law, undermines democratic equality, and demoralizes ordinary citizens. The editorial writers at *Le Monde* understood this, characterizing the underworld revealed by the Paradise Papers as "democratic hell."[2]

The Panama and Paradise Papers were leaked illegally and anonymously. Could the whistleblowers have been fulfilling their duty of justice? I believe so. The natural duty of justice is a common basis for the moral duty to obey the law. In this chapter I argue that it also grounds political obligations to resist injustice, including through principled, uncivil, and covert disobedience such as leaking.

To say that the duty of justice is natural is to say that it is grounded in our nature as moral beings and binds us all equally, regardless of our relations or voluntary undertakings. According to Rawls, the duty of justice has two components: "First, we are to comply with and to do our share in just institutions when they exist and apply to us; and second we are to assist in the establishment of just arrangements when they do not exist, at least when this can be done with little cost to ourselves."[3] The first part of the duty of justice implies a moral duty to obey the law of one's just or nearly just state. Where institutions are unjust, the second part of the duty of justice implies a duty to help repair or replace them.

Since Rawls, inspired by Kant, made the case for this duty in *A Theory of Justice*, it has been the most widely embraced source of political obligation. Jeremy Waldron, Thomas Christiano, Anna Stilz, William Smith, and Daniel Viehoff, among others, have defended their own accounts.[4] Although these theorists' accounts of political obligation differ, the structures of their arguments are similar. Each contends that the natural duty of justice requires submitting to the state and each places a limit on the duty to obey the law at the border of legitimate (liberal, democratic) states. That is, the duty of justice both grounds and limits the duty to obey the law. It addresses individuals as free and equal citizens and therefore cannot obligate them to maintain legal and sociopolitical conditions that deny people that free and equal status.

CONTEXTS OF INJUSTICE

If the duty to obey is dissolved by serious injustice, we need to know what constitutes that sort of injustice. Existing theories give us a number of boundary conditions to work with. Rawls stressed that the moral duty to obey extends to unjust laws, unless they are grave and entrenched. Stilz argues that citizens are morally bound to obey laws they consider unjust, "as long as these laws do not violate core aspects of external freedom," which she conceives of as the sphere of basic rights that constitutes persons' independence or self-determination.[5] According to Smith, the duty binds citizens so long as an unjust law "can be defended in terms that are reasonable"—that is, so long as the law is not blatantly unjustifiable.[6] Beyond these limits, however one might draw them, injustice defeats the duty to obey. Within these limits, the duty to obey obtains.

How do we know which side of the limit we are on? There will of course be disagreements over whether particular laws are unjust, and to what degree they are. But we can try to achieve greater clarity on the content of injustice. Doing so enables us to specify the target of resistance, which is in turn essential to assessing particular acts of principled disobedience. A typology of injustice is thus an important tool in our examination of political obligations within broadly legitimate societies.

Smith provides one in *Civil Disobedience and Deliberative Democracy*. He distinguishes three kinds of injustice that can be appropriate objects of civil disobedience in legitimate democratic states. *Deliberative disrespect* occurs "where a democratic majority tolerates or enacts blatant injustices," publicly denying some of citizens free and equal status. *Deliberative disagreement* designates unjust outcomes neither "blatant" nor "obvious." *Deliberative inertia* arises when certain issues or discourses are blocked from the public sphere.[7] According to Smith, Rawls considers only deliberative disrespect, thus overlooking the possibility of justifiable civil disobedience whose object is not obvious and egregious injustice. Civil disobedience undertaken against the first two kinds of injustice guards and enhances justice, while disobedience against the third kind of injustice can promote democracy.

However, the inevitability of disagreements about the severity of injustice makes Smith's distinction between deliberative disrespect and disagreement less helpful than it might otherwise be. I shall propose merging these two categories under the simple label *disrespect*, and carving out another category, *wrongs to nonmembers*, to designate states' commission of injustice against noncitizens at home or abroad. Smith's typology is also incomplete because it emphasizes the democratic assembly and neglects other institutions of government. We must keep in mind another context of injustice, *official misconduct*, cognizant of state officials' conduct, which I will describe. Finally, I will identify a fifth context of injustice, *public ignorance*, to mark cognitive deficits in the public sphere distinct from those of deliberative inertia.

Disrespect

Deliberative disrespect, according to Smith, consists of democratic majorities' enactment or toleration of laws that publicly and blatantly deny some citizens free and equal status. This category is meant to capture both isolated iniquitous laws and systematic injustice that impedes citizens' participation in public life. Smith's examples of deliberative disrespect are denial of the right to vote or stand for office and failures to secure the law's equal protection. These injustices— such as slavery, racial segregation, and women's disenfranchisement— are unjustifiable and thus cancel the duty to comply.[8]

Smith's second context of injustice—deliberative disagreement— designates outcomes of democratic debate that are unjust, even seriously unjust, but not clearly and obviously so. Therefore, they do not override the duty to comply.[9] Gender inequalities, institutionalized homophobia, and inadequate protections for workers and immigrants exemplify deliberative disagreement. These injustices are permissible and appropriate targets of civil disobedience, but they are unlikely to strike everyone as blatant and they can be defended in reasonable terms. Deliberative disrespect, in contrast, produces clear-cut cases of oppression in the form of indefensible laws.

But history suggests the inadequacy of this criterion. Even as slavery, women's disenfranchisement, and racial segregation were being scrapped, they had plenty of articulate, reasonable proponents. The Supreme Court defended racial segregation in publicly reasonable terms in *Plessy v. Ferguson*. Jim Crow laws stood for decades precisely because they were facially race-neutral and therefore arguably not unconstitutional under the Fourteenth Amendment. Today we see these injustices as blatant and egregious, but they may well have exemplified deliberative disagreement in their time. Of course, the test of time is not a useful standard, since we want to assess the gravity of current injustices.

For this reason, we should fold the category of deliberative disagreement into that of disrespect, and understand disrespect as public denial of citizens' free and equal status. We should also drop the "deliberative," which wrongly suggests that these injustices result from a process of free deliberation among equals committed to advance the common good. Respecting citizens' free and equal status means treating them as full moral agents, with equal standing in the social institutions and political processes, and endowed with dignity (more on this in chapter 6, which develops a dignitarian account of associative political obligations to resist injustice).

Some cases of disrespect are more serious and more obvious than others, although obviousness does not necessarily track seriousness. Recent examples of disrespect in the more encompassing sense I propose include the U.S. Defense of Marriage Act (1996), which denied same-sex couples the right to marry (struck down by the Supreme Court in *Obergefell v. Hodges*[10]); anti-trans bathroom policies such as North Carolina's HB2, which conditions bathroom access to sex assigned at birth; the French Riviera's "burkini bans" prohibiting the full-body swimwear some Muslim women wear at the beach[11]; solitary confinement of prisoners (including juveniles); and exploitation of prison labor. Grave economic injustices, including low or nonexistent minimum wages, efforts to debilitate labor unions, and laws facilitating the concentration of wealth and power can also fall in the category of disrespect, if citizens can claim that their free and equal status is threatened or violated by economic injustice.

Wrongs to Nonmembers

We also need to carve out another category involving grave injustice but not public denial of citizens' free and equal status. We need such a category because states may commit or tolerate egregious injustices against noncitizens. Policies that disregard the basic interests of authorized or unauthorized migrants, impose lengthy detention without charges, deport people for minor crimes, and break up nuclear families are contemptuous of the integrity of persons and appear seriously wrong.[12] Developed countries' recent refusals to take in more than very small numbers of asylum seekers displaced by conflict in the Middle East may provide another example.[13] I call the democratic enactment or toleration of violations of the basic rights and dignity of noncitizens, at home or abroad, *wrongs to nonmembers*. Such indignities may also be inflicted on nonhuman animals such as whales and dolphins held captive in water parks. Democratic states that license these practices may be found to be wronging nonmembers.

One might argue that what matters for political legitimacy and the moral duty to obey the law is how the state treats its own citizens, not how it treats migrants and animals in its midst or other people abroad. But this is debatable. Thoreau's case for the moral duty not to comply with U.S. law rested on the state's brutal domination of noncitizens—Native Americans and slaves. Justice did not demand full U.S. citizenship for indigenous people in Thoreau's time; instead it prohibited colonizing, displacing, and massacring them. In short, the gravity of wrongs to nonmembers and the extent to which they undermine political legitimacy is not necessarily tied to democratic exclusion. It relates to the harms inflicted on certain groups.

Deliberative Inertia

Deliberative inertia, a concept I borrow from Smith, designates breakdowns of public deliberation that occur when certain agendas and discussions are blocked from or fail to surface in the public sphere.[14] Such inertia inspired early environmental, animal rights, and alter-globalization activism, as well as the Occupy movement, which protested the lack of public attention to economic inequality while calling for democratic deliberation about the issue. According to Smith, deliberative inertia does not defeat the duty to comply with the law, but it is an appropriate target of civil disobedience.

Among other things, digital rights provide a significant current example of deliberative inertia. Increasingly, disobedient activism has targeted copyright laws, digital surveillance, and privacy violations enabled by companies and governments that structure the internet with little democratic input (and flawed input at that, since issues that do come up for democratic deliberation are poorly tackled due to representatives' basic lack of understanding of the issues[15]). Lawrence Lessig has shown how the United States shaped the digital world into a surveillance- and commerce-friendly space by exporting, through technology product sales, an "architecture that facilitates control."[16] Bernard Harcourt has recently argued that the internet is governed by a "tentacular oligarchy" that ties private and public institutions in state-like "knots of power" and engages in increasingly sophisticated surveillance of people's on- and offline behavior.[17]

Freedom of speech does not extend to the online world since speech is constrained by the decision-making of corporate intermediaries, including internet service providers; web hosting providers; and social network operators such as Facebook, Amazon, PayPal, and Apple. Ethan Zuckerman dubs this phenomenon the "threat of intermediary censorship": the ability to speak online is always mediated by commercial entities, whose terms of service generally give a great deal of discretion to the content host and few protections to the end user.[18] In *Consent of the Networked*, Rebecca MacKinnon makes a persuasive case for the democratic deficiencies of laws governing cyberspace, all the while expressing faith in the internet's potential to invigorate democracy, and come itself under democratic control.[19]

Official Misconduct

To Smith's typology, I believe we should add another form of injustice: official misconduct. This occurs when state authorities routinely violate the duties associated with their office. Official misconduct was one of the central pillars of Jim Crow, as local authorities— including police, prosecutors, and courts—failed to apply the law for the protection and benefit of African Americans. Police brutality was essential to the systematic production of terror. Bombing, assault, and murder were more or less officially sanctioned and often encouraged. Many state officials, judges and police, as members of the Ku Klux Klan, engaged in lynching. That and other forms of violence against Blacks were outlawed under Jim Crow, but they were rarely prosecuted. Blacks were prevented from serving on juries, and when Whites were prosecuted for crimes against Blacks, they could be confident that White jurors would vote to acquit them. These illegal practices were routine and occurred in the open. Officials who did not conform were intimidated, harassed, or worse. Efforts were made, sometimes successfully, to turn such illegal practices into law.[20] David Lyons dubs this "the legal entrenchment of illegality."[21] I simply call these wrongful executive and judicial practices "official misconduct."

One might object that official misconduct is but a facet of disrespect, since the latter, on Smith's account, includes the toleration, not just the enactment, of blatant injustice and encompasses the failure to secure protections of the rule of law. But the illegal or extralegal nature of official misconduct goes beyond majority enactment or toleration of blatant injustices. Its inclusion in a separate category thus underscores the different loci and mechanisms of injustice in contexts such as Jim Crow. Of course, carving out this category does not prevent us considering ways in which these distinct mechanisms of injustice can work in tandem.

Official misconduct similar to that of the Jim Crow era continues in the United States. Police brutality is common and might plausibly be deemed officially tolerated, as police departments tend to protect their own, and courts are reluctant to prosecute police officers. The Bureau of Justice Statistics estimates that between June 2015 and May 2016 police killed approximately 1,200 people.[22] Mapping Police Violence found 1,167 known police killings in 2014 (including 1,067 arrest-related deaths and 100 unintentional, off-duty and/or inmate deaths) and 1,123 police killings in 2013.[23] In 2015, which has since been deemed the year of reckoning for police, more than a dozen officers were charged with murder or manslaughter in fatal on-duty shootings, up from an average of five a year in the previous decade. Since 2005, however, only thirteen officers have been convicted of murder or manslaughter. No officers were convicted in 2014 or 2015: in the overwhelming majority of cases, police killings are ultimately determined to involve the lawful use of deadly force.

This low rate of convictions is not surprising given that the law requires adopting the subjective perspective of the officer on the scene to determine whether their use of lethal force was justified.[24] The legal standard invites (White) people to put themselves in the officer's shoes and imagine their "reasonable" fear when faced with criminal- and dangerous-looking (Black or Brown) people. A one-sided exercise of empathetic imagination that is firmly rooted in oppressive stereotypes is thus deployed to justify homicides. The problem is structural and compounded: official misconduct works in tandem with disrespect—from stop-and-frisk policies, which disproportionately target Black and Brown people, to the set of laws that govern police accountability—and is (ideologically) justified and sustained by racist cultural stereotypes that inform police officers, their superiors and peers, and the judges and juries asked to evaluate their actions.

We see another example of official misconduct when states violate international law in the conduct of war. The routine, illegal use of torture, and efforts to legalize it during the "war on terror," especially under President George W. Bush, are cases in point.[25]

Lastly, corruption presents an archetype of official misconduct. In Joseph Nye's influential conception, corruption is "behavior that deviates from the formal duties of a public role (elective or appointive) because of private-regarding (personal, close family, private clique) wealth or status gains."[26] For our purposes, though, it is important that corruption be widespread. While individual acts of corruption, such as former Illinois governor Rob Blagojevich's solicitation of bribes in exchange for political appointments, are wrong, contexts of official misconduct arise only when that sort of behavior is publicly perceived as common and more or less tolerated.[27]

Different contexts of official misconduct involve different wrongs: official illegality sometimes conspires to deny citizens free and equal status, as in the case of Jim Crow; endemic corruption assaults the integrity of the legal system, thereby harming everyone's fundamental interest in being governed by just institutions; states' human rights violations abroad implicate citizens of the perpetrator state in these wrongs. Official misconduct stains political legitimacy and weakens, perhaps even dissolves, the duty to obey the law.

Public Ignorance

The final type of injustice concerns governments' concealing from the public certain facts about their programs and policies and trying to cover up officials' misconduct. Calling this injustice public ignorance emphasizes the democratic wrong involved in such secrecy: the public ought to know what the government does in its name. What it keeps hidden may be clearly wrong and/or illegal, or there may be disagreement about its wrongfulness and/or illegality. Examples of government programs objectionably concealed from the public, whether they were illegal or not, include the Federal Bureau of Investigation's elaborate program of spying on dissident groups, known as COINTELPRO; the Central Intelligence Agency's use of

"Black sites" to torture detainees in the war on terror; and the NSA's dragnet surveillance programs. Official misconduct was covered up at Abu Ghraib and in postwar Bosnia, where American personnel were revealed as perpetrators in an international human trafficking ring.

Public ignorance differs from deliberative inertia with respect to the cause of the cognitive deficit in the public sphere. While inertial breakdowns are typically the result of many factors affecting the deliberative environment, public ignorance is a result of intentional government secrecy and/or cover-up: it is induced and cultivated by state officials. Although assessing contexts of public ignorance is tricky given the government's real and weighty interest in secrecy, as we'll see shortly, genuine cases of public ignorance seriously weaken the putative moral duty to obey the law by undermining democratic authority.[28] In other words, citizens have less trust in and respect for the state when they feel—and have to reason to believe—they are being deliberately kept in the dark while the state perpetrates injustice. Intuitively, we might say that the graver the informational deficit, the more serious the injustice of public ignorance, and the less trustworthy and legitimate the state.

The revelations from the Panama and Paradise Papers straddle deliberative inertia and public ignorance: thanks to offshore finance, the rich and powerful, including government officials and heads of state, are able to withdraw their wealth from national and fiscal scrutiny, while concealing the conflicts of interest that the public should know about. These conflicts of interest arise at multiple levels and hinder democratic governance. At a basic level, offshore finance benefits the rich and powerful; the rich are able to buy influence and power, in the United States and elsewhere; and those in power tend to be rich (44 percent of US Congresspersons have a net worth of more than $1 million). There is therefore little legislative interest in regulating that sector; indeed President Donald Trump's administration has determined to further deregulate banking. From this perspective, we might describe the situation exposed by the leaked financial documents from Mossack Fonseca and Appleby as deliberative inertia sustained by public ignorance. In addition, officeholders shroud in secrecy the particular conflicts of interest they have, and which the public should know about. For instance, the Paradise Papers revealed that Wilbur Ross, the commerce secretary under Trump, has extensive business ties with the Putin family, which he should have severed before taking office, in compliance with government ethics standards.[29] Conflicts of interest of the sort are a form of corruption that one may categorize under public ignorance.

To recap, disrespect consists of the public denial of citizens' free and equal status; wrongs to nonmembers involve democratically sanctioned violations of the basic rights and dignity of noncitizens at home and abroad; deliberative inertia occurs when issues and discourses are blocked from the deliberative agenda; official misconduct consists in routine illegal practices by officials acting on their authority; and public ignorance occurs when the state prevents the people from learning about conduct, programs, and policies they should know and deliberate about. These types of injustice can and often do arise in legitimate, democratic states. The typology is broadstroked and by no means exhaustive. It could have included historical injustice for instance. But it is sufficient to help us examine several implications of the duty of justice in unjust contexts within broadly legitimate societies.

(DIS)OBEDIENCE AND DEMOCRATIC AUTHORITY

Before examining these implications, I need to address a particular objection against my project, one that denies the very possibility of political obligations to disobey based on the natural duty of justice.

When we talk about political obligations, we are talking about the duties of individuals. But the natural duty of justice, as envisioned by most theorists, applies to public institutions, not personal conduct. If this is right, then the duty of justice makes no demands on citizens themselves.

This objection rests on an understanding of the duty of justice tailored for theories such as Rawls's, which focuses on the importance of society's basic structure: institutions with significant impact on citizens' life prospects. But while this stance may be warranted for the purpose of ideal-theorizing about justice, it does not follow that institutions alone are what matters for justice. To argue as much would be to set arbitrary restrictions on the pursuit of justice, excluding in particular non-institutional courses of citizen action. As Liam Murphy notes:

> The overwhelming practical importance of institutions in achieving the aims of justice in the typical case should not blind us to the fact that what matters to us, ultimately, is not whether our institutions are just, in the sense that they achieve our aims, but rather simply the extent to which those aims are achieved, however that might be done.[30]

While institutions are crucial, perhaps indispensable, vehicles of justice, social movements and conscientious individuals can act, too.

But well understood, the objection from institutional mediation is not that the duty of justice makes no demands on citizens: it does, and what it requires is their obedience to the law. Proponents of the duty of justice argue that justice cannot be achieved if individuals decide privately what its achievement requires, that they must set aside their own judgment of the matter and follow the state's determination, taking its directives as providing what philosophers call "content-independent" and "preemptive" reasons. The law provides content-independent reasons for action insofar as it is its source or pedigree (how it came about, the fact that it is issued by the authority) and not *what* it directs that gives a reason for action. That it provides a preemptive reason for action means that it purports to exclude from deliberation other reasons for action.

The argument is not simply that people's compliance with a single set of authoritative rules is needed for justice and stability. People deeply care how these rules are achieved. On many accounts, what gives people a reason to take the law as binding in these ways—that is, as providing content-independent and preemptive reasons for action—is the fact that it is the outcome of a democratic procedure that gives everyone an equal say in the decision. Political equality gives democratic procedures their authority. This is why the duty of justice requires the establishment of just democratic institutions, and grounds citizens' moral duty to obey democratically made law, even when they find it unjust.

However, modern liberal democracies fail to generate a comprehensive moral duty to obey the law insofar as they are affected by the kinds of injustice and democratic deficits outlined above. Few decision-making procedures in democratic states may be deemed to produce morally authoritative outcomes. Viehoff's account of democratic authority is especially well suited to understanding why.[31] On his view, it is the egalitarian character of democratic procedures and institutions—the fact that they are not shaped by unequal power advantages—that gives us a reason to treat their outcomes as authoritative. Democratic equality requires not only that parties have equal rights and that they accept that their respective interests are equally significant—as is standard in accounts of democratic authority—but also that parties have, and be committed to having, equal control over the relationship, and that they exclude the influence of unequal power advantages (Viehoff calls this the requirement of *nonsubjection*).[32] But many democratic states' institutions and procedures are insufficiently egalitarian, and shaped by unequal power, thereby giving citizens reason to scrutinize the content of these procedures' outcomes (rather than accepting blindly their supposed content-independence), and to include consideration of other reasons for action besides the one provided by the law (thereby challenging their preemptiveness).

Still, this does not mean that anything goes so long as institutions lack political authority. We often have reason to follow imperfect institutions' directives rather than acting on our own judgment in order to come closer to the ideal of democratic equality. For Viehoff this is so in part because actual or threatened disobedience menaces democratic equality by signifying willingness to defy it. Yet, as he recognizes, principled disobedience may sometimes better advance justice, too.[33]

Indeed, as we will see later on, principled disobedience can not only advance justice but can also promote democratic equality itself. Viehoff conceives of democratic equality in light of an ideal he calls "relational equality," and which requires us to "set aside and not act on unequal power advantages in shaping our interactions and the norms and expectations governing them."[34] Precisely: principled disobedience can shed light on and alert the public to the power differentials that threaten relational equality. This aim has been central to the Occupy and BLM movements, for instance. Principled disobedience of this sort is then justified on the basis of the duty of justice itself and as an expression of respect for democratic authority.

For acts of principled disobedience to be justified on the basis of the duty of justice, it is not enough that they seek to promote the realization of democratic values; they must further be constrained in ways consonant with democratic equality. Agents must show concern for the interests of the parties potentially affected by the disobedient acts and not seek to dominate or intimidate them. In particular, attempts to retaliate against those on the winning end of power differentials cannot be explained away by the duty of justice, and nonviolence should be favored. But the targeted and selective use of coercion is compatible with the imperative of nonsubjection: for instance, organized workers can justifiably deploy some force in their effort to balance out the unequal power advantage, in the context of labor strikes. And as we shall see, uncivil types of principled disobedience such as vigilantism and government whistleblowing, though they appear to threaten relational equality, may be wholly justified under certain unjust conditions.

With these goals and constraints in mind, let us turn to the inquiry into our duty of justice-based political obligations in the face of injustice and democratic deficits.

POLITICAL OBLIGATIONS

So then, bound by the natural duty of justice, how can and, in some cases, how should citizens resist injustices of the type I've just laid out? Through the following methods: education; protest, including civil disobedience; covert disobedience; vigilantism; and government whistleblowing.

Education

Citizens can promote justice by working to improve the community's understanding of its demands. This is especially the case in contexts of deliberative inertia, which can produce an uninformed or misinformed public. Consider anthropogenic climate change and rising economic inequality. In neither case is the injustice obvious. For citizens to be able to sense injustice, they must have a basic understanding of complex scientific and social-scientific issues, especially to rule out alternative explanations (e.g., that climate change is not happening or that it is not man-made). To achieve that basic understanding, the public must know certain factual information. Al Gore's 2006 documentary *An Inconvenient Truth* and Leonardo DiCaprio's 2016 *Before the Flood*, for instance, are important popular sources with respect to climate change. But facts alone are not dispositive. The social-scientific and economic facts summoned to explain the injustice of economic inequality are neither value-neutral nor undisputed among experts, and even well-informed citizens disagree sharply about whether inequality is unjust. Furthermore, people often only hear what they want to hear: we tend to surround ourselves with like-minded people who share our worldviews. This tendency is amplified online, as our social media feeds and news sources confirm our convictions and biases, and as search engines like Google are designed to direct us to material that is most likely to reinforce our preexisting beliefs.[35]

Internet governance is another context of injustice in which education is both valuable and challenging. The complexity of the issues involved—combined with the relative digital illiteracy of most members of the community, including their political representatives—significantly impairs both democratic deliberation on internet governance and the struggle for digital rights. The Electronic Frontier Foundation—a nonprofit organization devoted to defending free speech online, fighting illegal surveillance, and advocating for users and innovators—spearheads this struggle. The Wiki Media Foundation, which operates Wikipedia, is also out front. It has blacked out Wikipedia in protest against the Stop Online Piracy Act (SOPA) and PROTECT IP Act (PIPA) and posted messages explaining how these laws threaten to restrict computer and information access.[36] Such educational initiatives are crucial to improving the community's conception of the demands of justice in the digital world.

Although educational efforts are often entirely lawful, the duty of justice does not rule out unlawful activities that relate to educating and informing citizens. Thus hacktivists—whom Celikates has dubbed "the avant-garde of the digital publics"—can acceptably resort to principled disobedience in this domain, including digital trespass and DDoS actions, to protest and educate the public about digital rights.[37] And they have done so. Aaron Swartz condemned the paywall surrounding publicly funded scholarship by downloading millions of academic articles from JSTOR. Anonymous launched a DDoS attack against the Motion Picture Association of America and other organizations that advocate and depend on stringent copyright laws. One can appeal to the duty of justice to justify Swartz's and Anonymous's actions, even if these actions constituted acts of uncivil disobedience.[38]

In some contexts of injustice, what is lacking and what education needs to remedy is not so much, or not only, information but also empathetic imagination. The wrongs involved in anti-immigration policies are arguably such a case. One may plausibly contend that false beliefs about how immigration undermines local and national community—and negative stereotypes about immigrants and refugees as parasites, criminals, and terrorists—prevent citizens from imagining themselves in immigrants' shoes. This epistemic condition facilitates the wrongs to nonmembers. A number of people have "come out" as undocumented immigrants to raise awareness about their plight and invite empathy. For instance, Jose Antonio Vargas, a Pulitzer-winning journalist, told his story in the *New York Times* and described his predicament in poignant terms: "Even though I think of myself as an American and consider America my country, my country doesn't think of me as one of its own."[39]

A final example of justice-based political obligation to educate concerns the "burkini ban" in the French Riviera, which I have described as a case of disrespect. Though the Council of State eventually struck down municipal prohibitions as unconstitutional, a majority of French people support them and hope that the bans will be reenacted. Public support for the bans suggests that resistance to them ought to focus on illuminating their assault on justice. This requires both information and empathetic imagination. Muslim women offer powerful voices of protest, as they explain why they choose to wear modest clothing and speak to the injustice of laws denying them the right to do so.[40] This particular case also reveals the importance of educating the public about the values associated with the rule of law and necessary features of legality, including the necessity of laws' generality and applicability, which the burkini ban blatantly violated (insofar as rash guards and bodysuits were effectively exempt from the law's enforcement, for instance).

Protest

Because the duty of justice binds people in their capacity as free and equal moral agents, it cannot demand complying with laws, policies, practices, and institutions that flout this status in oneself or others. Compliance would amount to endorsing disrespect and violations of democratic equality, which is forbidden by the duty of justice. Beyond noncompliance, one might speak up against injustice and seek legal and structural reforms. Protest and civil disobedience are often critical ways to register opposition to unjust laws, express respect for one's and others' dignity, denounce the unequal power advantages that distort the production of law, and call for reform. The duty of justice thus provides grounds for the duty to protest and sometimes civilly disobey, on the basis of these acts' communicative nature and potential to bring about reform (I present in the next chapter some social-scientific evidence supporting the effectiveness of protest and civil disobedience campaigns to usher in reform).

King's branch of the civil rights movement embodies a commitment to the duty of justice, which vindicates both its institutional demands and its affirmation of Blacks' dignity in the face of egregious violations of democratic equality. But let us look to anti-trans bathroom bills for a current and more controversial example. Regardless of the true motivation behind them—proponents cite the safety of women and children—these bills disrespect trans and gender-nonconforming people and leave them more vulnerable to trans- and homophobic violence. The duty of justice demands that citizens respond through protest, and, indeed, a significant movement now denounces such laws as discriminatory and hateful and calls for their abolition. While cisgender people are likely to unreflectively comply with bathroom laws, they may be bound to disobey them if a large campaign urged them to do so. In any case, speaking up, signing petitions, partaking in hashtag activism, and demonstrating offer citizens the means to discharge the duty of justice in this case.

Empirical factors matter to determine how the duty to resist and protest injustice should be discharged. Boycotts can be tricky in this way. Some powerful corporations such as Google are boycotting North Carolina, refusing to set up shop or host events there in response to the passage of HB2. In addition to their direct economic effects, these boycotts attract media attention, raising awareness about transphobia and serving to condemn anti-trans laws. But consumer boycotts, which encourage people to cancel trips to North Carolina or refrain from spending money there, may be less successful. This boycott has had adverse effects on small businesses, including LGBTQ-owned and LGBTQ-friendly shops.[41] These adverse effects seem remote from the goal of denouncing HB2. In this respect, the consumer boycott does a poor job of realizing the demands of justice, though it may contribute in important ways to improving the community's conception of justice. Such impacts must be weighed against each other in deciding the best course of action.

Covert Disobedience

The goal of protest is legal and structural reform to correct democratic deficits and bring about justice. But what is one to do before unjust arrangements are rectified, while they continue to wrong people? Think of slavery. Countless people of African descent were enslaved, brutalized, worked to death, and murdered even as activists devoted their lives to abolition. The duty of justice did not merely require opposition and protest. One also had a moral duty to rescue enslaved people, when one could, even if that meant disobeying egregious laws, such as the Fugitive Slave Law. Many abolitionists understood this and fulfilled their duty by assisting Blacks fleeing to the North and to Canada via the Underground Railroad. Note the difference between the enterprises of rescue and protest: the purpose of the Underground Railroad was to ensure the freedom of individuals, not to abolish slavery. Rescue fulfilled a non-institutional demand of the duty of justice. And it did so covertly, not communicatively, thereby violating civil disobedience's norm of publicity.

The sanctuary movement offers a contemporary example of principled disobedience designed to satisfy the demands of justice outside institutions, again covertly. This large political and religious campaign, active in the United States in the 1980s and 1990s, violated federal immigration law by providing safe haven for Central American refugees fleeing civil conflict. Sanctuary members secured shelter, material goods, and legal advice for refugees refused asylum under restrictive immigration policies.[42] Similar sanctuary movements have emerged in Europe in response to the global refugee crisis. For instance, French inhabitants of Breil-sur-Roya, near the Italian border, assist undocumented migrants by helping them cross the border into France, and providing them with food and shelter. Threats to unauthorized migrants, as well as escaped slaves, also require us to fulfill our Samaritan duty to aid people in dire need, as we'll see in chapter 5. French courts draw a line between Samaritan assistance and justice-based activism, excusing the former but firmly outlawing the latter: Eric Herrou was swiftly released in August 2016, soon after his arrest, when a judge ruled that he had acted on humanitarian grounds by helping a group of Eritreans into France. But when he was arrested again in mid-October for opening a shelter in a disused holiday camp to house fifty migrants, prosecutors insisted that his actions should be treated as a form of activism, and not as a humanitarian endeavor.

At the very least, the duty of justice prohibits complying with laws that make us agents of wrongdoing. Arizona, Alabama, and other U.S. states increasingly conscript citizens to enforce immigration laws by imposing legal duties on them to monitor, report, and refrain from employing, transporting, or aiding unauthorized immigrants, including children.[43] If these laws are unjust and violate migrants' rights, as some have argued, then citizens who comply with them contribute to violating the rights of migrants. And since the duty of justice prohibits contributing to rights violations, it prohibits citizens from obeying immigration laws, demanding disobedience instead.[44]

Disobeying immigration laws is a principled act, but not a civil one. It must be covert in order to succeed. Public disobedience would not serve to protect unauthorized migrants from the harms of arrest, detention, and deportation. Although the principled disobedients can also be outspoken critics of unjust immigration laws, they disobey covertly and their primary aim is not to condemn the law (such communicative aim would require publicity). Instead they defy the law because they wish to attend to vulnerable people's needs and express respect for the dignity and freedom of those whose equal moral standing is denied. This what the duty of justice requires; it is a duty that calls, when necessary, for uncivil disobedience to frustrate disrespect and wrongs to nonmembers of the state.

Vigilantism

When faced with official misconduct, as in contexts of disrespect and wrongs to nonmembers, protest and civil disobedience may be effective tools of reform. And some forms of uncivil (including covert) disobedience may be appropriate in the meanwhile, to frustrate ongoing wrongs. Vigilantism numbers among the types of uncivil disobedience that can be justified by the duty of justice in some contexts of official misconduct. It consists of the use of force or threat of force by nonstate agents for the purpose of controlling (preventing and/or punishing) conduct perceived as criminal or immoral. Vigilantes usurp law-enforcement functions. They wrongfully hold on to the natural right to punish, which John Locke insisted one must surrender upon entering civil society and transfer to the sovereign. In doing so, they wrongfully transgress the state's monopoly on violence, which makes this form of action a particularly subversive one.

Most vigilantism cannot be justified. The Ku Klux Klan's vigilante activities were egregiously immoral. They involved unjustifiable means—murder, torture, and terrorism—in the service of unjustifiable ends—the maintenance of White power. The vigilante killings perpetrated in San Francisco, California, in the 1970s, by a group of Black Muslims who called themselves the "Death Angels" cannot be justified either. They murdered at least fifteen people, perhaps closer to one hundred, simply because they were White.[45] But those vigilante groups, such as the Deacons for Defense and Justice, that arose to defend African Americans against White supremacist violence under Jim Crow—illegally and with force—could be justified in the context of grave official misconduct, as the state deployed its force against some of its people and failed to protect them from lethal violence inflicted by other subjects.[46] The Deacons exercised their fundamental right of self-defense and protective defense of others. The group, which grew to several hundred members in the 1960s and had twenty-one chapters in the South, protected members of the Congress of Racial Equality, Blacks registering to vote, and White and Black civil rights workers. They also provided security for King at speaking events all over the United States.

Malcolm X also defended Black vigilantism as a form of justified self-defensive force in the context of authorities' failure to protect Blacks:

> [I]n areas where the government has proven itself either un-willing or unable to defend the lives and the property of Negroes, it's time for Negroes to defend themselves . . . If the White man doesn't want the Black man buying rifles and shotguns, then let the government do its job.[47]

Thus a certain kind of vigilantism—the organized use of self-defensive force such as that practiced by the Deacons for Defense and Justice and the Black Panthers under racial segregation, and the Lavender Panthers in San Francisco—may be justified in contexts of entrenched institutional inefficacy that leaves some people vulnerable to grave harm, so long as it involves the justified use of force in defense of self or others. That is, the harm inflicted by the vigilante must be a proportional (necessary and fitting) response to an immediate threat. Wounding or killing a Klansman about to lynch someone is justified rather than, say, fleeing and calling the police; parading with weapons to publicly demonstrate one's willingness and capacity to respond to violence with violence can be justified too; but the use of deadly force cannot be used preemptively or indiscriminately or in response to future probable threats. Nor can it be used as a form of payback after an attack.

Vigilantism is often associated with retaliation and vengeance: Batman not only protects innocents from criminals but punishes the latter, under the guise of both retribution and deterrence. The Ku Klux Klan presented its lynchings of Blacks as punishment for alleged (invented) crimes. Quentin Tarantino's Revenge Trilogy, which includes *Inglorious Basterds* (2009), *Django Unchained* (2012), and *The Hateful Eight* (2015), represent retaliatory vigilante missions against sadistic wrongdoers from the ranks of Nazi officials, slaveholders, and Confederate army generals, respectively. The duty of justice cannot support vigilantes' use of deadly violence as punishment or vengeance. But consider the case of *digital vigilantism*. In Operation: Payback, Anonymous launched a series of retaliatory DDoS attacks against various entities they saw as inimical to digital rights, to alert the public to some of the unjust constraints on the free flow of information online.

As a protest seeking to raise awareness, the campaign could be justified by the duty of justice. However, hacktivist participants intended to inflict serious economic damage to pro-copyright and anti-piracy organizations as retaliation to previous cyberattacks against torrent sites. The British Recorded Music Industry (BPI), the International Federation of the Phonographic Industry (IFPI), and the Ministry of Sound estimated the financial impact of the attacks to total £33,000.[48] Whether the duty of justice can justify Operation: Payback depends on the legitimacy of the campaign's goal—it can be justified as a protest but not as a punishment—and on the justification of its means. In particular, one ought to take a close look at the costs inflicted: Did the companies overestimate the financial impact of the attacks? Did they unfairly include indirect costs such as those related to security systems' updates? Were the costs reasonable—small enough to be easily absorbed but large enough to garner publicity? Justifying Operation: Payback would require a positive answer to all three questions—the case can be made, in short, though making it requires a thorough investigation, which I won't undertake here.

However, the duty of justice cannot be used to support Operation Ferguson, in which Anonymous threatened and then hacked into the Saint Louis Police Department to release (what they incorrectly thought was) the identity of the officer who had shot Michael Brown in August 2014. They exposed the wrong officer and his family to death threats and mob violence—an expected but unacceptable result of Anonymous's doxxing (stealing and release of private confidential information), which would have been wrong even if it had targeted the right person. The duty of justice cannot justify exposing someone's family to such severe threat of harm.

Government Whistleblowing

In cases of public ignorance, when the government hides from the public some official misconduct or a particular program or policy about which the public should know, the duty of justice generates special obligations on the part of witnesses or participants. Public ignorance is a serious impediment to democratic deliberation. Those who have access to the wrongfully concealed information ought to alert the public about it. Agents who are in a position to diagnose public ignorance and its attending injustice are usually, though not necessarily, participants in the concealed programs or activities, in their professional or official capacities.

Reporting wrongdoing and corruption within one's organization is already employees' duty according to many professional codes of ethics—especially that of civil servants. But I want to argue something stronger, namely, that where the information in question is in the public interest, and when officials repress agents' attempts to blow the whistle through designated channels, agents may incur a moral duty to blow the whistle illegally, through unauthorized disclosures to the public. And this duty derives from the duty of justice.

Denouncing and reporting corruption and other abuses is indeed critical to the promotion of just democratic institutions, as public denunciation can serve several of the purposes we have focused on: improving the community's conception of justice and understanding of democratic equality, communicating protest, and frustrating wrongs through exposure that may lead to cessation. The duty of justice can thus support special obligations to blow the whistle against public ignorance, even if doing so involves breaking the law by disclosing state secrets. Snowden's leaks educated the public about digital rights infringed upon by government surveillance, and the Panama and Paradise Papers exposed systematic tax evasion by the wealthy and politicians' conflicts of interest. Government whistleblowing can remedy significant cognitive deficits in the public sphere, thereby enabling a deliberative environment. It can also frustrate injustice by halting or diminishing the wrongdoing in question as soon as it is exposed. These functions make it a particularly powerful way of addressing democratic deficits (in the form of public ignorance) and enhancing justice and the rule of law (when the state uses secrecy in order to conceal its own wrongdoing). Government whistleblowers can thus appeal to the duty of justice to justify their actions.

Of course only justified, suitably constrained government whistleblowing is mandatory: agents ought to seek to expose serious government wrongdoing or programs and policies that ought to be known and deliberated about; they ought first to undertake lawful, internal attempts to alert the public; and they ought to take serious precautions in the disclosure so as to minimize the harms that could potentially ensue, including by carefully choosing the leaks' recipients and editing the information disclosed.[49] Examples of whistleblowers whose unauthorized disclosures successfully combated public ignorance, were suitably constrained, and plausibly fulfilled the duty of justice include Ellsberg, whose leaks of the Pentagon Papers to the *New York Times*, as I mentioned earlier, revealed that the United States committed war crimes in Vietnam and lied at home; the Citizens Commission to Investigate the FBI, who exposed the illegal program of spying on dissident groups known as COINTELPRO; and Snowden's NSA leaks. While the Iraq and Afghanistan War Logs leaked by Chelsea Manning exposed war crimes—a clear subject of public ignorance—WikiLeaks's decision to publish the classified documents without editing them arguably sapped the justification of Manning's whistleblowing.

Ellsberg and Snowden are often praised as civil disobedients. The framing of government whistleblowing as civil disobedience rightly points to agents' principled motivations and communicative intent: whistleblowers, like civil disobedients, address themselves to the public. However, it is a mistake to conceive of government whistleblowing as a form of civil disobedience. Whistleblowers obtain classified documents covertly and without authorization. They often disclose the information they have gained access to anonymously, though some whistleblowers like Snowden make a point of publicizing their findings. Many whistleblowers seek to evade punishment. Government whistleblowers transgress the boundaries of state secrets for the purpose of challenging the state's use of secrecy. Unauthorized disclosures do not only challenge executive decisions to keep certain information out of the public realm, but they also unilaterally reverse these decisions. Civil disobedients do no such thing: their lawbreaking challenges but does not undo unjust laws.

OBJECTIONS

I have argued that the duty of justice does not simply ground a duty to comply with the outcomes of just democratic institutions but that it also supports a duty to resist injustice, by civil and potentially uncivil means, when the law violates justice or undermines democratic equality.

Two sets of objections arise from what I've argued, which I will examine in the pages ahead. First, one may wonder if political obligations based on the duty of justice are too demanding, difficult to satisfy, and generally undesirable. Do we really want ordinary people to undertake such obligations, when they might be mistaken about what justice requires? Likewise, one may object that only lawful protest and, at the limit, civil disobedience can be morally required in a basically legitimate society. Uncivil types of principled disobedience like the ones I defended above should be excluded.

Demanding, Difficult, and Undesirable

It is difficult to satisfy political obligations based on the duty of justice because these obligations are, I admit, demanding in nature. Indeed it is daunting to consider the extent of the deeds we might be required to do, especially if the duty of justice does not stop at the merely legal. How is it realistic to ask so much of ordinary citizens? Making matters worse, it can be confusing to tell exactly what the duty of justice requires us to do. Rawls qualified the duty of justice, arguing that it need be fulfilled only at "little cost to ourselves." But action requires time and energy and, in some cases, significant sacrifice. And while the duty to obey the law is straightforward—laws themselves more or less clearly specify the content of our duty— political obligations to resist injustice can be taxing. To fulfill such obligations, one must assess the moral merits of laws, evaluate their effects on people's standing and on the integrity of the legal system, and choose among methods of resistance.

There are hazards at each stage. We may err in assessing the merits of laws, their effects, the injustice of these effects, and the available and appropriate responses. We also may fail to perceive injustices. Our mistakes may reflect mistaken convictions about justice. But even when we understand the injustice of situations properly, our solutions may be misguided. In short, agents must be wise and virtuous in order to satisfy political obligations in the face of injustice, whereas the moral duty to obey the law supposedly can be met by anyone. Given that people could easily miscalculate and end up causing more harm than good, perhaps they shouldn't make judgments about the existence of, and solutions to, injustice on their own.

These objections, which also apply to political obligations based on other normative principles defended in this book, seem to strike a serious blow to the project. Chapter 7 tackles these issues. For now, let me briefly address each in turn.

First, are political obligations in the face of injustice too demanding? It is true that we possess limited time and cognitive and financial resources and may have many other valuable projects to pursue. But this just means we cannot be expected to devote ourselves entirely to struggles for justice and democracy. It does not mean we can shrug off all political obligations as excessively demanding and therefore do nothing. The duty to obey the law makes burdensome demands on citizens—to pay taxes, sit on juries, and, if conscripted, serve in the military. There is no reason political obligations in the face of injustice cannot be equally demanding. And just as one can reasonably be blamed for refusing the burdens of obedience to law (when it is morally required), one can be blamed for refusing the burdens of addressing injustice.

Second, can and should these political obligations—and the duty of justice from which they derive—guide action? Yes, assuming certain conditions prevail. Agents must be able to perceive injustice before they can assess the situation properly and take action. This presupposes good information, some intellectual capacity, and moral dispositions. In chapter 7 I propose that we supplement the account of political obligations in the face of injustice with two additional responsibilities: one, to form one's beliefs responsibly and exercise the civic virtue of vigilance; two, to engage with others in dialogue and foster the civic virtue of open-mindedness. But this does not mean that nothing is to be done until all the conditions for the possibility of satisfying one's political obligations are in place. In particular, those agents who are able to help improve others' conception of justice and aptitude for assessing injustices have a weighty responsibility to educate and inform others.

I also want to stress that I do not defend the view that all citizens should try to work out for themselves what the duty of justice—or any other important normative principle—demands in the face of injustice. My argument is that it is wrong to presume that the duty of justice solely requires compliance with the law in states like ours. Instead it demands resisting injustice so as to respect people's rights and make institutions more democratic. Satisfying the demands of the duty of justice unquestionably is complicated and difficult, but that does not mean we don't have to try to do so.

Against Uncivil Disobedience

One might see no problem with the resort to lawful protest and civil disobedience in the effort to advance justice and democratic equality, but point to the potentially destabilizing effects of uncivil disobedience. Covert disobedience can habituate citizens to illegality, thereby undermining the rule of law. Vigilantism usurps one of the state's most crucial prerogatives: its monopoly on the threat or use of violence in order to protect people. Government whistleblowing can put national security at risk. Each of these actions may manifest disrespect for democratic institutions and is likely to scare and antagonize the majority, erode the civic bonds, and compromise future social cooperation. We therefore must think carefully about whether the duty to support just institutions can be realized through uncivil disobedience.

But as I argued in the previous chapter, uncivil disobedience does not necessarily undermine or express contempt for democratic authority. As a form of self-defensive action in contexts of widespread state-sanctioned violence, justified vigilantism affirms the full and equal status of those under attack and thereby promotes democratic equality. What of the concern that covert disobedience habituates people to illegal behavior, potentially spilling over to totally unjustifiable, unprincipled criminality, thereby disserving the duty of justice? This is an empirical matter, and there is no evidence to support such fears. Consider drug and alcohol prohibition, a constant arena for covert disobedience. Between 1919 and 1933, Americans routinely and covertly disobeyed statutes banning alcohol use without suddenly turning to criminality. Today, many people in the United States and elsewhere quietly disobey legal prohibitions against marijuana use with no further effect on disobedience. Drug prohibitions do breed serious wrongdoing, but only because they encourage black markets and organized crime—not because of some disobedience contagion.

Noting his evasion of punishment, Snowden's critics suspect that he was disloyal to the United States and reject the claim that he was motivated by respect for the rule of law and democratic authority.[50] But this condemnation does not withstand scrutiny. Against journalists' advice to remain anonymous and thereby evade the possibility of punishment, he chose publicity. Since coming forward, he has been a relentless and eloquent advocate for electronic freedom and privacy, demonstrating his sincere commitment to the public interest. He has worked to strengthen democratic ideals by emphasizing their role in online governance. Not every whistleblower is as conscientious as Snowden, but his example shows that whistleblowing need not be disrespectful of democratic institutions, antagonize the public, or disrupt civic concord. All in all, we cannot discount the role of principled disobedience in realizing the duty of justice.

TRANSNATIONAL OBLIGATIONS

I focused in this chapter on how the duty of justice affects political obligations in nonideal legitimate, democratic states, which present a harder case for principled disobedience. We should also reflect on obligations with respect to illegitimate states. The central political obligation of citizens in such states is to resist illegitimate authority—be it autocratic or colonial—and establish in its place a government based on self-determination. Fulfilling this obligation typically requires mass struggle and coordination internally. But outside forces, including citizens of legitimate states, can help. Are they obligated to do so?

According to Rawls, the duty of justice binds us to help establish just institutions where they don't exist. Allen Buchanan has defended a "robust natural duty of justice," which specifies that obligations extend universally.[51] On this version of the duty, people living under just institutions must help those subject to unjust institutions, wherever these are. I want to suggest three main sites of action.

The first, and by far the most important, is supranational: international organizations such as the United Nations have a crucial role in helping war-torn and developing countries end conflicts and establish well-functioning institutions. Methods of assistance may include humanitarian intervention, financial aid, consulting, election-monitoring, and criminal prosecutions under international law.

Second, individual states can do their part in international humanitarian efforts. For better or worse, the United States is leading the international effort to fight transnational corruption by applying its anti-bribery law—the Foreign Corrupt Practices Act of 1977—internationally.[52] Insofar as corruption undermines the integrity of legal systems and thus constitutes an indirect assault on people's dignity and vital interests, one may plausibly argue that the United States is upholding its duty to support just institutions everywhere.[53]

Third, individuals themselves may also be bound by the duty of justice to help establish just institutions in other countries. One central transnational political obligation is to express solidarity with and, to the extent possible, contribute to, other people's pro-democracy movements. Examples of solidarity include demonstrations against global labor injustice and consumer boycotts of low-road producers in foreign countries. Financial and technical support can also help activists' and rebels' freedom struggles in illegitimate states. For instance, the hacktivist group Telecomix develops and provides Digital Care Packages, including anti-censorship, anti-surveillance, and internet-backup software, to pro-democracy groups the world over. Telecomix recently "mapped" Syria (i.e., scanned the state's networks and servers for surveillance equipment) and established encrypted connections to help local activists make their online activity harder to monitor.

Why should people obey the law? Champions of the duty of justice answer that citizens' compliance with the law is necessary for the state to uphold its peace-keeping and rights-preserving mission and that the duty of justice morally binds citizens to obey the outcomes of democratic decision-making procedures. But as we saw, the duty of justice can also support political obligations to resist injustice, institutionally and non-institutionally, at home and abroad. Even in legitimate democratic states, the duty of justice cannot bind people to comply with the law when doing so would contribute to denial of fellow citizens' free and equal status or support corrupt institutions. Instead, the duty of justice demands resisting injustice, bettering institutions, and frustrating wrongs, and it supports principled disobedience in the process. Given our less-than-ideal polities, obeying the law is neither the sole, nor necessarily the most important, of our political obligations.

Because the natural duty of justice is such a well-established source of justification for the standard understanding of political obligation, it serves as exhibit A in the case for revisiting that standard. But we can draw on other "evidence." In the next chapter, I turn to fairness. Like the duty of justice, the duty of fair play is frequently adduced as a ground for a political obligation to obey the law. But it, too, can ground an obligation to resist when systemic injustice arises.

Chapter 4

Fairness

Imagine you are an adult White man in Mississippi in the 1950s, under Jim Crow. You are deeply rooted there, and racial segregation is all you have ever known. You consider yourself a patriot and believe you are morally bound to respect the government and obey its law. By all accounts, you are a good person—you are generous and kind, beloved by your family and friends, respected in the community. Nonetheless, you are part of a profoundly unjust system that brutalizes and discriminates against Black people.

You go through your day benefiting in myriad ways from discrimination and witnessing its injustice. On your way to work, you comfortably sit at the front of the bus while Black passengers are crowded in the back. You have an interesting and lucrative job that roughly half of your fellow Mississippians cannot apply for or stand no chance of getting. Wherever you go, you are served before Black people are, no matter who got there first. You are always treated with respect and called "sir," while Black men your age are called "boy." Your children go to a good public school; have access to a good public library; play in a big, clean swimming pool in the summer; and can sit wherever they want in the cinema. You are well aware that Black children attend poorly funded schools and have limited access to the library, swimming pool, and theater.

What are your obligations under these profoundly unfair circumstances? H. L. A. Hart, George Klosko, and the early Rawls, among others, used the principle of fairness to ground the moral duty to obey the law in cooperative social schemes.[1] I will show that, under nonideal conditions such as those of Jim Crow, fairness demands something else. For our hypothetical Mississippian, and for others similarly situated, the principle of fairness imposes a political obligation to resist injustice, even when doing so means flouting the law.

Fairness imposes different demands, depending on context: fair judges are supposed to treat like cases alike; in fairly splitting a bounty, equal partners take equal rewards. When applied to mutually beneficial cooperative schemes, such as labor unions, neighborhood associations, and states, the principle of fairness yields a duty of fair play, which demands reciprocity. Through cooperation, which typically involves following the same set of rules, participants assume equitable shares of the burden associated with producing benefits. The duty of fair play (or principle of fairness—I use these interchangeably) proscribes taking advantage of other people's willingness to comply with the rules of the scheme for the benefit of all—a kind of foul play known as free-riding. Fairness guards against participants' noncompliance with the rules, because free-riding could affect the supply of benefits and increase other members' burden. Imagine shipwrecked sailors who have to row their lifeboat to shore: one free-rider on the boat increases other sailors' efforts. But the duty of fair play is supposed to hold even when noncompliance on the part of some of the participants would neither affect overall benefits nor require more sacrifice to offset. For instance, the subway goer who jumps the turnstile to avoid paying the fare does not affect other passengers, so long as this kind of free-riding is relatively rare.

FAIR PLAY AND INJUSTICE

Fair-Play Arguments for the Duty to Obey

Fair-play theorists of political obligation understand citizens of a good—near-just, legitimate—society as participants in a mutually beneficial cooperative scheme. Society provides stability, peace, rights protection, safe roads, clean water, military security, and other public goods (understood as collectively produced goods that are available to all), but only if enough citizens comply with laws requiring that they pay their share of taxes, refrain from committing crimes and report those they witness, drive on the appropriate side of the road, serve on juries, vote, serve in the military, and so on. (The particular list of duties varies from state to state and need not worry us.) Because (and to the extent that) the benefits of political authority are indispensable public goods, secured at a reasonable cost that is fairly distributed among the population, everyone is morally bound to do their part in sustaining the state. This moral duty is owed to fellow citizens—not to oneself, the state, or some other entity—and met through obedience to the law.

This argument for political obligation has its critics, who object that one must be a willing, knowing, and acknowledged cooperator in a given scheme before one can be bound to contribute one's fair share. Citizens do not generally satisfy this condition, critics argue, unless they take an oath of allegiance to the state, as naturalized citizens and state officials do. According to this "voluntarist" critique—posed by philosophical anarchists Robert Nozick and A. John Simmons, among others—participation in the scheme requires consent, and only then do individuals incur a duty of fair play. But because citizens cannot reject certain state benefits even if they wish to, their acceptance of benefits does not imply consent. Or so the voluntarists argue, against "nonvoluntarist" fair-play champions like Klosko.

Theorists also disagree about how the duty of fair play works in unjust societies. Some theorists, usually nonvoluntarists like Rawls and Klosko, argue that citizens cannot be bound to obey the law in a society fraught with pervasive, grave injustice, even if that society provides some important public goods such as security and order. I share this view (which I call the disjunctive view) but not the further, widely shared implication that citizens in unjust societies are relieved of any fairness-based political obligations. Others, voluntarists and nonvoluntarists alike, maintain that unjust schemes may still impose fair-play obligations on their participants, to the extent that they consent to the scheme (in Simmons's view) or enjoy benefits (in Garrett Cullity's). Call this the unified view.

Each of these views is supported by different, plausible intuitions: proponents of the disjunctive view ("disjunctivists," for short) stress that there cannot be any moral obligation to do wrong, while proponents of the unified view (or "unifiers") insist that there is such a thing as honor among thieves and that whoever willingly cooperates with others in a mutually beneficial scheme—even an immoral one—incurs fair-play obligations to do their share. However, unifiers add, such fair-play obligations are weak and typically, or always, overridden by countervailing moral considerations. Against disjunctivists, I intend to show that fairness demands resisting an unjust scheme, even (indeed, especially) if one benefits from it. Against unifiers, I will argue that fairness generates obligations to resist and reform unjust schemes, even if one has agreed to cooperate in them.

Injustice

Two kinds of unjust cooperative social schemes will be important in understanding the role of fairness in one's duty to resist: *exploitative* and *harmful schemes*. Exploitative schemes distribute burdens and benefits in a systematically objectionable way, as one group toils more than another that nonetheless benefits from the fruits of the first's labor. Iris Marion Young conceives of exploitation as an inherently wrongful set of structures sustaining "the transfer of the results of the labor of one social group to benefit another."[2] The capitalist economy, in Marx's analysis, is a stark example, as the bourgeois class, which owns the means of production, exploits the workers, who must sell their labor power to survive.

Harmful social schemes of coordination distribute benefits and burdens justly among their participants, all the while imposing negative externalities or harms on nonmembers. The harms I am especially concerned with here are those of oppression. In Young's analysis, they include marginalization (basically, social exclusion), powerlessness (inhibition of the development of one's capacities for autonomy), cultural imperialism (universalization of a dominant group's experience and culture), and violence (which is systemic and institutionalized when directed at members of a particular group specifically because of that membership). Colonial domination is a strong example of a harmful social scheme: the colonizer imposes powerlessness, marginalization, cultural imperialism, violence, and exploitation on the colonized. Cisgender heterosexist prejudice is another such scheme. Though typically less lethal than colonialism, heterosexism also tends to involve all four oppressive harms considered here: marginalization via exclusion of LGBTQ people; imposition of powerlessness via the inhibition of opportunities for development; cultural imperialism via universalizing of the cisgender heterosexual experience; and violence, including sexual assault.

Although the distinction between exploitation and harm is helpful in highlighting certain defects of social schemes, the two forms of oppression in fact overlap to a large extent. For instance, exploited groups are often at the same time discriminated against, powerless, and vulnerable to violence. As I conceive of it here, whether a given social arrangement is exploitative or harmful depends in part on how one assigns membership in the scheme. So one might describe workers in the capitalist economy as participants in an exploitative scheme, insofar as they consent, and are not forced, to work for particular employers, or instead as victims of that scheme, to the extent that they are forced to sell their labor to survive.[3]

But I do not mean to say that membership in the scheme *merely* depends on its description. It may well be obvious where one stands. For instance, victims of human trafficking are victims, not members or participants in the human trafficking ring. Ann Cudd describes women in Western labor markets who decide to opt out of the workforce (for rational reasons as far as their households are concerned) as willing participants in exploitative, sexist schemes, who perpetuate women's oppression "by choice."[4] Since the schemes of coordination we are considering here involve social groups, it may be the case that some individual members of these groups are appropriately described as willing and knowing participants where others are not. The point is that the framework's porous line between exploitation and harm is a desirable asset rather than a defect, I think.

Jim Crow, the racial caste system prevailing in the American South from the 1880s to the 1970s, in which Whites were beneficiaries and Blacks systematically oppressed, was both exploitative and harmful. How could it be both? Jim Crow was exploitative because it distributed burdens and benefits unjustly among Whites and Blacks. It was harmful, if one draws membership narrowly, because it subjected nonmembers—Blacks—to domination, humiliation, objectification, and violence. These two facets of the scheme based on two ways of delineating membership aligns with Robert Dahl's description of Jim Crow as a "dual system" in which White members cooperated on fair terms (so the scheme was internally fair but harmful), while Black nonmembers were forced to acquiesce to unfair terms (making the scheme exploitative or internally unfair, from another perspective).[5]

In this way, Jim Crow allows us to analyze two kinds of unfairness in one picture.

Free-Riding

Free-riders choose to receive or accept certain goods without paying the costs of producing these goods. Examples include going to a pot-luck picnic empty-handed, driving one's car on the bus lane to avoid a traffic jam, and regularly listening to public radio shows without ever donating any money. (Further details must be fleshed out for these cases to illustrate free-riding, such as that one is able but choosing not to bring something or contribute in some other way to the pot-luck picnic, one isn't facing an emergency justifying the decision to bypass the traffic jam, and one can afford to donate some money to one's favorite radio programs.)

Free-riding is generally considered wrong. In seeking benefits, the free-rider depends upon the willingness of others to subject themselves to a contribution requirement she is herself unwilling to accept. As Garrett Cullity observes, "If a person receives a net benefit from a scheme, then her unpreparedness to meet its requirements, when she depends for the benefits she receives on others' meeting them, is unfair."[6] The unfairness derives from giving oneself "objectionably preferential treatment"—putting one's own interest above others', making oneself an exception.[7] This is a form of wrongful ("reverse") discrimination: the imposition of an arbitrary and illegitimate advantage at others' expense.

Additionally, free-riding is conceived as wrong because it is a form of exploitation.[8] There are many accounts of exploitation, not all of which conceive of exploitation as inherently wrongful: some argue that exploitation is wrong, when it is, because it is coercive, or degrading, or fails to protect the vulnerable. According to Robert Mayer, to exploit is to unfairly take advantage of someone else, to gain at another's expense.[9] Again, gaining at another's expense is not always wrong—for instance, athletes take advantage of their opponents' vulnerabilities in order to win competitions—but exploitation, along with theft and cheating, are species of wrongful gain.

I favor Cullity's account over Mayer's for two reasons. One is that not all forms of free-riding appear necessarily exploitative in the sense of wrongfully gaining *at another's expense*. In many cases, free-riding is unnoticed by other participants and will not affect their share of burdens (think of my boarding the bus through the back to avoid paying the fare and suppose no one notices). In those cases the wrongful gain does not disadvantage others. However, such forms of free-riding would still constitute cases of objectionable preferential discrimination. Another reason to prefer Cullity's account is that one could plausibly argue that what is wrong with wrongfully gaining at another's expense is that one gives oneself an unfair advantage, so that the conception of free-riding as wrongful exploitation boils down to objectionable arrogation of privileges.

But whether or not Mayer's account is ultimately reducible to Cullity's, they both help illuminate what makes free-riding reprehensible. The free-riders objectionably grant themselves special privileges they are not entitled to and exploit others' cooperation to the scheme while shirking their duty to cooperate. With this basic outline of the wrongfulness of free-riding in hand, let us turn to the case for fairness-based political obligations of resistance.

THE NEGATIVE ARGUMENT

Can fairness require cooperating with an exploitative or harmful scheme of coordination? As we have seen, disjunctivists answer no, while unifiers answer a qualified yes. Either way, fairness allows all participants to refuse cooperation with exploitative or harmful schemes—on the disjunctive view, because the scheme does not distribute burdens and benefits justly, thereby violating one of the conditions necessary for fair-play obligations to arise; on the unified view, because the fair-play obligations to cooperate generated are weak and typically defeated by other moral demands (e.g., based on justice).

But I go further, arguing that, under certain circumstances, fairness not only allows all participants to refuse cooperation with exploitative or harmful schemes but also *prohibits* beneficiaries of such schemes to cooperate. The Negative Argument thus targets beneficiaries in particular (some and not all beneficiaries as we'll see shortly), while I will address victims' fair-play obligations later. This prohibition is compatible with the unified view that holds there are fair-play obligations to cooperate in unjust social schemes: if we accept the unified view, then we can say that the principle of fairness may sometimes be the source of conflicting sources of obligations—cooperation and noncooperation—which should be weighed against each other.

Here are the Negative Argument's barebones:

(1) Fairness prohibits free-riding, given the deontic wrong it involves.

(2) Benefiting from an exploitative or harmful scheme, under certain conditions, involves the same deontic wrong as free-riding.

(3) Therefore, under these conditions, fairness prohibits benefiting from an exploitative or harmful scheme.

We just saw that the wrong of free-riding may be understood as a form of objectionable preferential discrimination or exploitation and wrongful gain. Unsurprisingly, this is also how we can describe certain sociopolitical injustices, such as exploitation and discrimination, which epitomize unfairness. The idea is that benefiting from unfair social schemes, on the one hand, and free-riding, on the other, share a common deontic wrong. By definition, to benefit from wrongful exploitation or harms is to wrongfully gain at another's expense. But, as voluntarists point out, this is not sufficient to make beneficiaries morally like free-riders: they must further *intend* to take advantage of others' oppression. Intent is demonstrated by consenting to participate and through awareness of the injustice attending benefits or by occupying a position where one ought, reasonably, to be aware of that injustice. To accept a benefit in a consent-implying way typically requires receiving and enjoying the benefit and having the opportunity to refuse it at reasonable cost to oneself. Voluntarist critics stress that since the putative benefits of life under political authority are free and nonexcludable, states don't satisfy the latter condition—they don't offer benefits that agents can refuse.

But the voluntarist test—call it the "excludability test"—stacks the deck against the state by, in effect, stipulating that one cannot genuinely accept free and nonexcludable benefits. Pasternak has recently proposed a fine-grained framework to think about wrongful beneficiaries, which shows, against the excludability test, that consent-implying acceptance of free and nonexcludable goods is possible. She offers a fivefold categorization of wrongful beneficiaries ranging from involuntary to voluntary depending on four factors:

(1) Knowledge: does the beneficiary know, or could and should she have known, that she is enjoying the fruits of wrongdoing? (2) Desire: does the beneficiary welcome the benefit? (3) Activity: has the beneficiary deliberately put herself in a position where she stands to profit from wrongdoing? (4) Freedom: can the beneficiary avoid receiving the benefit without incurring unreasonable costs?[10]

On one end of the spectrum are "involuntary beneficiaries" who score negative on all questions; then come involuntary beneficiaries who know that they are enjoying the fruits of wrongdoing yet do not desire, did not seek, and cannot avoid receiving the benefits. "Welcoming beneficiaries" know the source of their benefits and welcome them. And at the other end of the spectrum, "voluntary beneficiaries" exhibit all the relevant factors, or all but activity. In sum, there are two sorts of involuntary beneficiaries, one sort of welcoming beneficiaries, and two sorts of voluntary beneficiaries.

Both welcoming and voluntary beneficiaries accept the fruits of wrongdoing in the relevant, consent-implying sense, whether the goods were excludable or not: they desire or welcome the benefits, all the while knowing that they were produced by wrongdoing. In some cases they actively seek them. One can reasonably say about these agents that they would not have refused the benefits even if they could have, would have sought them even if they were not free, and would gladly do their part to ensure that these benefits continue to be produced. Welcoming and voluntary beneficiaries, insofar as they accept the benefits produced by social schemes that they know to be wrongfully exploitative or harmful, take intentional advantage of others' disadvantage. Thus they may be deemed morally on par with free-riders and criticized for violating fair play.[11] On the other hand, involuntarily benefiting from injustice does not produce the deontic wrongs involved in free-riding. Whether agents are voluntary, welcoming, or involuntary beneficiaries of exploitative and harmful schemes, and thus whether they are morally akin to free-riders, can only be determined through a case-by-case examination of particular unjust schemes and participants' positions within. But as the case of Jim Crow shows, many citizens may be implicated.

Let us conceive of southern Whites as the beneficiaries of racial domination, and African Americans as its victims. (By drawing this simple line, I set aside many moral complexities of the situation, including the intersecting nature of classist, sexist, and racist oppression, the benefits to northern Whites, and the moral and psychic harms suffered by those implicated in wrongdoing.) Southern Whites' wrongful gains were numerous and multifaceted: economically, Whites gained in the form of better work and higher wages; psychologically, through heightened sense of self-worth; socially, through their higher status; and politically, by having full and equal capacity to participate in public decision-making.

The benefits of racial segregation—White privilege chief among them—were fundamentally free and nonexcludable for White people: they could not avoid benefiting from the better treatment and opportunities afforded by the color of their skin and the texture of their hair. Still, many Whites could be categorized as voluntary or welcoming beneficiaries of Jim Crow, as they supported the system with their actions and words: they voted for White-supremacist representatives and officials; expressed racist beliefs; mistreated Black people with whom they interacted; were active members or friends of the Ku Klux Klan, which counted four million members by 1925; perpetrated lynchings or attended public lynchings, which were often advertised in newspapers prior to the event (the public burning of Black teenage farmhand Jesse Washington in Waco, Texas, in 1916 attracted a crowd of fifteen thousand); refused, while serving on juries, to convict White defendants clearly guilty of crimes against Blacks; and so on. In the 1950s and 1960s, as the civil rights movement turned to direct action, some Whites condemned the Montgomery bus boycott, joined the mobs that attacked the Freedom Riders in South Carolina and Alabama, spat on student activists who sat at Whites-only restaurant counters, and demonstrated against school integration. They were clearly endorsing the benefits of racial segregation, and willing to take action to preserve it. Therefore, it is clear that they (i.e., some or many southern Whites) genuinely accepted its benefits, even though these were nonexcludable.

However, one may object that southern Whites, by and large, could not be reasonably expected to have known that the benefits they enjoyed resulted from serious injustice. Indifference, naivety, and moral blindness, encouraged by prevailing ideas of the time, including racist stereotypes and White-supremacist ideology, could explain their ignorance. Like privileged people in general, Whites under Jim Crow were prone to deceive themselves into thinking that they deserved their status and had earned their gains through personal talent and effort. In turn, seeing Blacks' lower socioeconomic position seemed to demonstrate the natural superiority of Whites. Simone de Beauvoir quotes George Bernard Shaw on the mechanics of this ideology: "The American White relegates the Black to the rank of shoeshine boy; and he concludes from this that the Black is good for nothing but shining shoes."[12] The injustice of subordination remains unseen as long as the privileges of the dominant group and the lot of the subordinated appear deserved. What is more, the privileged are often ill informed about the experiences of deprivation and oppression and little motivated to learn about them. (I return to this phenomenology of injustice in chapter 7, where I discuss the major obstacles to recognizing our political obligations of resistance.)

These mechanisms were undoubtedly at play in the Jim Crow South, at least for some people. However, identifying the psychological and ideological obstacles to understanding, compassion, and attention to social reality does not amount to absolving anyone of responsibility. Southern Whites who supported the system in the face of federal law demanding the end of racial segregation and vocal opposition from civil rights activists were well aware of what was at stake for them in abolishing the system. It is especially clear at that point, when opposition and dissent was widespread. However, the same could plausibly be said about the period before the federal government began ordering desegregation. Insofar as southern Whites chose and implemented racial segregation in the 1870s, deviating from the path toward racial equality that Reconstruction had set them on, they understood the rationales against Jim Crow. To the extent that Whites remained (fully or somewhat) sympathetic to White supremacy and contributed to maintaining the system, they were thus morally analogous to free-riders. They deliberately took advantage of Blacks' subjugation, in violation of the demands of fairness.

Does this conclusion extend to southern Whites who opposed Jim Crow and realized that the benefits they collected as Whites were unearned and wrong? Nonvoluntarist fair-play theorists, who do not consider acceptance of or desire for the goods necessary for fairness to generate obligations, would extend this conclusion to White opponents of Jim Crow, while proponents of the voluntarist view would categorize White opponents as involuntary beneficiaries, and thus deny their free-rider-like status. It is worth noting that the nonvoluntarist view aligns with how White opponents of Jim Crow felt and spoke, as they affirmed that their benefiting from an unjust system violated fairness, and that they had a moral duty not to support the system.[13] They could not always refuse these benefits, but they could highlight their unearned nature, extend some basic goods to Blacks (show respect, pay a fair wage, etc.), and speak up and act against racial segregation. Indeed, as I shall argue shortly, fairness demanded that they do so.

What about those beneficiaries who neither supported nor opposed the Jim Crow regime? One could reasonably expect them to be aware of the unjust mechanisms producing benefits they received, yet they did not exactly endorse these benefits. Think back on the White father we opened the chapter with. What is his reaction to the federally mandated integration of his children's school? Many White parents vehemently protested against racial integration, carrying signs that read, for instance, "Integration is a Mortal Sin," "Race Mixing is Communism," "Keep Our School White," and "Go Back to Africa Negroes." But let us say that, even if he is aware of the numerous injustices Blacks suffer under Jim Crow, our Mississippian may not have deplored or protested against the federal order to integrate his children's school—and this ought to make a difference, one might think. Perhaps he just went on living his life. What should we make of him and other "passive" White folks like him?

Fair-play theorists with nonvoluntarist commitments should conceive of the passive receipt of wrongful benefits as a violation of fairness, to the extent that compliance with the law indicates something like acquiescence to, if not endorsement of, these benefits. Southern Whites who neither supported nor opposed Jim Crow still cooperated with racial segregation and routinely enjoyed undeserved benefits, often blatantly at the expense of Blacks. Throughout the day, southern Whites saw Blacks waiting in long lines, crowding at the back of the bus, being called by their first names or as "boy" into old age, refused access to shops, theaters, hospitals, cemeteries, and entertainment parks (King speaks of the time "when you suddenly find your tongue twisted and your speech stammering as you seek to explain to your six year old daughter why she can't go to the public amusement park that has just been advertised on television, and see tears welling up in her eyes when she is told that Funtown is closed to colored children"[14]), and so on. Whites saw these humiliations and could imagine what they felt like. Passivity in the face of such obvious deprivation amounts to support.

But a voluntarist might be more ambivalent. Passive participants of Jim Crow did not seek the benefits of the system and thus never demonstrated intent to gain at someone else's expense. Whether one should extend the Negative Argument to these passive beneficiaries, then, depends on one's basic intuitions or meta-ethical commitments about what acceptance really involves. In my view, though, doing nothing is often blameworthy.

This illustration of the Negative Argument by means of Jim Crow should give a sense of how it might be applied to other unjust social schemes, including within legitimate societies. For instance, it can be applied to patriarchal societies, to show that men unjustly benefit from exploitative practices that diminish the opportunities and capacities of women at work, at home, and in the public sphere. If it can be shown that men's cooperation with sexist structures involves the kind of wrongs that make free-riding reprehensible, then an argument can be made that they are thereby prohibited by fairness to comply with these sexist structures.

A case-by-case approach must be taken to the question of whether agents accept benefits in the robust sense—whether, per Pasternak's framework, they know the source of the benefits, welcome them, deliberately sought them out, and could avoid receiving them at reasonable cost. And, in each instance, we must assess citizens' particular social situations, attitudes, and opportunities, and their level of cooperation with and support of the system.

THE RADICAL REFORM ARGUMENT

How does one cease benefiting from an unjust—exploitative or harmful—scheme of coordination? The answer is simple but demanding. One has no choice but to pursue radical reform. It is in effect the sole way to cease benefiting from an exploitative or harmful scheme of coordination, and resistance is crucial to bringing about radical reform. In brief:

(1) Under certain conditions, fairness prohibits benefiting from unjust (exploitative or harmful) schemes of coordination.

(2) There are three possible ways of not benefiting from an unjust scheme: exit, restitution, and radical reform.

(3) Exit is often excessively difficult and is generally undesirable.

(4) Restitution is complicated and insufficient.

(5) Radical reform offers the most straightforward way to cease benefiting from an exploitative scheme of coordination.

(6) Resistance is often crucial to bringing about radical reform.

(7) Therefore, under certain conditions, one ought to resist the unjust scheme of coordination from which one benefits.

Premises (1) through (5) form the Radical Reform Argument, and claims (5) through (7) the Resistance Argument. Let me examine the Radical Reform Argument and the Resistance Argument in turn.

The Radical Reform Argument is an argument by elimination. By examining and rejecting other candidates, it establishes radical reform as the most straightforward way of discharging one's fairness-based obligation not to benefit from an unjust scheme of coordination. Premise (1) is the conclusion of the Negative Argument; premises (2), (3), and (4) are descriptive claims in need of empirical support.

Premise (2) seems straightforward, although I may have overlooked other options. As far as I am aware, the only ways to cease receiving benefits from a scheme are to withdraw from the scheme, refuse ongoing benefits and return past ones, and transform the scheme so that it ceases producing benefits unjustly. I refer to the transformation in the latter option as "radical reform" to underscore the magnitude and scope of change required to eliminate the unfair privileges and wrongful gains of unjust social coordination.

In political cases, exit or withdrawal generally involves emigration. Blacks or White opponents of the unjust practices in the Jim Crow South at that time had the option to relocate to the North, Midwest, or West of the United States, but this is not strictly speaking emigration. For the sake of this discussion, let us assume that Jim Crow was a self-contained, independent system. As a matter of fact, some White opponents of Jim Crow, and many victims, found it impossible to stay in the South and chose to leave. More than six million

African Americans and thirteen million Whites left during the Great Migration, between 1916 and 1970.[15] However, the price of emigration may be too high to be required by fairness alone. As David Hume pointed out in response to John Locke's claim that continued residence in a state's territory amounts to tacit consent to its law, emigration carries enormous transition and adjustment costs.[16] These costs are not only financial and practical, as Hume emphasized, but also psychic, insofar as most people have strong feelings of attachment to their geographical roots and birthplace.

But, setting aside the cost and disruptiveness of relocating, one cannot enact change from within if one opts to exit. In this sense, even if leaving a place because of unjust practices taking place there were a viable and reasonably costly option, it would not be a desirable one from a practical and moral standpoint, since it leaves intact the scheme's arrangements. White beneficiaries, if they are from a privileged background, may be well situated to influence the scheme. In addition, since those who would seek to escape it are probably most critical of it, it is better that they stay within the scheme and work toward changing it. Hence premise (3), exit from an unjust scheme, is often not only excessively difficult but undesirable.

People can also choose to seek restitution, reparation, and compensation for victims in order to cease benefiting from unjust schemes. As recent work in reparative justice indicates, beneficiaries of injustice owe special duties to return ill-gotten goods and remedy the disadvantage suffered by victims. Robert Goodin argues that even where recipients and victims can no longer be identified, the holders of unjust gains have a duty to "disgorge" (expel or return) the unjust benefits they currently control, to be used for the public good.[17] Theorists recognize the complications of tracing, calculating, and returning benefits from injustice but usually consider cash payments and taxes decent ways of giving back. Affirmative action can be another method of restitution. (Exactly who should receive how much and in what form is controversial, and I will not focus on these issues here.)

The notion of a duty to give back seems implicit in fairness, whose root is reciprocity. But this appeal to restitution faces challenges, and not just practical ones. For one thing, establishing restitution rules doesn't ensure that anyone ceases benefiting from unjust schemes. Such rules do not address the scheme's system of entitlements but simply try to alleviate some of its adverse impact. In fact, restitution rules may even reinforce structural injustice by giving the scheme a more "humane" appearance while further entrenching and stabilizing privileges and wrongs. (This is the gist of Marx's critique of liberal reformists, and of the "pre-distribution" critique of welfare states, according to which welfare states attempt to equalize distribution of goods post facto but do not reorganize social and economic relations to ensure equal standing in the first place.[18]) Jim Crow plus reparations plus affirmative action may be better than Jim Crow tout court (or not), but it is still structurally unjust. If, however, restitution occurs alongside termination of the scheme's wrongs, then we have moved beyond restitution to radical reform (and indeed some theorists prefer classifying affirmative action under reform rather than restitution).

The champion of restitution may finally appeal to the communicative function of affirmative action rather than its impact on the distribution of burdens and benefits. According to Thomas E. Hill Jr., the moral justifications put forth in defense of affirmative action—the messages it sends—matter just as much as whether it successfully gives back.[19] In his view, both exclusively forward-looking (utilitarian) arguments and exclusively backward-looking (reparation-oriented) arguments tend to express the wrong message, while a defense of affirmative action focused on "cross-temporal narrative values," such as mutual respect, expresses the right message.[20]

However, even this more sophisticated argument for restitution is unsuccessful. For affirmative action cannot express the right message unless it realizes, or at least shows a sincere commitment to realizing, the cross-temporal values appealed to in its justification. Simply adding a program of affirmative action to a racist scheme cannot really express mutual respect.

The defects of the argument for restitution speak to the necessity of eliminating the *source* of wrongful gains, which brings us to premise (5), the conclusion of the Radical Reform Argument. In the case of Jim Crow, fairness does not demand adding restitution rules to a regime of racial stratification but instead obliges terminating the regime. The only practical way of not benefiting from an exploitative scheme is to transform the structures and institutions of that scheme so that it ceases wrongfully privileging some at the expense of others. The necessary reform is radical because it addresses the root (*radix*, in Latin) of the unfair allocation of burdens and benefits, including the system of norms and entitlements that underlie the scheme's practices.

THE RESISTANCE ARGUMENT

Premise (6) is an empirical claim: resistance is often crucial to bringing about radical reform. There may be other ways of bringing about radical reform, besides resistance. It is possible to radically reform an unjust scheme through outside intervention—think of Germany after World War II—or by executive fiat. But it is reasonable to argue that resistance is a critical, if neither necessary nor sufficient, cause of extensive political change.

Recall that by "resistance" I mean a multidimensional continuum of dissenting acts and practices, all of which express condemnation of and/or refusal to conform to the dominant system's norms.

Resistance thus applies to a broad range of activities, including petitions, demonstrations, strikes, slowdowns, boycotts, and efforts to work within appropriate legal and political channels (and I will not focus on principled disobedience in this chapter). Although it is possible to correct an oppressive scheme without resisting it, this is highly improbable.

One of the goals of resistance is to communicate condemnation of a wrong. As we saw in the previous chapter, it is difficult to see how radical reform could be achieved without first raising awareness about the injustice to be corrected, especially in cases of structural injustice, since privilege tends to be invisible to the privileged. Jean Harvey thus insists that educational initiatives such as consciousness-raising workshops and teach-ins, in which the privileged listen to victims speak about their oppression, qualify as acts of resistance.[21] Everyday resistance in the household and the workplace, such as challenging racist jokes and stereotypes, also falls in this category of educational resistance, as do information campaigns designed to improve the community's conception of justice, which we discussed in the previous chapter. As we'll see in chapter 7, one also has a duty to resist self-deception, by educating oneself against unconscious biases and exercising due care in reasoning.

In addition to seeking and spreading awareness, resistance highlights the wrongfulness of a scheme's system of entitlements. The resistor communicates disavowal of the scheme's values and rules, draws attention to the structural roots of injustice, and conveys the urgent need for a radical reform. Educational initiatives and expressions of dissent help pave the way for sustained collective action, which is critical to instigating reform. Indeed history suggests, and social and political scientists have recently demonstrated, that civil resistance campaigns—especially when they involve mass and persistent participation—help to overcome an unjust status quo and usher in peaceful democracies.[22]

To the extent that resistance—ranging from individual everyday resistance to organized collective action—contributes to, and is often critical for, reform, we can reasonably infer the conclusion stated in (7): under certain conditions, people ought to resist unjust schemes from which they wrongfully benefit, in order to reform the scheme and dismantle the production of benefits. The political obligation of resistance identified here is imperfect: it leaves individuals to decide how to discharge it. This does not mean that any act of resistance, however small, is sufficient to meet it. How much resistance is enough is of course a difficult question. People (including "allies") are prone to underestimate how much they should do and overestimate how much they do. They tend to feel contented with small acts, without bothering doing the more meaningful work they could be doing. For instance, Whites under Jim Crow wouldn't meet their duty to resist racial injustice simply by voting for equal civil rights. They also ought to contribute their money, time, and energy to the political efforts. They ought to treat Black people with respect; call out other Whites on their overt racism; and raise unprejudiced, nonracist children: their interpersonal and even familial relations should be transformed by their recognition of their duty to resist. In truth, only persistent action can demonstrate a commitment to cease benefiting from, and work to reform, an unjust scheme.

TWO ARGUMENTS FOR SOLIDARITY

What is solidarity? A good definition is this: meaningful cooperation and collective action to advance shared goals and values. The term seems best suited to describe bonds *among* the oppressed. Solidarity *with* the oppressed is sometimes referred to as "allyship" (or "allyhood"), to mark the different sociopolitical and epistemic situation of members of the dominant group—the fact that they can help but cannot identify with the oppressed and do not share their experiences. I explain in chapter 6 my concerns with the concept of "ally," and why I prefer that of "solidarity" to describe both in-group and out-group bonds, but I also identify significant differences between the two kinds of solidarity (within and toward oppressed groups).

There is, first, an empirical argument for solidarity in resistance, grounded in the need for sustained collective action to achieve radical reform. Indeed, organizing resistance increases the likelihood that volunteers' resources will be put to good use. Alliances and coalitions allow the sharing of resources and advantages and increase the chances of publicity. And once organized movements are in place, joining them is often relatively easy, as they simplify the individual's choice of how to discharge her moral obligations by presenting her with a specific agenda of activities.

In addition, numbers matter. For many or most forms of protest, such as civil resistance campaigns and labor strikes, the more participants the better. A thousand people rallying for a cause are more impressive than a hundred, and tens of thousands can turn a demonstration into a real "event" in the public's eye. Chenoweth and Stephan found that no civil resistance campaign failed that had achieved the sustained participation of just 3.5 percent of the population. They also stress that mass mobilization is especially effective when participation is diverse. The Montgomery bus boycott offers a powerful example of mass mobilization, while the Freedom Rides embody interracial solidarity.

Alongside this empirical argument for political solidarity, we can also make such an argument on the basis of fairness. Insofar as fairness prohibits free-riding and requires mutual cooperation, it can be understood to imply a requirement to do one's share in bringing about radical reform by joining efforts on its behalf. The activist social movement is itself a scheme of cooperation in which resistance is the cost and justice the main benefit. Who benefits from a successful resistance campaign? Both the victims and beneficiaries of the unjust scheme do: victims of the displaced scheme gain their freedom from oppression, and wrongful beneficiaries of the displaced scheme gain in moral terms, as they are no longer implicated in injustice and violating the demands of fairness. Both victims and beneficiaries may be tempted to free-ride on others' efforts to reform the scheme, since resistance is risky and costly in terms of time and resources. But fairness requires joining these efforts and grounds a demand for political solidarity both *among* and *with* the oppressed.

Victims of injustice, that is, exploited participants or harmed nonmembers of a social scheme, have a fairness-based duty to join existent resistance efforts that have a reasonable chance of success. Idle bystanders of such efforts would be free-riding on others' activism, in violation of fair play. Black residents of Montgomery, Alabama, for instance, had a fair-play obligation to join the organized boycott of the city's segregated buses in 1955–1956, despite the sacrifices it involved, insofar as the boycott represented a promising collective effort toward radical reform (75 percent of the buses' passengers were Black). Black taxi drivers, in their own show of solidarity with Black customers, charged the same fare as a bus ride.

For another example of collective resistance to exploitative schemes that demands solidarity on the basis of fair play, consider strikes. "An enormously disruptive form of collective action," according to Alex Gourevitch, strikes often involve unlawful actions, threats to and violations of owners' property rights (including property damage), and the use of coercive force (e.g., in confrontation with security forces and to prevent other workers from going to work). They impose economic costs and serious inconveniences to the wider community. Yet these risks, costs, and harms may be justified when the strike's goals are legitimate and, in Gourevitch's analysis, when it "looks like a credible attempt at reducing injustice."[23] Thus some strikes are justified while involving various dimension of uncivil disobedience (violence and coercion), as the textile workers' strikes did in Lawrence, Massachusetts, in 1912. Crucially, fairness can ground a duty of solidarity to join these strikes and share the burdens of cooperation.

In addition, fairness demands political solidarity *with* the oppressed, as a way to express the beneficiaries' commitment to fairness—to cease gaining from the unjust scheme and share in the burdens of reforming it. To put it in Hill's terms, political solidarity sends the right message. Avery Kolers has also recently argued that solidarity is a principal means for wrongful beneficiaries to affirm and act on the equal status of the victims, and an intrinsically valuable way to atone for having benefited from injustice and wrongfully gained at someone else's expense, whether they did so voluntarily or not.[24] In fact, these appeals to the expressive function and intrinsic value of solidarity suggest that solidarity may be appraised independently from its causal contribution to reforming the scheme, just as the wrongfulness of free-riding is independent of its effects on the production of goods.

Not just any act of solidaristic resistance is sufficient or appropriate to discharge this fair-play obligation. Activist and blogger Mia McKenzie notes that allies often wrongly assume that "one act of solidarity makes you an ally forever,"[25] or, in our case, is sufficient to discharge one's duty of solidarity: it isn't. As we'll see in further details in chapter 6, there are wrong and right ways of acting in solidarity with the oppressed. Kolers identifies the right way when he argues: "Solidarity demands that we [wrongful beneficiaries] join in collective action for justice by organized out-groups"—it is important that intended beneficiaries (*viz.*, the victims of injustice) be the ones organizing this effort—and "that we do so in a way that defers to their best judgment about our role in supporting them."[26]

Beneficiaries ought to follow the lead of oppressed people and offer solidarity and support on the terms defined by the latter.

In this way, fairness demands and constrains political solidarity. To take the example of the Montgomery bus boycott again, Whites had an obligation to act in solidarity with Blacks—all Whites (or at least, on voluntarist grounds, all welcoming and voluntary beneficiaries of Jim Crow), and not just beneficiaries of that city's segregated bus system, because racial segregationists everywhere (knew they) had to lose, and civil rights activists everywhere (knew they) had to gain, from Montgomery's desegregated public transportation. This obligation could be discharged through various acts of resistance. White residents of Montgomery could join the bus boycott, offer to carpool, and intervene when Black boycotters were assaulted in the streets. Whites across the country could publicly support the boycott, send money to the Montgomery Improvement Association (MIA) that guided the boycott under King's leadership, and donate shoes to replace the worn footwear of those who walked for miles rather than board a bus.

COSTS OF RESISTANCE

One might object that the fair-play duty to reform and resist unjust social schemes is too demanding of beneficiaries. Unjust social schemes typically attach heavy costs to noncompliance, even (sometimes, especially) for their beneficiaries. In the United States, many if not most of the 1,300 Whites lynched by White-supremacist mobs between 1882 and 1959 were seen as threats to the racial caste system, often in their capacity as civil rights activists.[27]

I concede that dangerous courses of action are not morally required. But when fairness is used to ground the moral duty to obey the law, it is understood to require substantial sacrifices, such as paying taxes or fighting in a conscript army. If discharging the duty of fair play can involve substantial sacrifices, the same may be presumed about the fairness-based duty to resist.

Nevertheless, the fair-play duty to resist cannot demand sacrificing one's life or exposing other people to significant risks. This is not to say that fair-play obligations are morally weak. In particular, a person cannot reject a promising (from the standpoint of effectiveness) and morally justifiable course of action on the grounds that it jeopardizes some of the benefits that he or she wrongfully gained in the first place, such as social status or a cushy job. The duty to resist demands taking positive steps, such as engaging in everyday resistance against cultural practices, learning about oppression from the scheme's victims, joining protest marches, and boycotting certain social events. Although the individual has discretion when it comes to discharging the demands of fairness, he or she can be blamed for failing to take any positive measures. Moreover, beneficiaries often have special access to the workings of the unjust scheme, which can improve the effectiveness of their resistance efforts.

Fair-play theorists argue that citizens of legitimate states are participants in mutually beneficial cooperative schemes, and they owe fellow participants to do their part in sustaining the scheme by complying with its rules. Failing to do so is then morally wrong—an instance of free-riding. Voluntarist critics object that citizens rarely count as willing and knowing cooperators, so that they cannot in general be morally bound to comply with the state. At the same time, some theorists submit and others deny that consenting participants can be bound by fairness to cooperate with unjust social schemes. Both camps only think of the demands of fairness in terms of cooperation, so that where fairness does not require cooperation, it does not demand *anything*, in their view.

This chapter argued instead that under certain conditions, fairness prohibits benefiting from, and requires reforming and resisting, exploitative or harmful schemes of coordination. This means that fairness can ground both obligations to cooperate with a social scheme (just or unjust, depending on one's meta-ethical commitments) and obligations to reform and resist unjust social schemes from which one benefits. In addition, victims of exploitative and harmful schemes are also bound by fairness to join resistance efforts, under certain conditions. These political obligations of resistance can be met by undertaking various types of action, including principled—civil and uncivil—disobedience.

In conclusion, the principle of fairness, which is one of the grounds most commonly used to support the moral duty to obey the law, also supports political obligations to resist injustice. This important finding constitutes the second pillar of the case for revisiting our concept of political obligation and paying greater attention to the ways in which living under and participating in unjust conditions affects our political obligations. Under nonideal, all-too-often unjust conditions, obeying the law is neither the sole, nor the most important, of our political obligations.

Chapter 5

Samaritanism

Cubbon Park is a large, lovely public garden in the heart of the southern Indian city of Bangalore. It hosts a library, museums, an aquarium, a tennis academy, and several pavilions. In November the park explodes with the purplish-pink, trumpet-shaped blooms of the Tabebuia tree. On a Saturday afternoon, Vira Mistry, twenty-four years old, strolls through the park and settles on a shady, grassy area. She tries to take a nap: "I lay there and couldn't sleep," she later recalled.

> I realized that there is a learned subconscious fear of being so exposed and vulnerable. You wonder who's looking at you, what they are thinking, are they taking pictures? When you're so used to walking around and having men stare at you all day, it is hard to let go of that anxiety of being in a public space.

Mistry was attending her first Meet To Sleep event. Blank Noise, the Indian activist group that organized the event, protests widespread sexual violence against women in an effort to "shift the fear based relationship we have been taught to have with our cities" and to "initiate a dialogue on trust." On their Facebook page, Blank Noise writes:

> We will Meet To Sleep for our will to be fearless.
> We will Meet To Sleep for our right to be unwarned.
> We will Meet To Sleep to build new memory with our very own
>   public parks.[1]

One evening, two weeks before Mistry lay down on the grass, a thirty-year-old woman who was on her way to play tennis was raped by two of the park's security guards. Blank Noise reported the reaction of the head of the Ministry of Home Affairs, or Home Minister, who is responsible for India's internal security: "Why should a woman go play tennis at 9:30pm?" In response, the group denounced ubiquitous victim-blaming with the slogan, "I Never Ask For It."

Hundreds of women have participated in sleep-ins around India, in a collective effort to reclaim public spaces. "I want to 'Meet To Sleep' because in three years, I've never been in a public space without being afraid for my safety," one participant explained. "I want to reclaim this city and the places that are as much mine as they are anybody else's." Women do not nap in India's public parks. They avoid them, or pass through them hurriedly, on guard. India's streets, buses, trains, workplaces, prisons, and homes are dangerous for women, too. Rape is rampant, if still underreported.[2] As Blank Noise founder Jasmeen Patheja put it, the project aims to revise these conditions, to make India's public places safe for "women who are relaxed, asleep, defenseless, not hurried, and not rushed."[3]

Meet To Sleep participants call themselves Action Heroes. I contend that they are good Samaritans. They may not sound much like the "original" Samaritan who, according to the biblical parable, stopped in his tracks to help a man left nearly dead beside the road after being attacked by robbers. Mistry and her fellow activists also don't cut the figure popularized by Peter Singer—the Samaritan who steps in a shallow pond to save a drowning child. Yet Samaritans these activists are, in the sense that matters to our duties to each other.

THE SAMARITAN DUTY AND THE DUTY TO OBEY THE LAW

The Samaritan duty requires us to aid persons in peril or dire need when we can do so at no unreasonable cost to ourselves.[4] Although scholars disagree on the nature or source of the duty of easy rescue (is it a duty to prevent harm or a duty of beneficence?), and on questions surrounding its legal enforcement (e.g., regarding liability, sanctions, clumsy Samaritans, and potentially unintended consequences), nearly everyone accepts its existence and stringency.[5] Like the duty of justice, the Samaritan duty is a *natural* duty, which means that it is grounded in our nature as moral beings and binds us all equally, regardless of our relations or voluntary undertakings. The Samaritan duty is generally deemed among the most stringent requirements of ordinary and critical morality. According to Joel Feinberg, it is "virtually as stringent" as the duty not to harm or put someone in harm's way.[6] Feinberg casts the duty as a duty to prevent harm, while others, like Peter Unger and Liam Murphy, conceive of it as a duty of beneficence.[7]

The Samaritan duty arises in situations in which (1) some fundamental human interest or noncontingent basic need—including, minimally, life, security, and bodily integrity—is threatened; (2) the threat is immediate, imminent, or probable; and (3) someone else—typically an innocent passer-by or bystander—is able to help at no unreasonable cost to herself and others.[8] The severity of Samaritan perils depends on the magnitude of the harm threatened or inflicted, as well as the probability that a threat will be realized.

Per condition (3), one unable to help, or unable to help at a reasonable cost to herself and others, is not a potential Samaritan rescuer. But the cost qualification attached to the Samaritan duty shouldn't be misunderstood. "Reasonable" does not mean "trivial," and rescue need not be easy. I follow Cécile Fabre's illuminating account, in which a potential rescuer has a duty to help "only if the following three conditions obtain: (a) they are physically able to help; (b) the cost of doing so is not such as to jeopardize their prospects for a flourishing life; and (c) giving the required assistance would not put them at a high risk of incurring those costs."[9] Fabre notes that although individuals cannot be duty-bound to incur a high risk of dying for the sake of another, they can be duty-bound to incur some life-threatening risk.

So, if a toddler is drowning in a shallow pond as I walk by, I am morally bound to step in and rescue her. Pointing out that I am not the one who imperiled the child, that I am in a hurry, or that someone else will surely pass by the pond soon won't let me off the hook. I may be in a wheelchair, and unable to go the toddler's rescue myself, and I will still be duty-bound to assist her, by calling 911 and crying for help. Only if I am unaware of the child's dire straits, say, because of very poor eyesight or hearing, do I not have a duty to help her. Missing my classes and having mud on my shoes because I stopped to rescue the child are very reasonable costs. But suppose the pond is an ocean or a large river: could I be required to swim to the child's rescue? It depends on the particulars of the situation: perhaps I have a heart condition, or it is dark, the water is choppy and I am likely to drown, too. Presumably, lesser Samaritan perils demand lesser sacrifices: the cost of assistance in cases that involve less probable and/or less serious harm could be, let us say, far from jeopardizing one's prospects for a flourishing life.

The Samaritan duty grounds an influential account of legitimacy and political obligation propounded by Christopher H. Wellman.[10] The state has the unique capacity to protect everyone from the violence and chaos of the state of nature: it is legitimate when and to the extent that it rescues others from dire need and peril and achieves political stability. In Wellman's view, "my state may justifiably coerce *me* only because this coercion is a necessary and not unreasonably burdensome means of securing crucial benefits for *others*."[11] The move from the state's right to coerce me (state legitimacy) to my duty to obey appears straightforward: if my compliance with the law is necessary to the success of the state's Samaritan mission, then I have a Samaritan duty to comply with the law. The problem is that my compliance is not necessary for the state to achieve its Samaritan goal. In fact it makes virtually no difference whether *I* comply with the law or not: a well-functioning state requires only general, not universal, conformity and indeed tolerates a certain amount of noncompliance.

Wellman therefore supplements the Samaritan account of the duty to obey the law with nonconsequentialist considerations of fairness. "We understand our political obligations as our fair share of the communal Samaritan chore of rescuing others from the perils of the state of nature," he writes.[12] And this fair contribution to the Samaritan rescue can come only in the form of obedience to the law because political instability, which is fertile ground for violence, is fundamentally a coordination problem that cannot be solved without forcing everyone within a given territory to defer to the same authority and play by the same rules.

But what happens when the law itself is oppressive, even though the state is stable? Wellman recognizes that there can be reasons for disobeying the law and resisting injustice in otherwise-legitimate states. These reasons, in his view, stem from the injustice of particular laws. For instance, though the state imposes a Samaritan duty to obey the law, he argues that Martin Luther King "was morally at liberty to break the particular laws he disobeyed simply because they were unjust."[13]

But I go further. Many reasons for resisting injustice are Samaritan in nature, grounded in the duty to rescue people from peril. Indeed the Samaritan duty may obligate one to protest injustice or break unjust laws, under certain conditions, when unjust laws, institutions, and practices endanger people, by prohibiting Samaritan rescues or facilitating the incidence of violence on members of a social group.

ILLEGAL SAMARITAN RESCUES

States sometimes subvert fulfillment of citizens' Samaritan duties, either directly by outlawing performance of the duty itself, or incidentally, through unrelated laws that burden the Samaritan. My contention is that, under either circumstance, disobedience is required of those capable of it. If Samaritan duty holds at all, then it does so even if fulfilling it forces an agent to break the law.

Lawbreaking is incidental to the Samaritan rescue when the connection between the law broken and the endangerment of the person is accidental. For instance, a hiker may break into a cabin in the mountains, thus trespassing on private property, in order to find resources to take care of an injured companion. Per the so-called necessity defense, the law recognizes that a technical breach in an emergency situation sometimes averts a great evil or furthers some greater good, and that, in these cases, strict adherence to the law cannot be required.[14] I shall not address incidental Samaritan disobedience, as I am primarily interested in cases where the peril that calls for Samaritan rescue is causally connected to the law being broken.

Lawbreaking occurs directly when the law explicitly prohibits Samaritan rescue. An infamous example is the Fugitive Slave Act of 1850, which forbade aiding runaway slaves and instead demanded that people assist law officers in slaves' capture. Frederick Douglass describes the law as one that "makes mercy to [Blacks] a crime."[15] Yet any able resident of the antebellum United States was morally required to take care of wounded escaped slaves knocking at their doors, even though such assistance directly violated the law, unless they could be sure that they would be found out. For a recent example, take Alabama's 2011 HB 56, which criminalized "certain behavior relating to concealing, harboring, shielding, or attempting to conceal, harbor, or shield unauthorized aliens" (this provision was blocked in court months after the law went into effect), and France's immigration law L622-1, which punishes anyone who "facilitates or attempts to facilitate the illegal entry, movement or residence of a foreigner in France . . . by imprisonment for five years and a fine of €30,000 (over $32,000)." U.S. or French citizens who help undocumented immigrants—say, by serving them food at a soup kitchen, providing them shelter, or driving them to the hospital—could be charged with a felony. Yet such Samaritan assistance may be morally required.

Laws banning Samaritan rescues appear inherently unjust: they prohibit the exercise of basic moral duties and violate the fundamental dignity of individuals as agents capable of engaging in practical deliberation, pursuing moral ends, and taking responsibility for their actions. In France, a grassroots campaign seeking to repeal restrictive anti-immigration laws stresses that *sans-papiers* (unauthorized aliens) are human beings in dire need—"isolated and destitute men, women, and children."[16] It is citizens' duty to help them. The law, in their view, violates the dignity of immigrants by erasing them and that of citizens by prohibiting them from fulfilling their Samaritan duty. The campaign included a spectacular incident of civil disobedience, with 5,500 Samaritans turning themselves in to the police for their lawbreaking ("délit de solidarité" in French): "If solidarity is a crime," they proclaimed, "then we demand to be arrested for this crime!" Though they framed their campaign in terms of solidarity, they could as well have chanted: "If rescuing those in need is a crime, then we demand to be arrested for this crime!"

But unlike this particular public campaign of civil disobedience, note that Samaritan disobedience in the case of illegal rescues is not and cannot be public: to be effective, the Samaritan agent must break the law covertly, or else risk being arrested and putting the undocumented migrant at risk of being arrested and deported. Thus the Roya Valley citizens in the French Alps (mentioned in chapter 3) and other sanctuary groups, who assist unauthorized refugees with food, shelter, clothing, basic healthcare needs, transportation, and legal advice—all in violation of the law—are forced to act covertly in order to protect those they seek to aid.

SAMARITAN DISOBEDIENCE

The Samaritan duty may thus demand breaking the law covertly in the course of a rescue. I want to go farther and argue that the Samaritan duty also supports resisting injustice through protest and civil disobedience in some cases. The case for Samaritan civil disobedience extends the above reasoning, regarding cases of illegal Samaritan rescues, to more complex situations in which social and political conditions produce not just laws that prevent rescue but what we might call *persistent Samaritan perils*. In such cases, injustice generates, enables, or aggravates Samaritan perils, making them pervasive. Under these circumstances, citizens themselves are passers-by. They can best, perhaps only, fulfill the duty to rescue by promoting reform: rescuing people from persistent Samaritan perils involves eliminating or righting the injustice at the root of the peril—that is, reforming unjust laws, policies, or institutions. Finally, principled disobedience may be an effective tool against persistent Samaritan peril because it can signal to the public that such peril exists and because it can stimulate the reform necessary for rescue.

Persistent Samaritan Perils

What makes a Samaritan peril "persistent"? It is so because an interrelated system of norms, practices, and institutions repeatedly subjects members of given social groups to injustice. As we saw in the previous chapter, Jim Crow is a strong example: the racial caste system induced persistent Samaritan peril by excluding African Americans from political participation and subjecting them to conditions of extreme material deprivation. The system was maintained through coercion, intimidation, and terror, enabled and aggravated by police and officials.

Today's system of mass incarceration presents another such example that demands our attention urgently.[17] In 2017, there were more than 2.3 million prisoners held in the United States, with an additional 5 million on probation or parole.[18] How are prison inmates in peril? Prisons are overcrowded. The Supreme Court declared in 2011 that overcrowding in California penitentiaries had become so severe that it violated a prisoner's Eighth Amendment right to freedom from cruel and unusual punishment.[19] There is also a great deal of violence in prisons, whether routine physical assault by inmates and staff or endemic rape. The Justice Department estimates that, in 2008, nearly a quarter million people were sexually abused in prisons and jails, often repeatedly.[20] In "supermax" prison facilities—of which there are 350 in the United States, and none in the European Union—nearly all inmates are placed in solitary confinement for extended periods of time, sometimes decades. Prisoners in less secure penitentiaries may be held in solitary for lengthy terms as well. Many psychologists believe such treatment is a form of torture and precursor to insanity.[21]

American urban ghettos may also be described as sources of persistent Samaritan perils, perhaps especially for young men, whose interests in life and bodily integrity are under constant threat. First-person testimonies, such as Geoffrey Canada's description of growing up on the South Side of Chicago and Ta-Nehisi Coates's Baltimore memoirs, as well as social scientific research about life in poor, crime-ridden neighborhoods, portray a Hobbesian society of insecurity, violence, and stress.[22] Favelas and other types of low-income, crime-ridden, densely populated neighborhoods in Latin America, Southeast Asia, and Africa present similar climates.

Many of the Black and Brown residents of these neighborhoods and beyond suffer police brutality, sufficiently rampant in the United States to qualify as a persistent Samaritan peril. Scholars have generally concentrated on police brutality and patrol tactics in the urban ghetto. But, as BLM activists have emphasized, police methods threaten the basic interests of every Black and Brown person, regardless of socioeconomic status and sex.[23] A recent Justice Department report goes beyond race to expose the special vulnerability of women, sex workers, and LGBTQ people to assault and sexual harassment by Baltimore Police. Although the report focuses on one city, its authors expect that police departments across the country exhibit similar misogynistic and transphobic prejudices.[24]

Girls and women are under persistent Samaritan peril in many parts of the world, subject to gender-selective killing, male violence, sexual trafficking, rape, and enslavement. Even in the United States, women commonly fear for their safety. The Bureau of Justice Statistics estimates that a rape occurs every 6.2 minutes in the United States.[25] At least some female populations experience such a high incidence of violence that they ought to be considered in persistent Samaritan peril. The situation of American Indian women is so dire that President Barack Obama called it "an assault on our national conscience . . . an affront to our shared humanity."[26] It is estimated that one in three indigenous women is the victim of completed rape in her lifetime.[27]

Refugees and LGBTQ people also experience persistent Samaritan perils. Migrants' journeys are fraught with dangers.[28] Refugee camps are unsanitary, disease-ridden, depressing places with alarmingly high levels of violence and suicide.[29] Refugees' condition constitutes persistent Samaritan peril insofar as it is the result of injustice, and not mere misfortune. For their part, LGBTQ people are particularly vulnerable to hate crimes, sexual assault, violence, and suicidal ideation, especially in deeply homophobic and transphobic societies where such ill treatment is enabled or aggravated by anti-gay and anti-trans law.[30]

Identifying persistent Samaritan perils, as these examples suggest, requires some empirical knowledge about the incidence of violence and intimidation with respect to particular groups, its effects on members' well-being, and the social etiology of threats—that is, their correlation to injustice. Not all groups whose fundamental interests are under grave threat may be deemed in persistent Samaritan peril—it depends on whether an injustice gives rise to the enduring dangers. For instance, although wealthy Mexicans suffer a high rate of kidnapping-for-ransom, I don't think that they are in persistent Samaritan peril, because their vulnerability is not the result of injustice but instead of their wealth and status.[31]

Once we identify persistent Samaritan peril, what are we to do? We turn now to the passers-by who observe peril underway. They owe certain duties in light of threats that they may not themselves face, duties that may demand intervention and principled disobedience.

Citizens as Passers-by

Typical Samaritans, like the man in the biblical story from which the term takes its name, stop in their tracks when they see an injustice, and lend a helping hand. In modern life, we encounter strangers in need in a wide range of situations. Active bystander intervention constitutes one form of Samaritan assistance. When we (literally) pass by someone in Samaritan peril, or in a situation that could escalate into one, we can and ought to intervene as active bystanders to de-escalate the situation. Basic strategies for safe intervention include the "three D's." A Samaritan ought to (1) direct: confront the perpetrator or ask the victim if they are okay, (2) distract: defuse the situation by distracting either party, and (3) delegate: bring in another person to help.[32] Suppose you are in the bus and witness someone being harassed, insulted, and threatened, on the basis of their perceived Muslim identity: depending on your particular situation (sex, perceived social identity, physical attributes, company, etc.) you can tell the harassers to leave the victim alone or you can simply go sit by the person, pretend you know them, and start a conversation. If the situation continues to escalate, you can alert the bus driver, call on others to come help, ring the alarm, or call the police.

Active bystander intervention is very often called for in contexts of persistent Samaritan perils, where violence is common. Citizens ought to be informed about and trained in active bystander strategies in order to safely help victims. So there are Samaritan political obligations to be responsible bystanders, aware of our surroundings and ready to intervene and de-escalate threatening situations.

I want to go further here and examine a second, more abstract and more critical level of Samaritan assistance, which is citizens' responsibility in the face of persistent Samaritan perils. Citizens may be viewed as passers-by to persistent Samaritan perils anywhere in their (local, national, or global) societies where they encounter them, and they constitute potential rescuers insofar as they are capable of assisting the current and potential victims of Samaritan perils through political action.

But how does one "pass by" a persistent Samaritan peril (rather than one of its discrete occurrences)? Persistent Samaritan perils are structural and, as the student protesters famously put it on the blackboard of a Sorbonne classroom in May 1968, "structures don't go down into the streets." One can encounter particular, actual people in peril, but how does one encounter a persistent Samaritan peril? What makes one a potential rescuer? What kind of political action could rescue people from persistent Samaritan perils?

Let me first defend the claim that citizens could be deemed passers-by to persistent Samaritan perils, not just their discrete occurrence. Not every citizen is properly described as a potential rescuer, for some might not be aware of the peril or might be unable to help. But, I want to say, many—or most—citizens, including the potential victims themselves, are passers-by capable of assistance. Could this be? After all, there are at least three grounds of objection. First, it is widely assumed that passers-by must be close to the peril, yet many citizens will be far away. Second, passers-by must also be aware of the peril, which is not assured. Finally it may seem that even if citizens are generally deemed passers-by they are largely unable to help the imperiled. I'll respond to these objections in the following sections.

PROXIMITY

Classically, potential rescuers are innocent bystanders, who happen to be spatially near the imperiled person—they "stumble" into Samaritan situations, in Joel Feinberg's phrase.[33] Indeed, spatial proximity is often critical in standard cases of rescue. It makes plain the perilous situation and allows immediate assistance. One may therefore deny that citizens in general are Samaritan "material," as John Simmons does in his critique of Wellman, to which I return below.

If we accept this physical-spatial requirement, then citizens' Samaritan duties will be considerably constrained. Some will not escape their duties. Men live with women; Whites live close to and under the same social structures as Blacks. But while men and women share family ties and loving relationships, the same cannot often be said of Blacks and Whites in the "racial polity" (Charles Mills's term for the state established by the Racial Contract for the purpose of maintaining White privilege and non-White subordination).[34] There, Blacks and Whites share little: often, they are neither friends nor colleagues, neither kin nor neighbors. Interracial friendship and love is discouraged, workplaces lack racial diversity, and people live in different zip codes under de facto residential segregation.[35] At the extreme, persistent Samaritan perils may occur in isolated spaces, such as prisons and ghettos, not only distancing most citizens but also hiding the ills in need of repair.

That being said, in an age of safe, rapid travel and the seamless transfer of money and information, physical nearness is hardly critical to Samaritan potential. As Simmons notes, "The moral burdens of the rescue fall . . . on those who happen to be present at the emergencies . . . or have the knowledge that allows them to make themselves present."[36] Consider transnational cases of aid and rescue, such as disaster relief. The needy may be thousands of miles from potential rescuers, but electronic media have short-circuited the connection between spatial proximity and knowledge of the need for rescue, expanding the body of bystanders to vast numbers worldwide. For instance, international aid poured in Puerto Rico after Hurricane Maria in 2017, as the Trump administration failed to set up a speedy and adequate disaster relief plan (contrasting with the government's response to Hurricane Harvey in Texas and Hurricane Irma in Florida in the previous months). What matters here is knowledge of the problem and the ability to help solve it, placing many people in a position to provide Samaritan assistance to distant others as well as neighbors. This is the gist of Singer's case for transnational Samaritan duties in "Famine, Affluence, and Morality."[37] A similar logic may apply at home, even in nearly just societies. Citizens fall somewhere between Feinberg's literal passer-by and Singer's distant bystander, depending on their relation to the unjust institutions, practices, and laws inducing persistent Samaritan perils.

AWARENESS

Members of an imperiled group are likely to have suffered or witnessed Samaritan perils firsthand. They are probably aware of the problems and understand that their persistence results from injustice. However, it is sadly plausible to argue that the majority of those outside the group are not so aware. Much of the world follows a standard sort of imbalance, within nations and among them: wealthy people; White, male, cisgender, and heterosexual people; and members of dominant religious groups tend to be less aware of the persistent, structural endangerment of ghetto dwellers, Black and Brown people, LGBTQ people, indigenous women, undocumented migrants, and minority believers, among others.

Two factors may explain citizens' lack of awareness. One is citizens'—especially privileged citizens'—lack of basic information about the persistent imperilment, which can thus go unnoticed. The other is a failure to recognize the injustice that allows Samaritan perils to emerge, again and again. In this case, one recognizes the fact of imperilment but does not recognize it as persistent or unjust. The first factor presents an issue of visibility, the second of moral blindness or indifference.

Persistent Samaritan perils can go especially unnoticed when they occur in closed-off spaces such as prisons and ghettos (the next chapter further examines political obligations in the face of prisoner rights abuses). Authorities' failure to take victims' reports seriously, or to classify them properly as, say, rape or hate crime, as well as victims' failure to report (which could be in reaction to official misconduct—the kind of institutional inefficacy and untrustworthiness I identified in chapter 3); or the media's failure to inform the public about the high rate of peril, leading citizens to assume its coincidence rather than persistence all help to conceal these perils. Moral blindness may also be at issue when a culture's prevailing ideas encourage people to see pervasive perils as anomalies. And, even when peril is recognized as persistent, those ideas may motivate the belief that the peril is justified by the traits of the targeted group. For instance, because so many in the United States view Blacks as inherently criminal and menacing and police as well-trained community servants, police brutality against Black suspects is too often seen as justified.

Do invisibility and moral blindness get citizens off the Samaritan hook? Lack of awareness might, but its origin matters. If citizens truly cannot see—and cannot reasonably be expected to see—the persistent perils surrounding them, then they have no Samaritan duty to help. If, however, awareness can reasonably be expected, then citizens may have a Samaritan duty, whether they recognize it or not.

What about citizens who lack awareness because they fail to see injustice as the source of peril? Even where culture and ideology legitimize injustice, citizens may be blamed for their moral blindness and indifference. Jim Crow, again, offers a case in point. Under Jim Crow, there was no lack of visibility. The Ku Klux Klan regularly bombed homes and churches. Police officers failed to protect, and actively assaulted Blacks in public. Alongside countless lesser-known acts of violence intended to intimidate Blacks and draw bright lines of social division, researchers have documented more than four thousand "racial terror lynchings" in twelve southern states between 1877 and 1950.[38] Terror lynchings were major public events; White citizens knew about them and many attended. It would be implausible to argue that adult, mentally competent White southerners didn't know that African Americans were persistently imperiled and living in fear. Nevertheless, most White southerners supported racial segregation and failed to see Blacks' persistent imperilment as unjust. Prevailing ideas of the era made for a potent mix of self-deception, indifference, and denial.

But while the White-supremacist culture and ideology buttressing Jim Crow may explain people's ignorance, it cannot excuse it. This is partly because, as I will argue in chapter 7, people face "second-order" duties: we are obligated to do what we can to understand and implement our primary moral obligations, which are especially salient in contexts of oppression. These secondary duties include, for instance, duties to seek information, revise one's beliefs based on evidence, show due care in moral deliberation, exercise self-scrutiny, resist self-deception, and develop empathetic understanding. Many White citizens under Jim Crow could be blamed for failing to satisfy these duties. It is also difficult to claim lack of awareness amid widespread protest. Once demonstrators and others draw attention to injustice, awareness spreads. In this way, Samaritan duties may gradually bind more and more people: as more and more people become conscious of persistent Samaritan perils, those who continue to deny those perils become increasingly blameworthy.

Even when persistent perils are well known, Samaritan burdens do not fall equally on everyone. People are differently situated relative to the perils: among knowledgeable people, some are better positioned to help, owing to the resources they possess and the influence they exercise. Many citizens are well positioned to assist at no unreasonable cost to themselves or others. Most should do much more than they realize.

One may be concerned that those already oppressed are more likely to be Samaritan "material," and thus more strained by Samaritan political obligations, than privileged people. Not only are they closer to and more aware of the perils, but they have less to lose (in terms of prospects for a flourishing life) than privileged people. These undue burdens would be unfair. However, what I am arguing here does not imply such a thing. Being able to help—which is crucial to Samaritan potential—is not the same as having nothing to lose. One's ability to help is a function of one's opportunities and position in society, and the greater the ability to help, the weightier the duty to do so. This means that the privileged, not the oppressed, face the heaviest burden of Samaritan rescue.

Rescue through Reform

Samaritan perils generate duties of rescue. But when these perils are persistent, effecting rescue in every instance when it is needed is daunting, unending, and insufficient. It was certainly helpful and noble to assist assault victims under Jim Crow, but one-off rescue couldn't undermine White-supremacist norms and systematic failure to enforce the equal protection of the law. The same goes with police brutality today: aiding assault victims one by one does not change the institutional and cultural conditions of policing in minority communities where brutality is common. Instead citizens need to push for reform. Unjust laws and institutions must be scrapped or revised in order to correct or impede systematic endangerment.

This is a novel idea. No one questions whether the Samaritan duty demands physical assistance, but structural reform is another matter. Indeed, in the biblical parable, the Samaritan need only help the wounded man. The Samaritan does not concern himself with the injustice that allows the assailant to go free and perhaps recidivate. That is all right so long as the victim rescued by the Samaritan is not a member of a persistently imperiled group. But when he or she is, the Samaritan duty demands more than a one-off rescue: it demands structural reform of the law or institution that generates persistent Samaritan peril, in order to reduce the latter.

In cases of humanitarian intervention, we are used to associating Samaritan rescue with serious, sometimes prolonged, intervention, for the basic purpose of preventing atrocities (and not, say, establishing just institutions). The same reasoning is at play in the present case of persistent Samaritan peril, but it concerns rescuing groups of people from dangerous situations enabled by unjust sociopolitical conditions, and so it demands rectifying those. The Samaritan duty can thus also support reforming laws or institutions that entrench persistent Samaritan perils.

So what does this look like in practice? I noted earlier that Native American women face structural Samaritan perils, given the staggering rate of sexual violence they are victims of. Eradicating these perils entails extensive legal, social, and moral reforms, some of which are underway. Some nongovernmental organizations such as Anishinabe Legal Services and Indian Law Resource Center exemplify Samaritan assistance, as they work to ensure safety and freedom from fear for Native women, through the establishment of rape crisis centers and the provision of legal resources for victims.[39] One key issue is that 86 percent of rapes and sexual assaults upon Native women are perpetrated by non-Native men, and very few are prosecuted.[40] In her novel *The Round House*, Louise Erdrich draws a vivid picture of the tangle of laws that hinder investigation and prosecution of rape cases on many reservations in the United States.[41]

In 2011, President Obama enacted the Tribal Law and Order Act (TLOA), a comprehensive law designed to fill key gaps in the criminal justice system and improve the federal government's ability to work with Indian tribes in the investigation and prosecution of crime impacting tribal communities.[42] The TLOA marked a crucial effort in the Samaritan rescue. But inadequate laws and failures of enforcement are not the only structural factors enabling the imperilment of American Indian women. The issue is also one of norms and culture as Native women suffer from stereotypes that dehumanize and objectify them.[43] This demands radical reform, too—a change of mentality and perception—which involves fighting the relative invisibility of Native Americans in the media, exposing and debunking stereotypes, teaching about Native American cultures, and providing rich portrayals of American Indian identity in the media and cinema.[44]

Principled Disobedience

There are many ways of bringing about reform, and the etiology of political change is too complex to allow us to ascertain all of the necessary and sufficient conditions for it. But one step that surely is necessary, which I focus on here, is the call for reform, which names the peril and the injustice sustaining it.

Calls for reform come from social movements and can be relayed by well-situated individuals, who need break no laws in order to address the public or pursue legal change. For instance, public officials, journalists, and lawyers, because of their access to the political arena and the courts, are well positioned in this way, with ample opportunities for publicity and the tools to pursue systemic change through, for instance, impact litigation and smaller-scale cases that can highlight widespread problems. But most people lack such access to levers of power. For them, public protest and civil disobedience may be effective ways to reach the political forum. Blank Noise's Meet To Sleep events are a case in point as they raise awareness about women's fear for their safety in public spaces and purport to help women unlearn this fear. Action Heroes, as the participants call themselves, deploy lawful yet onerous tactics, whose power rests on women's visible vulnerability. Activist projects like these have abounded in the aftermath of Jyoti Singh's brutal gang rape in a public bus in Delhi, in December 2012. The harrowing details of Singh's hour-long ordeal, which she recounted before dying in the hospital where she was treated for her injuries, shocked the world. Responding to national and global outrage, and to activists' pleas, India has since enacted stronger laws and policies against sexual violence. However, human rights groups have shown that rape survivors continue to face significant barriers to obtaining justice and critical support services, largely because of the stigmatization of rape victims by police officers, physicians, and judges in particular.[45] This issue is not unique to India. Around the world, hundreds of protest marches and rallies such as Take Back the Night and SlutWalks have called for an end to rape culture and victim-blaming. Marches are not necessarily illegal, but they might be: once a police officer orders protesters to leave or disperse, a lawful protest can become civil disobedience.

The next chapter examines associative political obligations to inform and educate the public about injustices, and thus pave the way for reform; I detailed in the previous chapter some of the empirical evidence supporting the effectiveness of civil resistance campaigns. In this section I want to focus on principled lawbreaking, including civil and uncivil disobedience, and defend its viability and even necessity (within constraints) for drawing attention to persistent Samaritan peril.

History demonstrates that civil disobedience is often a method of drawing attention to injustices. In the United States, the civil rights movement's marches (in violation of court orders), sit-ins, and Freedom Rides exposed the persistent Samaritan perils of Jim Crow and thereby highlighted the need for reform. BLM activists have organized public protests, vigils, die-ins, sing-ins, and traffic disruptions across the country, demanding structural reforms and police accountability in the killings of unarmed Blacks. In July 2016, for instance, a BLM-affiliated group called the Let Us Breathe Collective organized a march in Chicago to demand police reforms. Some protesters marched down residential blocks (without a permit) and joined others who were chained together in front of the police station. After singing songs, chanting, and reciting poems, the crowd was asked to leave by police. The group, which was chained together, refused to move, and police took them into custody.[46]

We saw that Samaritan interventions must be reasonably devised to protect the interests under threat. How can civil disobedience qualify as a reasonable intervention to rescue members of persistently imperiled groups? Civil disobedience need not achieve immediate reform to be justified. Rather, the idea is that it can effectively contribute to the Samaritan mission, insofar as it sheds light on the injustice that generates or aggravates the repeated incidence of Samaritan perils and calls for structural reform. Succeeding at this basic level generally requires civil disobedients put forward a clear and salient message, and also, following the guidelines identified in chapter 4, that they strive to spur political change by forming coalitions and exerting pressure on politicians.

But I want to go further and argue that other forms of principled lawbreaking besides civil disobedience can also contribute to the Samaritan mission with respect to persistent Samaritan perils. For instance, prisoners in the United States undertook hunger strikes, against prison policy, in order to denounce the inhumanity and dangers of solitary confinement (more on this in the next chapter). Guerilla street art can also draw attention to persistent Samaritan perils: British artist Banksy, for instance, painted a series of graffiti to alert the public to the United States' appalling and degrading treatment of suspected terrorists. Banksy also installed an inflatable doll in an orange jumpsuit, on its knees, hooded, and hands cuffed behind its back, inside the Big Thunder Mountain Railroad ride in Disneyland to expose Guantanamo Bay.

For a last example, in September 2015, asylum seekers stranded in a makeshift refugee camp outside Budapest in Hungary decided to march toward the Hungarian border with Austria, ninety miles away, in protest against the camp's conditions and European states' inadequate response to the refugee crisis. Forcibly displaced people are undoubtedly suffering from persistent Samaritan peril. The march violated the direct orders of Hungarian authorities as well as various

European Union regulations regarding asylum-seeking. Although it was public, as the marchers invited media coverage, and nonviolent, it arguably did not qualify as civil disobedience given asylum seekers' lack of standing (since they are not members of the Hungarian political community).

Principled disobedience—be it civil or not—can thus contribute to the Samaritan mission of rescuing people from persistent Samaritan peril by shedding light on the injustice that enables the frequent occurrence of Samaritan perils for particular groups, and demanding the reform of such injustice. Citizens, as passers-by to these persistent Samaritan perils, may thus be required to do their part in the rescue by engaging in principled disobedience.

OBJECTIONS

Samaritans' Judgments

The first objection to the foregoing account of Samaritan political obligations contends that even if the Samaritan duty requires law-breaking in the course of a rescue, the duty to obey the law always outweighs such Samaritan political obligation. The duty to obey the law should always prevail because judgments about the Samaritan duty are too controversial to be left to individuals. Insofar as disagreements about Samaritan perils are inevitable, it should not be up to individuals to decide whether they are bound by the Samaritan duty. Take anti-abortion activism. Whether engaged in protests or bombings and assault on providers, anti-abortion activists claim to be acting on the basis of a Samaritan duty to rescue fetuses. Some opponents of abortion believe that fetuses have the same moral rights, and should be granted the same legal rights, as people. Therefore, in their view, the Samaritan duty requires resisting abortions by all means necessary. They insist that the Samaritan duty outweighs all other considerations, including the rights of pregnant women and clinic staff to be free from harassment and harm. They often use the necessity defense in court, to underscore that the situation involves an emergency or threat of death.[47] In some cases, they even claim that the Samaritan duty requires the use of deadly force against abortion providers.[48] This case suggests the dangers of allowing individuals discretion to judge Samaritan perils.

In response, I noted that coercive courses of action must pass a higher bar of justification than non-coercive ones. Illegal Samaritan rescues of undocumented immigrants often do not involve any coercion or interfere with anyone's rights. In contrast, militant anti-abortion activities interfere with or violate the rights of women and abortion providers. Good Samaritans may sometimes resort to coercion or violence in a rescue, but they must show that the course of action reasonably seems necessary for the rescue, is well designed to protect the interest under threat, and is suitably constrained (proportionate to the threat, among other things). Anti-abortion protests that do not involve harassment or intimidation of patients and staff could pass the bar of Samaritan justification, if we granted, for the sake of argument, that fetuses have interests in being born. But if Judith Jarvis Thomson's argument in defense of abortion is correct, unborn fetuses' putative right to life does not entail a right to use the mother's body, so that resorting to violence against women seeking abortions and physicians providing them could not be justified on Samaritan grounds.[49]

I do not intend to weigh in on the abortion debate here. Suffice it to say that Samaritanism alone does not tell us how to identify Samaritan perils: other facts and values regarding who counts as a person having a fundamental interest or noncontingent basic need must come into play when identifying Samaritan perils. But that people make mistaken judgments about what the Samaritan duty requires does not entail that illegal Samaritan rescues can never be morally obligatory. All it shows is that people disagree about what constitutes Samaritan peril and can make mistakes about the content of their moral duties.

Another version of this objection seeks to reconcile Samaritan political obligations of illegal rescues with the moral duty to obey the law: the idea is that the good Samaritan would assist the person in need and then report him or her to the authorities, as the law demands, thereby satisfying both the Samaritan duty and the duty to obey the law. Dudley Knowles argued that, being a law-abiding citizen, the good Samaritan would always seek legal ways to assist people in peril.[50] For instance, a law-abiding Samaritan in Alabama could rescue an undocumented immigrant from grave peril by driving him to the hospital, and then report the immigrant to authorities. In this way she would fulfill her Samaritan duty without flouting the law, assuming that one who reports after helping cannot be charged with a felony.

I am skeptical of this proposition's appeal. Note that no one would press this objection in the case of the Fugitive Slave Law, where reporting the runaway slave would return him to terrible Samaritan peril—slavery—or death. Similarly, if the detention and deportation of undocumented immigrants amount to peril, then the Samaritan duty to assist would prohibit reporting the undocumented migrant after the rescue, as the law requires. There is in fact evidence of serious abuse in U.S. detention centers.[51] And it is plausible to argue that forcing undocumented immigrants to return to the situation of extreme violence they were fleeing in the first place amounts to endangering them anew. A 2015 Guardian investigation and Amnesty International report found that dozens of U.S. deportees from Central America have been murdered days or weeks after their return to El Salvador, Guatemala, and Honduras.[52] Thus in cases like these, Samaritan illegal rescues must be covert—and thus uncivil.

Unreasonable Costs

A second objection focuses on the costs associated with Samaritan disobedience. Even if one agrees that laws criminalizing the exercise of moral duties or enabling persistent Samaritan perils are unjust, one might still worry that fulfilling our Samaritan political obligations jeopardizes or risks jeopardizing our prospects for a flourishing life. Recall the earlier example of aiding a fugitive slave in the antebellum United States. Colson Whitehead depicts in his historical novel *The Underground Railroad* the lynching of a North Carolina White couple who had given refuge to a young fugitive slave girl.[53] Punishments such as this were common—and very public—to deter people from helping slaves toward freedom. Today, helping undocumented immigrants is a felony in Alabama and elsewhere. One may recognize the Samaritan duty to aid an undocumented immigrant, but if a felony conviction jeopardizes one's prospects for a flourishing life, then one cannot be morally bound by that duty.

It is true, of course, that Samaritan rescues are sometimes too costly to be morally required. A state that harshly and systematically punishes disobedience appears to ensure that illegal Samaritan rescues cannot come at a reasonable cost. This suggests the limiting possibility that, in tyrannical regimes, there may never be a Samaritan duty to rescue people from persistent perils, given the costs of noncompliance with the oppressive system. This is tragic, since Samaritan perils are presumably most frequent—and Samaritan rescues most urgently needed—in tyrannical states. The Nazi regime offers a stark example, having routinely executed subjects for *Judenbeherbergung* (harboring Jews).

And yet, interviewed after the war, hundreds of rescuers in Nazi-occupied Poland reported simply fulfilling their Samaritan duty.[54] What made them feel this sense of duty, despite the hazards of opposing the Nazis? For one thing, even in tyrannical regimes, illegal

Samaritan rescues may sometimes involve a vanishing risk of being detected and good Samaritans of being caught. Furthermore, the weight of the Samaritan duty is proportional to the gravity and imminence of the peril, so that prudential considerations cannot always take precedence. Recall that, as Fabre argues, individuals can be duty-bound to incur some life-threatening risk. Hence one may assume that Samaritan duties to rescue people from peril in tyrannical states carry significant weight.

Individuals' Inefficacy

A third objection to principled disobedience is that individual acts make no difference to address persistent Samaritan perils. The Samaritan intervention must be reasonably calculated to protect the interest under threat, yet no one person's participation, in social movements and contexts of collective action, is necessary or sufficient to ensure the rescue's success. If there is no reason to think that one's efforts can make a difference, then why bother?

While it may be true that the actions of most *individuals* have no effect on persistent Samaritan perils, the actions of *people* do.[55] That is, mass actions can have significant impact, but there is no mass if individuals do not, on their own, participate. That the effect of mass action is not traceable to one person doesn't mean that individual decisions to participate are irrelevant. And, in this respect, particular acts of protest can make a difference by serving as examples. If an otherwise unremarkable community member engages in protest, she may inspire others, equally unremarkable, to join. This is one way movements grow to the point where they can have impact.

But while individuals do matter to collective rescue missions, their efficacy is not the only factor weighing against passivity. One might also appeal to fairness, as Wellman does in his account of political obligation, and as I did in the previous chapter. The fact that the rescue mission can be accomplished without everyone's participation enables free-riding—a tempting option, given the costs of Samaritan assistance. But fairness preempts free-riding on other people's Samaritan efforts. Every citizen may thus have a duty to contribute to the Samaritan mission, as their talents and opportunities allow.

Stretching the Samaritan Duty

RESCUE, CHARITY, OR JUSTICE?

One might object that my account stretches the Samaritan duty beyond recognition. This is one of Simmons's main objections to Wellman's theory: his Samaritan argument rests on conflating the duty of rescue with the duty of charity. Duties of rescue, Simmons insists, arise in response to one-off emergencies that occur nearby, typically in face-to-face situations. However, he writes, "The moral task to which Wellman thinks the [Samaritan] duty is addressed is an ongoing problem (of providing security for all), not the kind of local, occasional task to which duties of rescue seem to be addressed."[56] This objection might apply to my account of Samaritan principled disobedience, too, since I propose that the Samaritan duty is addressed to an "ongoing problem" of injustice at the root of persistent Samaritan perils. The moral task of reforming the system, for Simmons, would be a matter of charity or beneficence, not of rescue.

I agree that Simmons's objection threatens Wellman's theory, insofar as the perils of the state of nature constitute hypothetical or potential, rather than imminent, threats. Even Knowles, who aims to defend Wellman's Samaritan account, recognizes that "Wellman's talk of rescue" from the dangers of lawlessness "is hyperbolic."[57] However, the persistent Samaritan perils I address are appropriately and non-metaphorically described as emergencies. The perils described here may not always, or even often, be visible in face-to-face circumstances, but they are hardly theoretical. They arise when fundamental human interests or noncontingent basic needs—including minimally the interests in life, security, and bodily integrity—are immediately, imminently, or probably threatened.

In addition, I fail to see how eliminating the injustice sustaining persistent peril would be a matter of charity, though I see how it could be deemed a matter of justice. Insofar as Samaritan obligations and duties of justice are not mutually exclusive, claiming that eliminating persistent Samaritan perils through structural reform is a matter of justice does not undermine my account. At the outset of this chapter, I set aside the question of whether Samaritan rights exist—that is, whether the imperiled have a right to be rescued. An affirmative answer to this question would entail that Samaritan assistance is a matter of protecting people's rights—hence a duty of justice. According to Fabre, the duty to rescue *is* a duty of justice, owed to the imperiled and enforceable by the state.[58]

PERFECT OR IMPERFECT?

Another way of understanding the objection that Wellman, and perhaps I, conflate rescue and charity rests on the distinction between perfect and imperfect duties. Whereas the duty of rescue as standardly conceived is a perfect duty, owed immediately by those who can help to those in danger, the duty I describe in cases of Samaritan principled disobedience looks more like an imperfect duty, such as the duty of charity. If I encounter a child drowning in shallow water that poses little risk to me, then I cannot both leave the child and satisfy the Samaritan duty. The duty in this scenario is perfect. In contrast, I may refrain from participating in a die-in to highlight persistent Samaritan perils and still satisfy the Samaritan duty in other ways. Here, the duty is imperfect. The duty to engage in principled disobedience to rescue people from persistent Samaritan perils is therefore imperfect as well. But it does not follow that it is thereby less weighty, only that it can be discharged in many ways.

IDENTIFIED V. POTENTIAL VICTIMS

In standard Samaritan cases, the party in peril is an actual, identifiable person, whereas persistent Samaritan perils concern "statistical people" or potential victims. Though this is an important difference in some circumstances, I do not think it is relevant in determining our moral obligations.

Note first that persistent Samaritan perils engender a feeling of insecurity in *all* members of the targeted group, such as African Americans under Jim Crow. The situation of oppressed people is characterized by a climate of fear, which thwarts the possibility for a meaningful life.

In any case, let us assume that when it comes to intervention, the Samaritan is concerned only with whomever will predictably be assaulted, that is, statistical people. Research shows that people will pay an amount much greater to save an identified victim who faces a high risk of death than they will to save an equivalent number of statistical lives spread over a broader population.[59] But for many philosophers, this disposition to favor the interests of identified victims is a *bias*, not a justified moral judgment.[60]

Some philosophers have defended *moral actualism*, the view that only the interests of actual people are relevant for determining the moral status of an action, while those of merely possible people are morally irrelevant.[61] But Caspar Hare rebutted this view.[62] Hare has also recently scrutinized the problem of statistical people, arguing that the fact that we cannot identify the particular people who will be harmed or benefited by our actions is not particularly relevant to determining the strength of our obligations. If identifiability "does matter, it does not matter very much," Hare argues. "Our moral obligations are not significantly weakened by the absence of a person to whom we are obliged."[63] Careful thinking about the issue doesn't much support favoring the interests of actual people in peril over those of statistical people similarly imperiled.

Particularity

If there is a duty to obey the law, philosophers agree that it must bind us specially to our state. But, as Simmons shows, theories based on natural duties, such as the Samaritan duty or the duty of justice, cannot explain this special connection, since they bind people equally, regardless of their voluntary undertakings or relationships. Indeed, persistent Samaritan perils can arise anywhere, thus potentially binding us to help everywhere, not especially at home. This may be overwhelming for privileged people who could in principle be bound to rescue not only fellow countrymen who are imperiled but also people far away. But that is in fact the situation, and there is no reason to exclude transnational duties from our political obligations in the face of injustice. So numerous Samaritan duties may bind us at home and abroad. The interesting question, I think, is whether there may exist transnational duties to engage in principled disobedience.

I believe there are. There are situations in which one ought to engage in principled disobedience at home in order to highlight persistent Samaritan perils abroad, assuming this will help draw attention to the issue. Banksy did this in his London-based guerilla street art denouncing U.S. foreign policy. Another example came after the April 2013 factory collapse in Bangladesh, which killed more than 1,100 people. Protesters gathered in solidarity with factory workers to denounce the dangerous and unfair labor conditions in Bangladesh's booming garment sector. Though most of the protests were legal, some involved acts of civil disobedience, for instance, when protesters refused to comply with police orders to disperse or when activists violated restraining orders. For a last example, South Asian and Black women's organizations throughout the West, including the Freedom Without Feat Platform (FWFP) in the UK, have built solidarity with the protests against sexual violence in India and sought to counter Western media's racist vilification of Indian men (as "uncivilized," "murderous," and "hyena-like," among other epithets) and obfuscation of gender-based violence at home.[64] FWFP illustrates well the reality of transnational Samaritan duties.

If you believe there is a Samaritan duty to obey the law, then you should further affirm that this duty can require disobeying laws against Samaritan rescue and that it can require engaging in civil disobedience to protest injustices that imperil people. However, not all injustices trigger Samaritan duties. Thus there is a Samaritan duty to rescue undocumented migrants insofar as they are imperiled, but not simply in virtue of their being exploited. There is a Samaritan duty to rescue women from the perils of male violence, but not to fix the wage gap or increase political representation. To articulate a complete account of our obligations in the face of injustice, one that can ground citizens' responsibilities to address injustice beyond Samaritan endangerment, we need to look elsewhere. To this end, I now turn to political association.

Chapter 6

Political Association and Dignity

The sound of guards' footsteps in the corridor. "Bheith réidh anois," says one cellmate. "What?" the other asks. "Get ready." The guards open another cell and take a man out. He is Bobby Sands, wearing nothing but a blanket wrapped around his waist. The guards slam him against the wall and on the floor, beat him, and drag him through the corridor. They hold both his arms; Sands kicks back. He spits at a third guard, who punches him in the face. Sands ducks the second, more forceful blow, which lands on the wall. "Fuck," the guard screams in pain and anger.

Soon the other two have dragged Sands into the bathroom and are holding his head to the floor, while the third chops off his long brown hair and beard with scissors. His head and face are bruised and covered in blood, as are the guards' latex-gloved hands. Guards force him into a bathtub and hold his head and body under the water, which quickly turns red. A third guard frantically scrubs Sands' body and face with a deck brush. Eventually he is carried away unconscious.

This is not a scene from real life, but it might have been. The moment plays out in Steve McQueen's 2008 film *Hunger*, which stars Michael Fassbender as Bobby Sands, a member of the Provisional Irish Republican Army (IRA) and informal leader of the IRA inmates held at the Maze Prison in Northern Ireland, where the film takes place.[1] The events of the film follow the British government revocation of IRA inmates' prisoner-of-war-like status in 1976. In response, Sands and other IRA inmates engaged in the "blanket protest"; they went naked or dressed only in blankets rather than wear the uniform of an ordinary convict. In 1978, after particularly brutal attacks by guards, the IRA prisoners launched the "no-wash" or "dirty protest." They refused to leave their cells or to wash, instead smearing the cell walls with excrement and slopping their pots of urine under their doors and into the prison corridors. *Hunger* shows these horrendous conditions in great detail: the quarters fouled with a hand-mixed paste of garbage and fecal matter; guards mopping up the urine; guards clad in protective gear fit for radioactive waste disposal, pressure-hosing the cell walls.

In 1981, Sands—in real life and in the movie—organized a hunger strike. "There is no such thing as political murder, political bombing or political violence," British Prime Minister Margaret Thatcher said in response to the hunger strikers' demand of political status. "There is only criminal murder, criminal bombing and criminal violence. We will not compromise on this." Sands died after sixty-six days.

By most accounts, the grisly protests and hunger strikes accomplished nothing—and were even counterproductive. The prisoners debased themselves with grotesquery; the hunger strikes epitomized self-inflicted violence. Yet, I will argue, these protests were not wasted. There were uncivil efforts to realize the demands that dignity makes on political associates.

ASSOCIATIVE POLITICAL OBLIGATION

In previous chapters, we saw that the natural duty of justice, the principle of fairness, and the Samaritan duty, all of which have been used to support the moral duty to obey the law, ground political obligations to resist injustice—including by way of principled diso-bedience within decent, legitimate states. I now turn to another pos-sible source of political obligation: association. Associativist theorists ground the moral duty to obey the law in political membership. Just as parents ought to raise and nurture their children, and friends ought to support each other, so citizens ought to support their polit-ical institutions and obey the state's law: what matters is fostering the good of the group with which one is associated, whether that is one's family, informal community, or polity.

Associative obligations are special, not universal, differing according to one's role relative to others. We owe these obligations to people with whom we have special relationships, such as our family members, colleagues, coreligionists, and business partners—and our fellow citizens. Associative obligations constitute a third genus of moral requirements, besides natural duties and voluntarily incurred obligations. Unlike natural duties, owed to all of humankind, asso-ciative obligations obtain only among members of communities or groups. And unlike promissory or contractual obligations, they are in general neither voluntarily undertaken nor explicitly consented to. This is not to say that associative obligations never follow some consenting action. For instance, we typically take on professional obligations by choosing certain occupations, although we might not directly consent to the particular obligations associated with them. But even associative obligations that are not voluntarily incurred bind us, within limits.

Associativist accounts of political obligation have two main appeals. One is their conformity with ordinary moral thinking, es-pecially our experience as socially embedded beings. Associativist accounts recognize that membership in nonvoluntary groups is an integral part of who we are, as we identify with at least some of the roles we inhabit, feel bound by the responsibilities accompanying them, and value the relationships inherent in membership. Whereas the natural duty of justice, the principle of fairness, and the Samaritan duty ignore the feeling of being specially bound to one's country and compatriots, associativist accounts begin with the specialness of one's relationship to the political community.

The other appeal, as I see it, lies in associativist theorists' recognition of deficits within the traditional equation of political obligation and the moral duty to obey the law. Associativist theories also take seriously the possibility of political obligations—plural. Margaret Gilbert argues that political membership minimally entails acceptance of political institutions' authority but doubts that associative political obligations necessarily include, and are exhausted by, the duty to obey the law.[2] For Andrew Mason, political obligation mainly involves two types of special obligation: an obligation to give priority to the needs of fellow citizens and an obligation to participate fully in public life.[3] Hence at least some associativist theorists pave the way for thinking about types of political obligation beyond the moral duty to obey the law. The bulk of the associativist literature, however, strives to defend the thesis that citizens are bound to obey their polity's law.

Theorists offer different accounts of how political association (or membership; I will use the terms interchangeably) works to ground the obligation to obey the law. Some theorists hold that membership in a political community itself entails political obligation.[4] According to these conceptual arguments, following the law just is an institutional requirement. Others argue that political obligation grows out of not only membership full stop, but from the feeling of belonging and sense of identity that membership in the state provides.[5] Proponents of identity arguments hold that members who identify with the group they belong to are bound by its rules, regardless of what these rules require. Still others claim that associative political obligation is grounded in the value of political membership.[6] Arguments of this sort locate the source of associative obligations in the character, usefulness, or purpose of the relationship members share.

These three types of accounts, and the particular version each defends, are sufficiently different from one another that the arguments set forth in this chapter will not appeal to *all* associativist theorists. This is an inescapable difference from chapters 3–5, where my arguments could (sought to) compel any proponent of the duty of justice, principle of fairness, and Samaritan duty, respectively. In this chapter, I focus on one particular value-driven associativist account: that of the late Ronald Dworkin. It offers an attractive account of associative political obligation and has the additional advantage of drawing on dignity—a particularly powerful concept with great currency in politics and law. I thus hope that my arguments will appeal to both associativist theorists and champions of dignity.

DWORKIN'S LIBERAL-ASSOCIATIVIST ACCOUNT

According to Dworkin, if people have a moral duty to obey the law, they are subject to a special case of associative, not performative (i.e., voluntarily incurred), obligation, since we are usually born into political membership. The scope, content, and limits of special obligations are determined by contingent conventions, including what is customary in a certain social milieu. Dworkin denies that conventions and social practices are independent sources of moral duties, but he argues that they play an important role in clarifying and fixing the obligations that people standing in special relationships have. For instance, Western family practices assign the responsibilities of childcare and childrearing to children's parents, but in many kibbutzim, childcare is a collective endeavor. Social practices such as these are thus "parasitic" on underlying and independent moral facts, including children's needs.

Dworkin argues that special obligations, like other moral requirements, are grounded in the overarching interpretative value of dignity. As he explains in *Justice for Hedgehogs*, dignity requires both self-respect and authenticity. These principles govern and unify ethics ("living well," centered on the self) and morality ("being good," what we owe others). From the ethical perspective, the principle of self-respect demands accepting that how one's life goes is a matter of importance. From the moral perspective, self-respect demands recognizing the objective importance of other people's lives and showing respect for humanity in all its forms, thereby granting others the opportunity to satisfy the demands of self-respect. The principle of authenticity entails what Dworkin calls "ethical responsibility" and "ethical independence." According to the former, "Each person has a special, personal responsibility for identifying what counts as success in his own life; he has a personal responsibility to create that life through a coherent narrative or style that he himself endorses."[7] The latter forbids us from acting according to decisions and values that are not of our own making. Morally, authenticity demands we recognize and respect the responsibility of other people to design a life for themselves.

Dworkin deduces political obligation from the internal character of the political relationship, examined in conjunction with the demands of dignity. Although the principle of authenticity forbids subordination, it does not entail a blanket prohibition against deference to authority in decisions that affect us, including in the political realm. Dignity permits us to share our responsibility for our own lives with others—as we do in democracies—so long as the deference is in some ways reciprocal. Political association, especially in democracy, both contributes to the success of our lives and makes us vulnerable to a special kind of harm—namely, subservience, the indignity arising from unilateral deference. This "risky" relationship thus entails a special responsibility not to dominate the other party or parties. Political association, in short, must be structured by reciprocal concern so as not to compromise dignity.

Is political obligation a justified—that is, genuine—obligation? According to Dworkin, defective instances of valuable practices (e.g., family) and defective conventions such as honor among thieves impose no genuine obligation on those they purport to oblige. In the same way, not all political communities impose genuine obligations to obey the law. Only those that are legitimate—that respect the dignity of all parties involved—do. Thus, for Dworkin, state legitimacy entails political obligation: citizens are morally bound to obey the laws of their community when, and to the extent that, these emanate from a legitimate government.

Dworkin distinguishes legitimacy from justice, noting that governments may fall short of justice and still be legitimate, so long as

> their laws and policies can nevertheless be interpreted as recognizing that the fate of each citizen is of equal importance and that each has a responsibility to create his own life. A government may be legitimate, that is, if it strives for its citizens' full dignity even if it follows a defective conception of what that requires.[8]

Whether the community cares about its members' dignity and shows equal concern for them are thus matters of interpretation. According to Dworkin, "The interpretive judgment must be sensitive to time and place: it must take into account prevailing ideas within the political community."[9] In particular, legitimacy should be assessed on the basis of two criteria: first, the community's good-faith efforts to respect the dignity of its members; second, its amenability to change through politics. Assessing a community's legitimacy therefore involves determining whether it is generally structured in a way that expresses—or strives to express—equal and reciprocal concern; whether it contains particular laws, policies, or practices that threaten (some) members' dignity; and whether there are political channels for reform.

Where states contain the stain of domination and make political and legal processes of correction available, they maintain legitimacy and claims to political obligation. Where the stain is dark and widespread, political obligation may lapse entirely and revolution may be called for. Most historical and current polities fall somewhere between the two extremes. Slavery, colonialism, imperialism, and racial segregation, which characterize entire systems, generally constitute *lapses* of legitimacy. Particular laws and practices that threaten dignity, such as anti-immigration policies and the use of solitary confinement, express unconcern for members of certain social groups and thus *stain* legitimacy.

DIGNITARY ASSOCIATIVE POLITICAL OBLIGATIONS

There are various ways in which political associations can threaten their members' self-respect and/or authenticity. Paradigmatic violations include *denial of self-determination*, which consists in depriving an individual or a people of decision-making powers in their lives; *humiliation*, that is, demeaning physical or verbal treatment that undermines or denies a person's self-respect;[10] *objectification*, which reduces a person to her body or body parts or treats a person as a tool for the objectifier's purposes;[11] *discrimination*, that is, the wrongful imposition of disadvantage based on people's (perceived) membership in a particular social group;[12] *exploitation*, or unfairly taking advantage of individuals or groups;[13] *marginalization*, that is, exclusion from participation in major social activities;[14] and *violence* or the violation of a person's bodily or mental integrity, through, for example, assault and sexual abuse.[15] The list is not exhaustive. Having previously discussed discrimination and exploitation in some detail, I focus here on violations of dignity that involve denial of self-determination, humiliation, and violence—as Irish people in Northern Ireland suffered.

Both self-respect and authenticity forbid subservience, and an affront to one tends to be an affront to the other. To deprive someone of the background conditions for living authentically also violates her self-respect, and vice versa. Since the implications of the principles are practically interchangeable, I shall treat them together.

What does a person owe herself in the face of a polity's failure to treat her as an equal and valuable member? What does a person owe those in her polity who are not treated as equal and valuable members? Dignity demands recognizing one's and others' basic moral worth, taking one's own life seriously, and respecting others' ethical independence: it forbids dominating and unilaterally deferring to fellow citizens.

My contention is that political membership, in conjunction with the demands of dignity, also supports a general obligation to *resist* one's and others' violations of dignity. People who are not treated as equal and valuable members of their community—who are socially or politically subservient—have an ethical and moral obligation to themselves and others similarly situated to resist their own mistreatment. And members of a polity that violates some of its members' dignity have a moral obligation, owed to others, to resist such mistreatment.

The scope and content of the general obligation of resistance—what it requires in specific circumstances—depends on the kind and magnitude of indignity threatened and on the agent's abilities, opportunities, and particular position relative to the indignity.

I propose to distinguish and examine four related purposes of resistance, which can be deduced from the internal logic of dignity-threatening political relationships:

1. *Rectification*: fixing the flawed law, policy, institution, or system through reform or revolution;
2. *Communication*: publicly condemning a law, policy, institution, or system;
3. *Assertion*: affirming one's dignity; and
4. *Solidarity*: acting in and expressing solidarity with or among the oppressed.

These four goals of resistance are interrelated and not clearly demarcated: asserting one's dignity and expressing solidarity are communicative acts, and communication is the first step toward rectification. Citizens are bound to engage in resistance in order both to rectify dignity-threatening political conditions and communicate opposition to them. Asserting one's dignity is an ethical obligation that specifically arises in the face of subordination; and acting in and expressing solidarity with the oppressed is a moral obligation that can bind both the oppressed and the privileged members of society. These obligations to resist, which may be deemed "semi-general" in relation to the general obligation of resistance, are defeasible and imperfect. This means that they may be overridden by countervailing prudential and moral considerations, and that one has broad leeway in deciding how to fulfill them, within the constraints imposed by dignitary political membership.

In general, agents cannot insult or violate their own or other persons' dignity in order to resist illegitimate political associations. To do otherwise, by humiliating, objectifying, or brutalizing others, would be to wrongfully seek to dominate them. Dignitary political membership seems to require *dignified*—that is, public, non-evasive, nonviolent, and civil—resistance, and to prohibit, or at least place a presumption against, uncivil and *undignified*—that is, violent, offensive, and self-demeaning—conduct. But rather than trying to reinforce this presumption for civil (nonviolent, etc.) disobedience, I contend that dignitary political membership, under certain circumstances, justifies uncivil, violent and undignified, resistance.

Rectification

Dworkin's understanding of dignity demands that, when laws, policies, and institutions fail to express equal and reciprocal concern for all, they must be fixed or replaced. If the law's failure to respect everyone's dignity is sufficiently threatening or destructive, all people, not just those affected by indignity, may demand reform or revolution. Citizens can discharge the associative political obligation of rectification through nonviolent resistance or civil disobedience. However, I shall examine the range of uncivil, violent acts of resistance that dignitary political membership might permit and even require in efforts to rectify illegitimate associations.

Dignitary political membership does not demand that people ignore or react nonviolently to threats to their lives. In fact, a compelling argument can be made that self-respect demands standing up for oneself and others, as in Claude McKay's 1919 anti-lynching poem, "If We Must Die": "Like men we'll face the murderous, cowardly pack, / Pressed to the wall, dying, but fighting back!" Here, "men" can plausibly be construed to mean self-respecting agents. Frederick Douglass asserted his dignity—"manhood," "self-confidence," "determination"—when he resisted a slave-breaker's attack:

> It rekindled the few expiring embers of freedom, and revived within me a sense of my own manhood. It recalled the departed self-confidence, and inspired me again with a determination to

be free. He only can understand the deep satisfaction which I experienced, who has himself repelled by force the bloody arm of slavery.[16]

Frantz Fanon also argued that dignity prohibits passively absorbing oppressive violence and that, among the natives, responding to colonizers' violence with violence "restores self-respect."[17] Violence in self-defense, for these thinkers, is a moral right, a political obligation, and a therapeutic force, constitutive of political agency itself. It is not an exception to dignified conduct but, rather, what dignity demands.

The individual case for self-defensive violence can extend to the collective. A violent slave uprising can certainly be construed as a justified and dignified response to slavery, given the immediate and grave threats to slaves' lives, freedom, and bodily integrity. But disproportionate or retaliatory violence could not be justified as an exercise of collective self-defense.

The presumption in favor of nonviolence also is weakened when illegitimacy shows itself through the community's failure to respond to good-faith claims on behalf of the oppressed. This opens the door for justifying, on the basis of dignitary political membership, violent resistance to unjust and oppressive regimes. Consider the experience of the African National Congress (ANC), which struggled against Apartheid in South Africa. As Nelson Mandela recounts it, that effort began with serious and sustained attempts to bring about change through existing legal and political processes. Later, the movement pursued peaceful protests and civil disobedience. It took five decades for the ANC to decide that something more drastic than nonviolent resistance was needed, resulting in the formation of a military arm, Umkhonto we Sizwe (The Spear of the Nation), which organized sabotage actions and prepared for guerilla warfare.[18] The branch's manifesto read:

The time comes in the life of any nation where there remain only two choices—submit or fight. That time has now come to South Africa. We shall not submit and we have no choice but to hit back by all means in our power in defense of our people, our future and our freedom.[19]

The ANC's turn to violence can be cast in associativist and dignitary terms: submission would violate the ethical demand of dignity, so that the only acceptable course of action was to fight back in hopes of securing sociopolitical conditions expressing equal concern and respect for all. Appropriately directed and suitably constrained revolutionary violence was the last resort—a necessary and justified means to rectify oppressive political associations.

Could dignitary political membership justify violent resistance to rectify unjust political relations within an otherwise-tolerable regime (which South Africa wasn't)? What should we say, for instance, about the Attica uprising, from the associativist and dignitary perspective? In 1971, inmates at Attica Correctional Facility in New York held thirty-nine prison guards and employees hostage during a four-day-long standoff.[20] The inmates were armed exclusively with knives and makeshift weapons, and, contra state allegations, they did not kill any hostages. (One hostage, William Quinn, died in the hospital as a result of injuries he sustained during the takeover. Prisoners had released him so he could get medical care.) This is not to assert that the uprising satisfied the principles of necessity and proportionality, but at least the violence wasn't unbound. Many scholars further estimate that, in the vibrant activist climate of the time, the uprising stood some chance of success, at least in informing the public of prison conditions.

The uprising was spontaneous but quickly accrued leaders from grassroots organizations operating in the prison. These leaders called for thirty-three outsiders, including the *New York Times*'s Tom

Wicker (who went on to write his account of the uprising in the 1975 *A Time To Die: The Attica Prison Revolt*) and radical attorney William Kunstler, to visit the prison, and they demanded an end to unpaid and underpaid labor, prolonged solitary confinement, corporal punishment, extreme overcrowding, and racial hierarchy within the prison. They asked for educational programs, books, adequate healthcare, decent food, religious freedom, and amnesty for the takeover. They contested their exclusion from the political community and sought an institutional process through which to air grievances. Bespeaking illegitimate circumstances, prison conditions were not amenable to change through politics. But the prisoners seem to have presumed that local authorities would be willing to hear them out. All of their demands were reasonable.

Even so, on Governor Nelson Rockefeller's orders, the standoff ended in carnage. Twenty-nine inmates and ten guards were killed and eighty-three inmates were wounded. The state blatantly failed to respect inmates' dignity before the uprising, establishing miserable and degrading prison conditions; during, by refusing to meet any of the prisoners' reasonable demands and retaking the prison in a blood bath; and after, by torturing inmates and then publicly blaming the violence on the prisoners and, for decades, refusing to acknowledge wrongdoing. The prison can plausibly be treated as an isolated, illegitimate microcosm within the larger community—thereby weakening the presumption in favor of nonviolence—allowing us to conceive of the Attica uprising as a justified attempt to establish bonds of political membership against the civic death and egregious violations of dignity prisoners suffered. The uprising, in other words, flowed from, and sought to rectify, the perverse logic of the brutal and degrading treatment of prisoners.

The Attica uprising is instructive in another way. The state's cover-up of the massacre was successful because it comported with public expectations about criminals' animal nature and with the widespread

belief that criminals forfeit all their rights by breaking the social contract. These expectations and beliefs ensure that the general population largely does not care to find out how badly prisoners are treated.
Today, the two great challenges for prisoner-rights activists in the
United States are people's ignorance about systematic human rights
violations—from slavery-like labor to solitary confinement—that
plague prisons and their indifference to prisoners' fates. We should
thus take a step back and think about how to facilitate and bring
about rectification. A prerequisite, which the Attica uprising could
not fulfill thanks to the cover-up, is communication.

Communication

If we are to protect dignity in Dworkin's terms—by ensuring that
laws, policies, and institutions express equal and reciprocal concern for all—we will have to make sure people know that it is at risk.
But mistreatment may not be self-evident. In the case of structural
oppression, for instance, injustice hides within the normal workings
of the system. Resistance to it should aim in part to educate the
public. Whether we are talking about justice-based, fairness-based,
Samaritan, or dignity-based arguments for resistance, education is
essential. Dignity-threatening political relationships call for information and advocacy campaigns to improve the community's conception of what respect for dignity requires, highlight particular threats
to or violations of dignity, and communicate the need for reform.

The issue of prisoners' rights, again, offers a valuable case in point.
Successfully resisting mass incarceration and its allied abuses involves
not only informing people but also helping them to recognize
prisoners' dignity, instead of dehumanizing and demonizing them.
People need to have some respect for prisoners' dignity in order to
appreciate that it has been violated—with the active approval and
passive complicity of the polity at large. Journalists, scholars, lawyers,

prisoner-rights activists, nongovernmental organizations such as the Center for Constitutional Rights and the Vera Institute, and intergovernmental organizations such as the United Nations pursue this communicative mission lawfully every day, documenting and highlighting abuses, contesting their legality, encouraging critical debate and reflection, and proposing concrete policy reforms. For instance, historian Heather Ann Thompson not only uncovered incontrovertible evidence of the government's cover-up of the Attica uprising in *Blood in the Water*, but has also prompted people to realize that prison conditions have not improved since the 1960s, and in some ways have worsened thanks to privatization, increased incarceration rates, and even greater use of prolonged solitary confinement.

But efforts to expose and condemn dignity-violating relationships need not be lawful. They may also rely on principled, including uncivil, disobedience. This may be appropriate, within dignitary constraints, to the extent that it can capture public attention more readily than can a legal course of action, and especially when agents lack opportunities for lawful resistance. This tends to be the case for prisoners themselves. Certainly some can speak for themselves using regular publishing channels, as in the recent anthology *Hell Is a Very Small Place*, in which sixteen former and current prisoners give firsthand accounts of the devastating effects of solitary confinement.[21] (The book has been hailed as a catalyst for prison reform, an "ax for the frozen sea within us"—an apt metaphor, borrowed from Franz Kafka, for public indifference to prisoners' fates).[22] But most prisoners are not talented writers or do not have access to publishing platforms.

Given the challenges of reaching the outside world, many prisoners have turned to hunger strikes in the struggle for respect and recognition. Dozens have shaken U.S. prisons in recent years, especially to protest solitary confinement's inhumanity. During the 2013 California prisoner hunger strike, which began at the Pelican

Bay State Prison's Security Housing Unit and quickly spread through the state, thirty thousand inmates starved themselves.[23] Prisoners also coordinated a nationwide work stoppage in September 2016 to protest prison slavery; prisoners are paid between zero and $0.93 for twelve hours of work per day, and, even where they are paid, their wages are typically confiscated for "room and board."[24] An estimated twenty-four thousand prisoners in twenty-nine prisons across at least twenty-three U.S. states refused to work. The strike ended after three weeks, under threats of lockdowns and punishments, its demands unmet. But it succeeded in raising awareness about prison slavery. Hunger strikes and work stoppages, though not illegal, are against prison policy and thus qualify as principled disobedience (whereas civilians' political fasts generally don't). I do not think they fall under the umbrella of civil disobedience, despite being often labeled as such, because of the kind of coercion they involve (threat of suicide in one case, significant economic pressure in the other).[25] They might be deemed uncivil, yet dignified acts of principled disobedience in the face of agents' civic death—justified to discharge one's political obligation of communicative resistance.

I want to go further and argue that dignity can justify *undignified* conduct to communicate opposition to dignity-threatening relationships. The argument for dignity in conduct and against undignified resistance typically rests on the notion that oppressed people ought to demonstrate, and convince the public of, the moral standing they are denied. People whose dignity is violated by political associations are to *perform* dignity in their demands for it. But while I am sympathetic to the idea that undignified conduct might sometimes be counterproductive, this does not mean that dignity prohibits it. I broadly accept the presumption against undignified resistance, but there is reason to think dignity does not rule it out.

Let us return to the protests organized by IRA fighters at the Maze Prison. The no-wash protest involved disgusting and self-demeaning conduct. It was clearly—quintessentially, even—undignified. It was at the same time an effective symbol of the dehumanizing British treatment of IRA prisoners and so could be justified within the associativist dignitary framework. The protest was powerful because it dramatized Britain's failure to recognize the dignity of Irish freedom fighters and underscored the lack of dignified channels to express their grievances. The point was not to demonstrate their equal social standing and the fact that they deserved the respect they were denied. Instead, it was to represent the fact that they were treated without regard for their dignity. They demanded dignified treatment by sensationalizing its deprivation. The dirty protest illustrates undignified resistance justified by dignitary political membership, for the sake of communicating opposition to oppression. Ultimately, the prisoners can be admired for putting themselves through horrendous conditions out of respect for their dignity.

Assertion

The Maze protests are particularly interesting insofar as they slid from a *demand* for dignity to an *assertion* of it, in a way that could still satisfy the associative obligations of resistance. Padraig O'Malley carefully describes this transition in *Biting at the Grave: The Irish Hunger Strikes and the Politics of Despair*.[26] In 1980, after the blanket and dirty protests were harshly repressed, the prisoners organized a first hunger strike, which lasted fifty-three days. The British government refused to restore their political status and to meet any of their demands (including the right to wear their own clothes and not to do prison work).

When Bobby Sands began refusing food on March 1, 1981, the chances of accomplishing anything through a second hunger strike appeared nil. Or so the Belfast priest played by Liam Cunningham in *Hunger* tries to convince Sands (Fassbender) in a breathtaking unbroken seventeen-minute shot. But Sands knows the strike is unlikely to yield political concessions; he is nonetheless determined: "Putting my life on the line, it's the right thing." The protesters' demands for dignity had not been, and would not be, met—even though Sands was elected a member of Parliament during his fast, which culminated in his death at age twenty-seven. O'Malley shows that the second hunger strike did nothing but assert dignity. The prisoners had already communicated their grievances, and they had virtually no hope of achieving anything, reform-wise. Still, dignitary political membership makes sense of the urge to assert one's dignity in the face of its public denial, and even when one has no hope of righting the situation.

Bernard Boxill has argued for a Kantian duty to oneself to protest one's own subordination, even if there is no hope of rectifying it.[27] By protesting under these conditions, a self-respecting person manifests her conviction that she has worth, thereby reinforcing the conviction. She fends off the fear of losing her self-respect. "The self-respecting person wants to know that he is self-respecting," Boxill writes.[28] Unopposed injustice invites its victims to believe they have no value or rights, and therefore the self-respecting person is compelled to protest, over and above the hope that it will bring relief. Boxill's argument, made from Kantian premises, can be framed in associativist terms and support an ethical obligation to assert one's dignity in the face of political relationships that threaten or violate it.

These sorts of protests, asserting one's dignity to oneself, may be silent, internal, and invisible. They are failures from the standpoint of interpersonal communication and rectification. But this does not necessarily make them failures with respect to the assertion itself. Carol Hay has developed a Kantian account of duties to oneself to resist one's oppression, which is based on the recognition of the fundamental value of our rational nature and of oppression's damaging effects on our rational and agential capacities. Exploring ways to fulfill these duties, she notes:

> In some cases, there might be nothing an oppressed person can do to resist her oppression other than simply *recognizing that something is wrong* with her situation. This is, in a profound sense, better than nothing. It means she has not acquiesced to the innumerable forces that are conspiring to convince her that she is the sort of person who has no right to expect better. It means she recognizes that her lot in life is neither justified nor inevitable.[29]

Dworkinian dignity has much in common with Kantian rationality. Dworkin dubs the moral dimension of self-respect "Kant's principle," and his conception of authenticity is close to Kantian autonomy. Recent Kantian accounts of duties to oneself to resist oppression, such as Boxill's and Hay's, thus illuminate the present associativist account. Asserting one's dignity, by itself, is an important way to meet the demands of dignity when rectifying mistreatment seems impossible. And it can play an important role in thwarting some of the corrosive effects of oppression on one's dignity.

Solidarity

The ethical associative obligation to assert one's dignity has a moral analogue in solidarity. I discussed in previous chapters consequentialist and nonconsequentialist (fairness-based) arguments for solidarity in action. Dignity can also support a political obligation of solidarity among and with the oppressed. Recall Pankhurst's words about the suffragist movement: "To be militant in some way or other is . . . a duty which every woman will owe to her own conscience and self-respect, to other women who are less fortunate than she herself is, and to all those who are to come after her."[30] For the same reasons that the oppressed owe it to themselves to protest their mistreatment and assert their dignity, they owe as much to others similarly situated. The realization of common struggle gives rise to and constitutes solidarity among the oppressed.

Dignitary political membership also supports an obligation of solidarity on the part of privileged members of society. On Dworkin's account, the reasons you have to care about how your life goes are also reasons for you to care about other people's lives. Dignity's moral requirements thus mirror its ethical demands. If, for instance, prisoners are obligated to protest their degradation, then so are all of their fellow citizens. Even if I am not responsible for my fellow citizens' mistreatment, I have responsibilities to them in virtue of our co-membership in the polity; I must do what I can to correct the dignity-threatening relationship.

Dignitary political membership thus requires everyone to resist violations of some members' dignity. It further provides the rationale for the powerful notion that the demands of dignity cannot be fulfilled for *anyone* unless the community actually treats *everyone* with equal concern and respect. This is so because a citizen cannot be morally bound to abide by rules that systematically violate the dignity of her fellow citizens. If she were to accept an obligation to obey laws that denigrate certain groups, she would fail to recognize the objective importance of other people's lives, as authenticity demands. Solidarity in resistance is, then, a crucial way of expressing proper concern for everyone, undermining support for dignity-threatening political associations, and hopefully rectifying them.

Solidarity should thus be viewed as a moral obligation of both subordinated and privileged members of society. As I noted in chapter 4, where I also defended fair play obligations of solidarity, the term "solidarity," understood as meaningful cooperation and collective action to advance shared goals and values, seems best suited to describe bonds *among* the oppressed. "Allyship" is sometimes used to refer to members of the dominant group's solidarity *with* the oppressed. In Kendrick T. Brown and Joan Ostrove's definition, "Allies are generally conceived as dominant group members who work to end prejudice in their personal and professional lives, and relinquish social privileges conferred by their group status through their support of nondominant groups."[31] So men can be allies to women in denouncing rape culture, cisgender people can be allies to trans people in promoting trans rights and visibility, and so on. Talk of allyship is so widespread, especially in activist settings, that it has spawned recognition, and critique, of "ally culture."

Although allying with marginalized groups is an important way of acting in solidarity with them, I want to register some concerns with ally culture, which explain my choice to retain the concept of solidarity to describe both in-group and out-group bonds. These concerns also help frame some wrong ways of acting in solidarity with the oppressed.

For one thing, allyship can be disingenuous. The activist and writer Princess Harmony Rodriguez coined the term "ally theater" to criticize the way some allies perform on and off social media in order to reap the benefits of being seen as supporters of the cause— to get "kudos, likes, faves, shares, and even career opportunities"— without showing any actual concern for the marginalized people they are supposed to be allying with.[32] Rachel McKinnon has recently identified allies' bad *epistemic* behaviors, through the lens of trans women's experiences. One bad epistemic behavior consists in using one's self-identification as an ally as a defense against charges of bad behavior. This can reinforce gaslighting—an epistemic injustice in which "the hearer of testimony raises doubts about the speaker's reliability at perceiving events accurately" and "doubts that the harm or injustice the speaker is testifying to really happened as the speaker claims."[33] In her example, a trans woman reports to a self-described ally that her colleague repeatedly misidentifies her using a masculine pronoun, but the "ally" nonetheless doubts her testimony.

This testimonial injustice produces a special kind of harm, insofar as allies present themselves as trustworthy and invite victims' confidence: gaslighting is a betrayal of the marginalized person's trust. It can lead to loss of critical support and feelings of isolation and exclusion. Given these considerations, McKinnon contends that the epistemic and emotional harm of being gaslit by allies "can often be worse than the original harm that the person wishes to share."[34] In light of the observed tendency of allies to behave badly and the screen that allyship allows them to hide behind, she urges abandoning allies and allyship and instead focusing on "cultivating active bystanders." I am sympathetic to this proposal, as I underscored in chapter 5 the importance of active bystanders to Samaritan perils.

However, I believe that solidarity remains a valuable and compelling concept in establishing our associative political obligations toward oppressed people. The active bystander discharges responsibilities to intercede when a disadvantaged person is in harm's way. But the active bystander helps to remedy violations of dignity one by one, whereas solidarity points to the need for collective action to fix political relationships that systematically threaten people's dignity. Solidarity is thus a distinctive and worthy associative political obligation in the dignitary framework: it crystallizes the idea that violations of dignity are everyone's concern and that everyone ought to express their commitment to respecting everyone's dignity and join organized movements of resistance against oppression.

In the previous section, we saw that there can be an obligation to assert one's dignity even when the assertion will only be apparent to the agent doing the assertion. Can there be an obligation to act in solidarity with or among the oppressed when there is no hope of rectifying indignities? Perhaps. Even if there is no hope of rectification, it is not the case that solidarity would accomplish nothing: communication and assertion would still constitute significant goals of resistance. But what about cases that would achieve none of these things? I have in mind symbolic acts of private solidarity. They do not aim to bring about social change and may not be seen by anyone—exactly like certain invisible assertions of dignity. For instance, upon finding out that sugar was not available to French soldiers during the First World War, six-year-old Simone Weil gave up sugar in private solidarity with the troops. Nicolas Bommarito argues that acts such as Weil's "are themselves morally virtuous and can play an important role in moral development."[35] Private solidarity has clear expressive value from the dignitary-associativist perspective: it expresses, if only to the speaker, a commitment to dignity. Because there is usually some other act of resistance one can do that would contribute to achieving something, there is no associative political obligation to act in private solidarity. However, it may be that if and where there really is nothing productive one can do, private solidarity becomes obligatory, for the same reason that the oppressed agent ought at least to realize that there is something wrong with his situation and thereby assert his dignity.

To recap, dignitary political membership supports a general obligation to resist one's and others' violations of dignity. People who are not treated as equal and valuable members of their community—who are socially or politically subservient—have an associative political obligation to themselves and others to resist their own mistreatment. And members of a polity that violates some of its members' dignity have an associative political obligation to resist such mistreatment. This general obligation entails, depending on the agent and situation, specific obligations to protest in order to communicate opposition to the source of violation, to try to rectify the defects in question, assert one's dignity, and express solidarity through collective and individual action.

Let us now examine some objections to the foregoing associativist account of political resistance.

OBJECTIONS

Too Demanding

First, the account may be deemed to require too much sacrifice, since it binds every member of society to resist any dignity-threatening political relationship. Given the inevitability and ubiquity of threats to dignity in large political communities, the demands of Dworkinian dignity would constantly weigh on citizens and seriously impede their day-to-day activities and life plans. Some readers may consider this problem so serious as to constitute a reductio ad absurdum of my argument.

We have already examined versions of this objection. My response is basically that we shouldn't expect morality to be anything other than demanding in the nonideal, often-unjust circumstances in which we live. But, from within the dignitary-associativist perspective, the worry is a bit different: that the demands of political resistance would objectionably obstruct people's authentic self-realization.

This sets up a false dilemma. Authenticity demands that each person exercise independence in and responsibility for designing their own life. Political resistance often enacts values by which one lives and may even be central to the pursuit of responsibility. Daniel Silvermint argues that resisting one's own oppression can be an important component of well-being when living in oppressive circumstances.[36] The same should be said about privileged members of society, given the harmful effects of oppression on privileged people and bystanders, not just the oppressed—about which I'll say more in the next chapter. So political resistance does not have to impede my authentic self-realization. If attending to my associative political obligations to resist injustice would crowd out my life projects, then I have a choice to make. I may have much value to add to the world as an artist, for instance, but there is no reason to think that because my choice is aesthetically good I do not in fact have demanding political obligations.

Burdening and Blaming the Victim

The second objection contests the idea that those who are politically subordinated ought to resist their own oppression. Telling people whose dignity is threatened that they ought to resist and may be blamed for failing to do so amounts to objectionably burdening the victim as well as blaming her for failing to resist. These are two, tightly connected objections: that my account burdens victims with obligations and that it assigns them blame if they fail to carry out those obligations. As Marilyn Frye asks,

> Can we hold ourselves, and is it proper to hold each other, *responsible* for resistance? Or is it necessarily both stupid cruelty and a case of "blaming the victim" to add yet one more pressure in our lives, in each others' lives, by expecting, demanding, requiring, encouraging, inviting acts and patterns of resistance and reconstruction which are not spontaneously forthcoming?[37]

In response to the burdening-the-victim objection, I fail to see what is problematic with the claim that people whose dignity is violated incur special responsibilities to protect and assert that dignity. Our relations with others make us responsible and vulnerable in all sorts of ways, few of which we voluntarily take on. Recall this is part of the appeal of associativist accounts: where, for liberal contractualist theorists, what we owe others is mostly a matter of what we voluntarily undertake, associativists can account for the variety of involuntary and semi-voluntary obligations we incur in the course of forming bonds with others. The point is that victimhood and subjugation, even if entirely involuntary, may generate some responsibilities.

It is further noteworthy that the defense of ethical obligations of resistance accords well with the self-understanding of participants in many liberation struggles. W. E. B. Du Bois argued that self-respect was incompatible with silent submission to racial subjugation and required protest.[38] The Black Power movement encouraged racial pride and heightened self-esteem. This casts doubt on the implausibility, or unpalatability, of the idea of ethical obligations to resist one's mistreatment.

With respect to the objection of victim-blaming, it is important to keep in mind that even if we agree that subordinated people could be blamed for passively going along with their own oppression, this does not entail that it would be appropriate for anyone to blame them. Privileged people clearly lack the moral authority to do so and would be engaged in immoral victim-blaming if they were to chastise passivity. Only some people within the subordinated group can perhaps appropriately apply social sanctions to those who fail to resist, depending on their knowledge of others' particular circumstances and opportunities to resist.

Letting the Oppressed Fight

A third objection pushes in the opposite direction, stressing that dignity commands self-sufficiency and weighs against letting other people fight one's struggle. It demands that the oppressed resist alone. Assistance would be patronizing. This idea resonates with the third goal of resistance—asserting dignity—and has been prominent in liberation movements. For instance, Stokely Carmichael, former chairman of the Student Nonviolent Coordinating Committee (SNCC) and honorary prime minister of the Black Panther Party, refused the presence of Whites in the Black Power movement and insisted that SNCC "be Black-staffed, Black-controlled, and Black-financed." The demand for exclusively Black financing was especially burdensome given African Americans' relative lack of resources, but Carmichael insisted, "If we continue to rely upon White financial support we will find ourselves entwined in the tentacles of the White power complex that controls this country."[39] He thought that Whites could not relate to the Black experience, intimidated Blacks, and behaved paternalistically. "The charge may be made that we are 'racists,'" he wrote, "but Whites who are sensitive to our problems will realize that we must determine our own destiny."[40]

But while there is indeed great dignity in liberation by the oppressed themselves, it does not follow that others—oppressors, privileged, or bystanders—are not morally obligated to rectify oppressive arrangements. The slave rebellion led by Spartacus was certainly dignity affirming and awe inspiring. But it does not show that the abolition of slavery was the slaves' task. On the contrary, abolishing an unjust system such as slavery was everyone's moral duty—and, as I argued in chapter 4, those who benefit even involuntarily from injustice have an especially compelling duty to resist. So ethical obligations to resist one's own mistreatment are perfectly compatible with the moral obligations of the privileged to resist oppression, too, and with the latter obligations being weightier than the former. From this perspective, Carmichael's point should not be taken to exclude White resistance against racism but instead should be understood as emphasizing the importance of the composition and organization of oppressed people's own liberation movement.

Delineating Political Relationships

A fourth objection concerns the scope of political relationships. The dignity-threatening political relationships I focus on are laws, policies, practices, and institutions (including the government) that express contempt, or fail to express concern, for certain groups in the political community. But political relationships may not always be clearly delineated. There can be disagreements about whether a given power relationship is also a political one. For instance, most people deny that nonhuman animals are members of the moral community and therefore do not believe that considerations of justice apply to our treatment of them. The mistreatment of animals is not usually perceived as violation of their dignity, nor do people see their relations to animals as political. As another example, consider Americans' relationship to people in developing countries where the goods we consume are manufactured. Economic decisions made in the United States profoundly affect these countries, yet we are usually blind to the political nature of our relationship with, say, Bangladeshi garment workers.

It is appropriate to worry about all the power relationships left out of the liberal-associativist account. But I am not convinced that these observations actually amount to an objection against it. Instead, they suggest extending the account of special responsibilities and associative obligations of resistance beyond political membership and across borders. Dworkin's framework may accommodate such an extension. He explains how the obligation to obey the law flows from political membership, but this is premised on particular features of political membership that conceivably could expand beyond national and species borders. Namely, what makes political membership valuable is that it reduces vulnerability to subservience. There is no reason we could not extend the principles of dignity to account for associative obligations flowing from relationships that do not take place within the boundaries of a political community.

In conclusion, dignitary political membership grounds a general obligation to resist one's and others' violations of dignity, including by way of rectification, communication, assertion, and solidarity. I argued that dignitary political membership can justify violent, undignified, and hopeless resistance, and that it supports a political obligation of solidarity among and with the oppressed. One important point to infer from the foregoing account, as in the previous chapters, is that citizens' political obligations are *plural*. Under nonideal conditions, the obligations of resistance that flow from the responsibility neither to dominate nor to unilaterally defer to others are more central to the role of citizen than the obligation to obey the law—or abide by prison rules.

Chapter 7

Acting on Political Obligations

Perhaps you now feel overwhelmed by the number and extent of our political obligations, if not also skeptical of their demands and feasibility. It is difficult to act on them, to judge what they require us to do, and even to recognize them in the first place. Individuals are left to decide for themselves when they have an obligation to resist injustice, how they ought to discharge that obligation, and whether they are still bound by the obligation to obey the law. Given cognitive limitations and unconscious biases, citizens may make mistakes in good faith. They may feel the weight of an obligation that does not in fact exist and, in so doing, reject what is just and legitimate. They may destabilize and divide society by engaging in unnecessary acts of resistance. As I've noted before, that one may be wrong about one's duties and may fulfill them inadequately or irresponsibly does not rebut my arguments. But the problem of discretion does speak to an important general concern about the complicated demands of morality under nonideal conditions.

In this final chapter, I want to examine in more detail this concern. Simply put, correctly identifying and being motivated by our political obligations in the face of injustice presupposes many conditions unlikely to prevail. These include good civic and moral education; unbiased, readily accessible information; and strong civil-society institutions. Too often, these conditions don't obtain.

What are some of the major obstacles that hinder citizens' recognition of their political obligations? Are they insurmountable? How can individuals respond to their defective environments? My answers will point inward to individuals' responsibilities to exercise due epistemic care and outward to the collective: together we think; together we resist.

OBSTACLES

Authoritarian regimes and liberal democracies raise different worries for an account of duties to resist. The main difference between the two lies in the visibility of injustice. In autocratic states, injustice tends to be either glaring or intentionally hidden. In liberal democracies, it tends to be concealed behind the normal workings of social structures, divorced from agents' intentions.

In many cases, autocratic subjects may be barred from publicly naming an injustice, but it is nonetheless there for all to see. Think of public executions in Iran and kangaroo courts in Apartheid South Africa. Often, however, the wrongdoing that takes place in authoritarian regimes is concealed. When the injustice is not clearly discernable, it is likely a result of the government's lies, deception, and propaganda, not of the inherent difficulty of grasping that injustice. Either way, overt or covert, the harms of "agent oppression," to use Sally Haslanger's terminology, are intentional.[1]

In contrast, subjects of liberal democracies really may be unaware of injustices affecting fellow citizens, compromising and staining state legitimacy. In cases of "structural oppression," the harms are the unintended results of structures that work systematically—but not intentionally—to impede some groups' capacities for self-realization.

Each kind of injustice generates different obstacles to citizens' recognition of their political obligations.

Seeing and Denying

A routine aspect of life in tyrannical states is fear for one's safety and the safety of loved ones. Historical examples unfortunately abound. Imagine being Jewish, Roma, gay, or disabled under the Nazis; or living in Cambodia under Pol Pot's communist rule, when 1.5 million Cambodians—a fifth of the population—died of starvation, execution, disease, or overwork. Closer to the United States, it is estimated that thirteen thousand people disappeared in Argentina during the 1976–1983 military dictatorship.

Totalitarian regimes reinforce this basic fear for one's life by encouraging distrust among subjects. For example, denunciation flourished in police states such as Nazi Germany and the Soviet Union. Robert Gellately's study has shown that the Gestapo numbered only about 7,500 at its peak, while the real instruments of surveillance were the citizenry, who reported everything from Jews holding hands with non-Jews to Germans listening to foreign radio.[2] Gellately found that denunciations enabled individuals to draw on the state's coercive power to settle private, often petty, grievances and advance their own interests. The same sort of thing happened in the Soviet Union, where denunciations aimed at securing a larger or better living space were so common that they spawned the coinage "apartment denunciation." What these phenomena show is the corrosive effects of injustice on our moral capacities: some people wrongfully and even deceptively expose others to grave harms for their own petty benefit. Pervasive grave injustice can habituate and desensitize us to itself. The Grimké sisters, who grew up on a slave-owning plantation in South Carolina, suggested that slavery, insofar as it left people morally estranged from one another and thwarted compassion, eroded everyone's moral capacities.[3]

Along with desensitization and advantage-seeking, denial is a common reaction to and coping mechanism for grave injustice.

It offers a psychological "solution" to the horrors of witnessing or participating in state atrocities. In his sociological study of denial, Stanley Cohen speculates of the ordinary Reichsbahn employees in charge of transporting Jews to their final destination: "These booking clerks and train drivers must have recognized that something abnormal, if not morally wrong, was going on. They must have eventually slipped into a state of dulled routinization—as if this was more or less business as usual."[4] This slippage, he suggests, could come from an unconscious defense mechanism, or from a conscious decision to proceed as if everything were normal.

Despotic governments facilitate subjects' denial by denying the facts (e.g., that a massacre has taken place), denying their proper interpretation (that certain actions are grave human rights violations), denying their value (that the actions are morally abhorrent), or denying responsibility for the truth of these facts.[5] Officials themselves often engage in denial, despite the cognitive dissonance involved. Albert Speer, a high-ranking SS officer in Nazi Germany, famously denied knowing about the Final Solution until his death in 1981, all the while accepting some responsibility owing to his senior position. Speer's wife later explained her husband's denial as a kind of willful ignorance: "If one had known, one would have had to question it, one would have had to face the reality of it and . . . one would have had to question one's own attitude toward it."[6]

This conundrum applies to perpetrators, accomplices, beneficiaries, and bystanders, and the lines between these categories can be porous. Just witnessing acts of injustice may leave a stain on the spectator's moral conscience because bearing witness inevitably raises the question of what one could have done to prevent the acts and, as Speer's wife suggests, can foster a sense of guilt for having done nothing. This is a crucial reason why people shut their eyes to injustice around them. Visual metaphors are telling: they pretend they just don't see, as Bob Dylan sang.[7] This is pretense more than blindness, and it arguably involves both deception—of oneself and others—and moral cowardice. Yet it may also be that people close their eyes because they feel helpless or endangered, or because what is in front of them is too horrible to be watched. And all of these possibilities may be tied up together, such that we pretend not to see injustice because it is unbearable to do so, because we fear for our lives, and because we think there is nothing we can do.

Claude Lanzmann masterfully represents these complexities and tensions in *Shoah*, which recreates the life of the concentration camps through nearly ten hours of interviews with Jewish survivors; German executioners; and Poles from the villages of Chelmno, Malkinia, and Auschwitz.[8] While the film's main subject is the extermination process, it also offers a powerful examination of responsibility and blame. The Polish villagers present themselves as victims of the Nazi occupation, helpless witnesses to the mass murder of Jews. In some respects, this defense is plausible. What could ordinary Poles have done? The Nazis conquered and occupied Poland, and routinely executed Polish subjects for sheltering Jews. Poles were by and large powerless.

As the movie unfolds, however, some of the villagers demonstrate callousness so appalling that they appear as complacent spectators rather than as helpless would-be Samaritans. For instance, Lanzmann asks one farmer whether the villagers weren't afraid for the Jews. The farmer replies, "Well, it's like this: if I cut my finger, it doesn't hurt you, does it?" A number of villagers laugh as they recall drawing a finger across their throats at the sight of passing cattle cars full of Jews unaware of the fate before them. Pervasive anti-Semitism coexists with heartbreaking testimonies from those left horrified by what they saw and by their inability to prevent it.

This is the case even among those who causally contributed to the evil, such as the Treblinka locomotive driver who transported Jews to their deaths. He appears irreparably broken by what he saw and especially by what he heard, which cannot be ignored with a turn of the head: the screams, followed by total silence, which Lanzmann makes him describe meticulously. In this way, the film illustrates the range of subjective experiences between witnesses, bystanders, spectators, and contributors, and suggests that evaluating witnesses' moral roles—determining when observer becomes accomplice— can be complicated. *Shoah* also shatters the myth that people didn't know about the genocide until after the war. Many people knew but felt it wasn't their concern, or that there was nothing they could do about it.

One takes from the film a disturbing lesson: no one living amid grave injustice comes out unscathed. Denunciation makes one an agent of or direct contributor to wrongdoing; moral integrity is diminished by denial, however understandable as a coping strategy; helpless bystanders must live with traumatic memories and the guilt of having done nothing; victims' sense of their own worth is diminished and their trust in others broken, leaving grief, suffering, and sometimes survivor's guilt. The effects of injustice, reactions to it, and obstacles to recognizing it are thus intertwined in the phenomenology of injustice. This is important as it suggests that precisely where resistance is the most needed, some forces hinder recognition and attribution of political obligations of resistance, by facilitating mechanisms of denial and rendering difficult the determination of people's moral role in atrocities.

Not Seeing and Justifying

In contexts of agent injustice, the horror afoot is noticeable because it is abnormal. In cases of structural injustice, the problem is the opposite: nothing unusual happens. The harms of structural injustice are primarily consequences of the normal interplay between social institutions, processes, and norms. By default, these harms are harder to detect than those resulting from the intentional, egregious actions of individuals. Of course one can hardly resist injustices one does not perceive.

The harms of structural injustice consist in hindering people's capacities for self-realization by virtue of their perceived membership in a social group. As it diminishes some people's capacities, structural injustice benefits others through privilege. On Alison Bailey's conception, privileges are "unearned assets conferred systematically."[9] They are unearned because the members of the privileged group enjoy them as a result of sheer luck—the luck of belonging to a social group whose race, sexuality, gender, or class confers privilege. One of the functions of privilege, according to Bailey, is to "structure the world so that mechanisms of privilege are invisible—in the sense that they are unexamined—to those who benefit from them."[10] Privilege thus breeds blindness and blindness reinforces privilege, since being privileged is being able, even encouraged, to fail to see the oppressive system and the privileges it grants. The privileged are prone to deceiving themselves into thinking that they deserve their status and benefits, that they earned their gains through talent and effort.

As privilege is invisible to the privileged person, so is oppression in general invisible to him or her, and sometimes to the oppressed themselves. The unjust situation of those who occupy a subordinated position in the social structure remains unseen as long as the privileges of the dominant group appear deserved. Bailey describes this phenomenon:

> The maintenance of heterosexual, White, or male privilege as positions of structural advantage lies largely in the silence surrounding the mechanisms of privilege. . . . Whites are not encouraged to recognize or acknowledge the effects of racialization on White lives, men have difficulty seeing the effects of sexism on women's lives, and heterosexuals rarely

understand the impact of homophobia on gay, bisexual, and lesbian communities.[11]

The privileged often lack basic understanding of the experience of deprivation and oppression, and further lack the motivation to learn about it.

Marxist notions of ideology and false consciousness help explain how decent people can deny the existence of structural injustice without necessarily being credulous or ill willed. Ideology—understood here as a widely shared worldview that stabilizes sociopolitical conditions by representing them as just—and its arsenal of stereotypes and biases assure that structural injustice remains concealed by providing simple, alternative explanations for disparities. For instance, the stereotype of African Americans as drug users and criminals is taken as an explanation of their disproportionate representation behind bars, thereby concealing racist criminal justice policies and practices.[12]

Ideology in turn produces false consciousness. According to Tommie Shelby, "To hold a belief with a false consciousness is to hold it while being ignorant of, or self-deceived about, the real motives for why one holds it."[13] The individual who suffers from false consciousness believes that she accepts a belief solely because it is epistemically justified, when in reality noncognitive motives influence her belief without her awareness. Shelby gives the following examples of noncognitive motives for embracing certain beliefs:

> Though presumably we do not do so consciously, we sometimes believe things because to do so would, say, bolster our self-esteem, give us consolation, lessen anxiety, reduce cognitive dissonance, increase our self-confidence, provide cathartic relief, give us hope, or silence a guilty conscience. When these

and other noncognitive motives are psychologically operative, we easily fall into epistemic error.[14]

So not only are members of the privileged group encouraged to think that they earned their higher status, but members of the subordinated group, too, can find (unconscious) solace in the dominant ideology, for instance by believing that it is in their power to climb the social ladder in a capitalist meritocratic society. Denying structural injustice with false consciousness can also serve as an anxiolytic against the uncomfortable feeling that one ought, but is not willing, to fulfill one's responsibilities in the face of injustice.

Structural injustice thus corrodes our moral capacities in the following respects: the dominant ideology, buttressed by stereotypes, infects us with bias and obstructs our reading of social reality and of our own and others' conduct. Hay argues that it even damages our rational capacities.[15] It makes us prone to various kinds of conative, cognitive, and affective errors when assessing complex situations.[16] By encouraging self-deceit, then, privilege and false consciousness further hinder the development of moral conscience and critical thinking, which are crucial to perceiving injustice and recognizing our political obligations.

Some Caveats

So various cognitive, conative, and moral capacities are essential to countering injustice. But pervasive injustice compromises these faculties. Prejudice and propaganda infect perceptions of social reality and moral conscience, and they corrode our abilities to see, and our emotional responses to, injustice. Moral conscience cannot always be relied on as a guide to right action. Think of Mark Twain's

story, in which Huckleberry Finn experiences a kind of agony when
he frees Jim from slavery:

> Jim said it made him all over trembly and feverish to be so close
> to freedom. Well, I can tell you it made me all over trembly and
> feverish, too, to hear him, because I begun to get it through
> my head that he was most free—and who was to blame for it?
> Why, me. I couldn't get that out of my conscience, no how nor
> no way.[17]

Huckleberry sincerely believes he is acting against his conscience.
The drollness of the passage lies in part in the tension between
Huckleberry's objectively right action and his feelings of guilt
born from the conviction that he is doing wrong. Yet, while Twain
recognizes the corrosive influence of pro-slavery ideology, morality prevails thanks to Huckleberry's natural feelings of shared
humanity. Twain thereby suggests that the point about injustice's
corrosive effects—indeed, the general notion that moral conscience is a product of society's ethos, cultural norms, or economic
superstructures—should not be exaggerated.

In "What to the Slave Is the Fourth of July?" Frederick Douglass
derides the very idea that abolitionists need to argue the point that
Blacks are fully rational humans, and that White slaveholders really
believed otherwise.

> Must I undertake to prove that the slave is a man? That point
> is conceded already. Nobody doubts it. The slaveholders them-
> selves acknowledge it in the enactment of laws for their govern-
> ment. They acknowledge it when they punish disobedience on
> the part of the slave. There are seventy-two crimes in the State
> of Virginia, which, if committed by a black man, (no matter

how ignorant he be), subject him to the punishment of death; while only two of the same crimes will subject a white man to the like punishment. What is this but the acknowledgement that the slave is a moral, intellectual and responsible being? The manhood of the slave is conceded. It is admitted in the fact that Southern statute books are covered with enactments forbidding, under severe fines and penalties, the teaching of the slave to read or to write.[18]

Douglass denounces slavery's apologists' hypocrisies and contradictions and shows that slave laws were predicated on the guilty knowledge of slaves' full humanity.

Similarly problematic is the common, relativist idea that people don't know and have no way of knowing that an immoral practice is wrong when it is widely established and buttressed by ideology. Kwame Anthony Appiah debunks this idea in *The Honor Code*, as he shows that immoral practices are deplored and seen as immoral from their inception, though it often takes a very long time before they are reformed or abolished.[19] His case studies are dueling, Chinese foot-binding, and British chattel slavery. Contradicting a common understanding of moral revolutions, Appiah shows that arguments about the wrongfulness of these practices circulated widely from the start. In each moral revolution, according to Appiah, "It wasn't the moral arguments that were new; it was the willingness to live by them."[20] Recognizing the injustice of a state of affairs is often insufficient to redressing it. For Appiah, moving people to action is a greater challenge than getting them to recognize injustice.

All of this is to say that we should be wary of arguments emphasizing the obstacles to recognizing injustice. Failure to act on the basis of our best-considered moral judgment is a familiar problem. How many of us eat meat all the while believing the carnivore diet to be morally wrong? But even if recognition of the manifold obstacles to satisfying our political obligations of resistance does not necessarily weigh against my account, it does underscore the need for additional, second-order responsibilities.

IMPLICATIONS

We must cultivate in ourselves the civic virtues of vigilance and open-mindedness. These matter especially for privileged citizens—indeed, while vigilance is often second nature for oppressed subjects, demanding them to be open-minded would be unreasonable and condescending; rather, they should be the recipients and beneficiaries of privileged persons' open-mindedness. At the same time, the intersectional nature of oppression suggests that most people have to practice vigilance and open-mindedness on some level, say, as White, middle class, educated, native-accented, cisgender, male, heterosexual, or able-bodied. Vigilance and open-mindedness, as I understand them, are generic virtues: they implicate a host of capacities, dispositions, and habits, such as critical thinking for the former and empathetic imagination for the latter. Through these civic virtues, citizens can form correct beliefs and engage in critical dialog about justice, practices necessary to discharging the obligation to resist injustice. Dialog is essential in no small part because our thinking and motivation are developed with, and political obligations owed to, others.

Belief

"It is a task to come to see the world as it is," Iris Murdoch wrote.[21] This chapter has discussed several obstacles to fulfilling duties to resist. But these are only part of the story: other obstacles derive from the complexity of our world. Assessing the merits of a particular tax policy or international trade agreement, for instance, requires understanding politics and economics. Our limited cognitive resources generate further challenges. We commonly make mistakes in reasoning, as we use heuristic devices and shortcuts that generally serve us well but that also lead us to make gross errors, including some that impede realization of our own interests.[22] In addition to these cognitive biases, our perception of social reality is tainted by implicit biases that produce, among other things, unconscious prejudice against certain social groups.[23]

Citizens make decisions that significantly affect others, especially in democratic contexts where they are the authors of the law. Jean-Jacques Rousseau highlights the implication of this authorship in his opening to *The Social Contract*: "Born a citizen of a free State, and a member of the Sovereign, the right to vote in it is enough to impose on me the duty to learn about public affairs, regardless of how weak might be the influence on them."[24] Since citizens of a democracy make decisions on the basis of their beliefs, they ought to form their beliefs responsibly. They ought to recognize their own fallibility and biases and resist self-deception. They ought to be accurately informed, in particular about the state's laws and policies, society's institutions, and their effects on people. They ought to exercise due care in reasoning. It is essential that citizens seek trustworthy sources of information; think critically about that information; question received wisdom; listen to others, especially those situated differently from themselves; and adjust their beliefs according to solid evidence and reliable testimony. The responsibility to exercise due care in reasoning is especially weighty when one considers principled disobedience, but this does not mean that law-abiding citizens can just "cruise" along. Indeed injustice typically endures thanks to compliance. The choice to uphold the law, too, should therefore be given thoughtful consideration.

To fully grasp what is required of us, we need to expand how we understand vigilance as well. Vigilance exemplifies the right exercise of this responsibility and is a civic virtue. In political discourse, the idea of vigilance has been coopted to some extent by the right. Entertainer and conservative commentator Rush Limbaugh, whose radio talk show garners more listeners than any other in the United States, frequently urges vigilance against the media, Democrats, and elites, and has described conservatism as "an active intellectual pursuit" that "requires a constant vigilance."[25] Neighborhood watches and other vigilante groups identify their raison d'être in vigilance against criminals and illegal immigrants, often smokescreens for racism and xenophobia.

The left—and any movement concerned with liberation—should reclaim the term. Vigilance evokes dispositions, skills, and habits that make us attentive to self-deception and propaganda, much needed under nonideal conditions such as those presented by the presidency of Donald Trump. I am not the first to say so. Obama administration attorney general Loretta Lynch urged vigilance against Trump's potential abuses of the Justice Department as a weapon against his personal and political enemies.[26] John Oliver, host of the satirical TV show *Last Week Tonight*, also called for vigilance against Trump, whom he called a "Klan-backed misogynist Internet troll."[27]

One might object that generalized vigilance would sow distrust among people and thereby corrode civic bonds and increase society's divisions. But the attentiveness and alertness I defend entail nothing of the sort. For one, virtuous vigilance would be turned not against fellow citizens and residents, but inward, leading us to recognize our fallibility, tendency toward self-deception, and susceptibility to false consciousness. In addition, citizens who exercise virtuous vigilance scrutinize officials, which leads them to hold accountable people entrusted with state power. Institutional mechanisms of citizen vigilance, such as oversight committees, can further these goals. It may be perfectly appropriate for citizens to distrust officials or institutions when they have shown themselves to be untrustworthy, but distrust need not be the default attitude.

Some background elements are crucial for the flourishing of vigilance as a civic virtue. First, there should be good universal education, so that all citizens possess critical-thinking skills and basic knowledge of history and of the workings of government. People need free time as well—time that is not committed to meeting life's necessities—to develop their intellectual capacities, acquire knowledge, and generally pursue their chosen ends.[28] People living in abject poverty or working very long hours under strenuous and exploitative conditions are deprived of the time and energy necessary for the exercise of civic vigilance. They lack any sort of leisure—*skole*, in Greek, the root of the English word "school." Education and free time are tightly connected. Some form of welfare state may be a prerequisite to ensuring access to both, and both are prerequisites to virtuous civic vigilance. Third, because virtuous civic vigilance is impossible without reliable information, we cannot do without able, independent, trustworthy media organizations.

So the generic civic virtue of vigilance encompasses many subtraits—not only the duty to form one's beliefs responsibly, which itself implies the disposition to self-reflect and think critically, but also certain affective capacities and habits that are implicated in an attentive approach to our social world and alertness to its dangers. However, vigilance carries the risk of hypersensitivity, to wit, an excessive alertness to dangers and tendency to be quickly irritated by, and intolerant of, differences. We sometimes need to overlook differences that irritate us or to try hard to understand them. Vigilance needs to be selective and moderate: in particular, it should not target people in a way that denies their full and equal standing in the political or moral community (think of the way hyper-vigilance to terrorist threats can lead to Islamophobia). And Melissa Schwartzberg argues that liberals and democrats are committed to respecting fellow citizens' epistemic equality, that is, their standing as knowers and bearers of judgment.[29] In short, vigilance needs to be balanced by a certain kind of openness and epistemic respect for others I dub open-mindedness.[30]

Dialog and Ambivalence

Being informed and vigilant does not guarantee one will "see the world as it is." The right kind of perception is suffused with empathy and a yearning to understand others. One must be disposed to imagine others' experiences, to listen to their testimonies, and engage with them. Elizabeth Spelman argues that the privileged must exercise their imaginative capacities to put themselves in the shoes of the oppressed.[31] As with the previous responsibility, it is important to be aware of self-deception in this process. Recall marginalized people's critique of so-called allies discussed in chapter 6: when allies fail to believe a marginalized person's testimony, they not only inflict a serious kind of epistemic harm on her, but they also betray her trust. Proper moral learning about oppression requires that we exercise and cultivate imaginative self-projection, and listen to others.

Mindful introspection and imagination can only do so much; moral learning also requires empathy, as research in cognitive science has shown and as feminists have long argued through their defense of care ethics.[32] Moral learning is also an interactive enterprise, which we undertake with others. Laurence Thomas argues that the privileged must listen to the oppressed with an attitude he calls "moral deference," which counsels openness and attentiveness.[33] Engaging with others in dialog and collaborative projects, with empathy and an open mind, is crucial to perceiving oppression and developing the motivation to fight it. Many forums may promote this type of empathetic and open-minded moral learning, including interactive environments such as college campuses and community centers, projects committed to diversity and inclusion, and active-bystander training programs.[34]

The goals of practical and dialogical engagement go well beyond learning about oppression. These are practical endeavors that enrich our lives, stimulate creativity, and make us better decision-makers.[35] I submit that those who take up this sort of engagement practice the civic virtue of *open-mindedness*. This civic virtue combines a host of attitudes and dispositions, including moral deference to others, desire to engage in dialog and collaboration, and openness to one's own transformation in the process. Open-mindedness facilitates mutual understanding, which is vital to recognizing and resisting oppression.

The civic virtue of open-mindedness flourishes only amid social integration. There must be a range of environments favorable to meaningful interaction. When people regularly interact with others who look or act differently from them, they may shed their fears and prejudices about these "others" and stop thinking in terms of "us versus them." This phenomenon has been well documented in sociology and discussed in philosophy.[36] Instead of expanding on this, I shall examine an attitude that may appear at first glance pernicious but which in fact invites open-minded engagement: ambivalence.

Ambivalence is usually seen as a mark of a troubled or confused conscience whose inner conflicts undermine steadfast, responsible action. However, Amélie Rorty has recently pleaded in favor of ambivalence, arguing that ambivalence is inevitable given the multiple roles we inhabit, each with its distinct values and priorities, and further that ambivalence can be epistemologically grounded and responsible. Rorty distinguishes ambivalence from indecisiveness and vacillation. When we are indecisive, we are "in a maybe this/maybe that epistemic condition, with multiple distinctively ranked preferences among their various desirable options."[37] We vacillate when we are "in a now this/now that epistemic condition that expresses erratic and shifting preferences between distinctive and apparently incompatible options."[38] To be ambivalent is to be "in a both/and epistemic and motivational condition, endorsing all one's options while thinking them incompatible."[39]

Whereas indecision and vacillation call for stable guiding criteria, which we can arrive at by reflection, the best policy in the face of ambivalence, according to Rorty, involves first trying to identify and assess the sources and grounds of our ambivalence. When we have reasons to favor each alternative, so that our ambivalence is a fitting response to circumstances, Rorty deems our ambivalence "internally appropriate."[40] The framework illuminates the situation of citizens under nonideal conditions. Ambivalence will often be an appropriate attitude for those who sense conflict between their professional and political obligations or between the obligation to obey the law and the obligation to resist injustice. Ambivalence might also be appropriate for those uncertain about which course of action is best.

If we reflectively attempt to integrate the grounds for our appropriate ambivalence with our other commitments, Rorty submits, we are "responsibly" ambivalent.[41] We can also imaginatively reframe our choices in order to preserve the terms and rationales of seemingly conflicting commitments, thereby exercising "constructive ambivalence."[42] Thus the soldier who refuses to obey an order he perceives as immoral may come to see the order as illegal—as are orders to participate in war crimes—and realize that his professional, political, and moral obligations in fact align. The best strategy for constructive ambivalence is to expand the scope of our partners in deliberation and enlist their empathic cooperation in a shared deliberative effort. "Collaborative ambivalence," as Rorty calls this, enables us to envision different resolutions to our conflicts as well as to deepen our understanding of ourselves and our partners through practical and dialogic engagement.

Citizens trying to resolve their appropriate ambivalence about certain policies or practices therefore should get together in town hall meetings and social movements. In these contexts, they might work out sources of ambivalence and resolve conflicts by prioritizing and organizing the values at stake, choosing together courses of action, and following them through. Such dialogical engagement is also a propitious environment for responsible belief formation and a powerful countermeasure against the wide circulation of "fake news" and discrediting of true stories as "fake."

Thinking and Resisting Together

In Rorty's analysis, "The sources, the structures and resolutions of ambivalence reveal how much of our thinking—and so also how much of our motivational structure—emerges from the details of our collaborative and dialogical engagements."[43] We come to think what we think, and are moved to act on the basis of what we think, as a result of our interactions. Rorty is not saying that our beliefs are influenced by what everyone else thinks, as reflected in the dominant culture and accepted worldview. She is saying that we think together: that thinking is a collaborative activity. When we talk with each other and act together, we reassess what we think, compel others to do the same, and further reflect and deliberate together. There is obvious normative significance here. It is a good thing to talk to others, and to really listen to them, as I argue in my defense of open-minded engagement. But Rorty's point is first and foremost descriptive: *this is how we think.*

There are at least two reasons why we may not recognize the collaborative nature of our thinking. One is the tendency to think about conscience and responsibility as individualistic processes. Another is the apparent lack of genuine practical and dialogical engagement all around us. The latter is obvious in democratic societies, where deliberation often lacks in open-mindedness, inclusiveness, empathy, and mutual respect. But this does not entail that people "think alone" the way they "bowl alone," in Robert Putnam's phrase. Interaction is constant in the home; among friends; at school; in places of worship, voluntary associations, and workplaces; and online. Rorty's insight further suggests that deprivation of opportunities to practically and dialogically engage with others constitutes a special kind of injustice, one that affects the development of our rational capacities and self-realization.

Rorty submits that the notion of "thinking as an individualistic process" pervades "our folk-psychological and philosophical models of thoughtful deliberation."[44] Images of thinking—from Auguste Rodin's famed sculpture, The Thinker, to the archetype of the monk meditating in isolation—are deeply individualistic. This individualistic slant has warped discussion of political struggles in particular. Thus Hannah Arendt denounced as "the greatest fallacy" in the debates about anti-Vietnam war and Civil Rights activists "the assumption that we are dealing with individuals, who pit themselves subjectively and conscientiously against the laws and customs of the community," when "the fact is that we are dealing with organized minorities" formed "with the same spirit that has informed voluntary associations."[45] Michael Walzer also insisted, going against common thinking about the matter, that the basic unit of analysis for theorists interested in political struggles had to be the group, not the individual. As Walzer saw it, philosophers will never grasp what rebels and civil disobedients do and why they do it until they realize that "individual responsibility is always *to* someone else, and learned *with* someone else."[46] It is a matter of mutual commitments and undertakings. Rorty, Arendt, and Walzer show that together is how we think and resist.

But aren't there many individual exemplars of conscientious objection? And isn't the distinction between conscientious objection and civil disobedience so blurry that civil-disobedient groups may well amount to aggregates of conscientious objectors?

Indeed, the line is blurry. Thoreau's tax refusal, for instance, which is better described as conscientious refusal, became public when he later wrote and lectured about it, and is now seen as a paradigmatic method of civil disobedience. Whistleblowers also appear as obvious counterexamples to the essentially collective nature of thoughtful resistance, as they seem to stand alone against their peers and superiors. Thus Oliver Stone's *Snowden* and Sidney Lumet's *Serpico* represent their protagonists—the NSA whistleblower and the officer who exposed endemic corruption in the New York Police Department, respectively—as lonely men compelled and burdened by their consciences.[47]

In response, I would argue that this objection rests on a problematic contrast between conscientious objection and civil disobedience, with the former deemed an essentially subjective, internally compelled, individual decision. We should extend Rorty's insights to conscientious objection: agents do not undertake their principled, conscientious disobedience out of the blue. Even if they act alone, conscientious objectors often practically and dialogically engage with others similarly situated and rarely limit their activism to a single act of conscientious refusal. Thus Christian pharmacists opposed to prescribing plan-B contraceptive pills discuss, organize, and protest. When they refuse to honor their clients' prescriptions, it is generally with the encouragement and approbation of their fellow religionists and some of their professional peers. Emanuela Ceva has recently detailed the collaborative engagements of conscientious objectors and vindicated its role as a form not of recusal but of political participation.[48] In the final analysis, there is little reason to contrast civil disobedience and conscientious objection along the dimension of collaboration.

Nor is whistleblowing inherently individualistic. Consider the debate among government lawyers about whether to serve the Trump administration. The human rights lawyer David Kaye writes:

Ultimately, when serious illegality is taking place, who will blow the whistle but the lawyers and other civil servants who have the ability or willingness to resist?

You should also know that you have a network of lawyers outside who would support you, whether our professional networks like the American Society of International Law and the American Bar Association, academics from around the country, or the research and advocacy organizations from across the spectrum of issue areas.[49]

I venture that a close look at seemingly solitary whistleblowers will also reveal a multitude of engagements, small and large. Though viewed by many as a loner, Snowden collaborated with journalists Laura Poitras, Glenn Greenwald, and Ewen MacAskill. As soon as he stepped forward, the American Civil Liberties Union (ACLU) offered him pro bono legal assistance, and Daniel Ellsberg praised him. Ellsberg and Snowden now work side by side on the Board of Directors of the Freedom of the Press Foundation. And, far from presenting himself as a maverick, Snowden often places his actions among those of previous NSA whistleblowers, so that his leaks appear as the culmination of others' work. In short, subjective, individualistic resistance is not the norm—collaboration is.

Civic Virtues

Throughout this book, I have reconceived political obligation as encompassing resistance against injustice. I have sought to extend philosophical thinking beyond civil disobedience to other forms of principled disobedience, including uncivil ones. But it is not enough to show that principled disobedience is theoretically grounded. It must also be within our power. Thus, in this chapter, I have identified key obstacles to perceiving and satisfying our political obligations in the face of injustice and described second-order responsibilities to develop the dispositions necessary to face these obstacles. Through responsible belief formation and engagement with others, I believe these dispositions can be developed and these obstacles overcome. If we understand citizens' political obligations as learned with and owed to others, in line with philosophical insights about the collaborative structure of our thinking and motivation, then we overcome also the atomizing tendencies of individualist perspectives that would undercut solidarity.

Developing our capacities requires a commitment to civic virtue, cultivated by education (understood not merely in terms of schooling but in the widest sense of socialization of shared civic life). This can seem a bit old-fashioned. Civic virtue was a major concern of the founders of modern nation-states, but it seems far from public debate these days. Yet, civic virtues remain important. Prominent candidates today are patriotism and law-abidance, though only the former is typically framed as a virtue, while the latter is expected of citizens as a matter of course, rather than praised.

Many citizens and politicians, as well as some philosophers, argue that good citizens are patriots, loyal to their country. These same voices argue that patriotism should be inculcated in children.[50] As one of his first official acts, President Trump declared his inauguration day to be a "National Day of Patriotic Devotion."[51]

But Simon Keller has shown that patriotism entails bad faith and blindness toward the shortcomings of one's country.[52] He has argued that not patriotism but cosmopolitanism—or "worldly citizenship," which involves attachments within one's country and to other countries—should be deemed a civic virtue.[53] I agree: patriotism is a suspicious candidate for civic virtue, no matter how harmless, and even intrinsically good, feelings of belonging to and love of one's country might otherwise be.

Patriotism does not necessarily exclude political obligations of resistance—and many dissenters and their supporters in fact appeal to patriotism to justify their actions. Daniel Ellsberg and Oliver Stone call Snowden a patriot. Protesters at the Women's March in Washington, DC, and sister cities on the day following the inauguration of President Trump held signs that read "Dissent is patriotic" (the ACLU slogan). The kind of patriotism that makes room for dissent and resistance is different from that which entails bad faith and blindness. The latter reduces, while the former increases, the likelihood that one will satisfy one's political obligations of resistance responsibly. Yet I am skeptical of even the former kind of patriotism, on the grounds that it too can blind people to the dark tendencies of their community. Patriotic dissidents in the United States, for instance, tend to conceive of racial injustice as flawed implementation of the polity's principle of democratic equality, rather than as what it might in fact be: the natural manifestation of deeply entrenched racist principles. Ta-Nehisi Coates derides this tendency and the selective reading of history that sustains it: "To celebrate freedom and democracy while forgetting America's origins in a slavery economy is patriotism à la carte."[54] That being said, I consider patriotism a powerful tool in many liberatory struggles, especially in the U.S. context where characterizing a policy or position as "un-American" (not just illegal, immoral, and harmful) is often a very effective way to combat it. In short, I think that patriotism has a potentially crucial role to play in resistance movements, although it should not be counted as among our civic virtues.

Especially as far as governments are concerned, law-abidance may be an even more important candidate for civic virtue than is patriotism. Philosophers have generally paid little attention to law-abidance as a civic virtue, but William Edmundson is an exception. According to Edmundson, law-abidance always involves respect for authority and the rule of law. Configuring law-abidance as civic virtue means endorsing a moral duty to obey "retail" orders—issued personally by an authority.[55] This is a civic virtue, in his view, because it makes for good citizens, who support the legal order. Law-abidance and compliance in general are taught in school and tend to be praised in children and adults alike. But I am skeptical that law-abidance is in fact a civic virtue under nonideal conditions. As I have argued, disobeying direct orders may be called for in some cases, yet virtuous law-abidance would prohibit such disobedience.

In place of these dubious civic virtues, I have recommended vigilance and open-mindedness. These by no means exhaust the civic virtues, and they do not, on their own, suffice to constitute good citizenship. But they are uniquely important in helping us to responsibly identify our political obligations. Where strong tendencies toward loyalty and law-abidance can result in credulity, laziness, self-deception, and close-mindedness, vigilance and open-mindedness nurture informed and empathetic understanding.

Conclusion

The Freedom Riders took enormous risks to denounce the injustice of racial segregation. They were insulted, tear-gassed, beaten, and arrested. The buses they rode were burned down. Yet they felt it was their political obligation to protest and hinder the racial caste system. They put their bodies on the line, in Thoreau's evocative description of civil resistance, to serve as "counter-friction" to the machine of the state. So did, in their own ways, the militant suffragists, Bobby Sands and other IRA inmates, Saudi female drivers, government whistleblowers like Snowden, Meet To Sleep's Action Heroes, and sanctuary workers like the French olive farmer Eric Herrou. *A Duty to Resist* sought to ground the political obligations they all felt they had, by providing a multi-principle account of political obligations in response to injustice, expanding in the process the concept of political obligation to include duties to resist injustice and disobey unjust law. It also sought to make conceptual and normative space for thinking beyond civil disobedience to other forms of principled, including uncivil, disobedience that may be called for even in near-just legitimate societies.

Although the arguments for political obligations to resist injustice based on the natural duty of justice, the principle of fairness, the Samaritan duty, and dignitary political membership stand alone, it is important to note the logical connections between them and within the general account. First, a number of the arguments overlap. For instance, the duty of justice, the principle of fairness, and political membership support a general obligation to resist oppression. Fairness and political membership imply an obligation of solidarity. That different principles separately generate the same obligations in the face of injustice reinforces the case that these are, in fact, political obligations. Second, because each principle can account for different kinds of situations (e.g., fairness illuminates our thinking about exploitation, and the Samaritan duty helps us decide what to do for people in peril), the four collectively cover a wide range of contexts. Third, some principles appear outside the chapters devoted to them, suggesting internal connections. For instance, I use the duty of fair play in order to solve collective action problems in the context of Samaritan rescues. Democratic authority is central to the duty of justice but also does some work in the associativist account. In these ways, each central chapter's single-principle arguments are best seen as working in tandem with the others to render the overall, multi-principle account more compelling.

If my arguments are right, it should be clear that citizens' political obligations are manifold. The obligation to obey the law is just one among many, and, in the real world, it is not the principal one. It is time, then, that philosophers forsake the equation of political obligation and the duty to obey the law. The problem is not mere semantics: it permeates what is discussed and how it is discussed. The duty to obey has long had the lion's share of philosophical attention, at the expense of other political obligations binding people, especially those binding them under injustice. And by and large, both camps in the literature on political obligation concentrate on the inferential logic of the arguments pro and con, without questioning the equation of political obligation with, or the exclusive focus on, the duty to obey the law. Framing the discussion this way has the effect of obscuring the role of noncompliance in impeding injustice and promoting democracy. In a way, the philosophical centrality of political obligation-as-obedience and relegation of principled disobedience to other corners (e.g., the question of whether liberal states should exempt conscientious objectors or be lenient toward civil disobedients) takes for granted and thus validates states' demand for compliance. This book sought to upend this framing and revisit political obligation, articulating a richer account that is attuned to real-world injustices.

The pressing political obligations I identify in the book often align with activists and dissidents' self-understandings and calls to others, whom they urge to join the resistance against injustice. To paraphrase King, the arc of the moral universe needs some pressure to bend toward justice. Undisturbed by resisters' and reformers' efforts, it does not run its course but is warped by those in power for their own advantage, and turned into ideology to sustain the status quo.

What may be surprising is that these manifold political obligations of resistance derive from well-established norms of liberal political morality, which radical activists such as socialists, anarchists, and Black feminists, tend to view as barriers to resistance. But basic liberal commitments can and do have far-reaching and radical implications for how we ought to respond to injustice around us.

History shows us that principled disobedience—from popular uprisings to draft dodging and from ordinary American citizens covertly aiding runaway slaves to Iranian women's posting photos and videos of themselves sans veil, in violation of the compulsory hijab law—is a force for good and a powerful check against authoritarianism and oppression. *A Duty to Resist* further argues that citizens, even in democracy, can and sometimes ought to engage in principled disobedience to fulfill their political obligations. Disobedience can obstruct, or signal opposition to, injustice, and, when done in large numbers, can assert the popular will against the state. Remember that Hannah Arendt viewed mass civil disobedience as an authentic political act—something people do together, ushering in new beginnings.[1]

Arendt's conception of political action as essentially an unexpected, free, and spontaneous creative rupture with the established order motivates the following general concern. From an Arendtian perspective, the instrumental thinking I deployed throughout the book (of the form: disobey, join movement, blow the whistle, etc., in order to resist injustice and further democracy) misrepresents political action, wrongly turning the praxis that it is (an event, a doing) into poiesis (a product, an artifact). This quasi-metaphysical objection can be reformulated a little more modestly: my account misrepresents political agency, assuming it involves agents' rationally weighing different courses of action against each other on the basis of their expected consequences. Laid bare, the problem is epistemological: I assume that we can know what effects our action will have in the world—which we can't.

Although most readers might not share Arendt's metaphysics of political action, her theory puts in stark relief the potential problems with my reliance on instrumental reasoning. For if authentic political action is a brute expression of freedom and togetherness; if it is spontaneous, unpremeditated, and unpredictable, as Arendt claims, then instrumental thinking is maladapted to it—it risks distorting and betraying it, stripping it from the elements that make it authentically political.[2]

To be sure, my account assumes agents' deliberation or premeditation and actions' relative predictability. It assumes that agents are self-reflective individuals who carefully assess their surroundings, identify injustice, and deliberate with others as to the most effective way to combat it. And it assumes that they can make reasonable efforts to anticipate the likely consequences of their actions. But I do not find these assumptions problematic. This picture of political action reflects activists' actual practices, as they deliberate, organize, and plan; write and distribute pamphlets; raise funds; give interviews and publish press releases; anticipate reactions to their actions; secure bail money in case of arrests; and so on. The need to deliberate about the right courses of political action is evident; it is the mirror image of critical reflection at the level of public argumentation. And strategic calculations are compatible with an Arendtian view of political action as channeling the spirit of the social contract (of disruption, creation, and new beginnings). Indeed they are necessary for successful political action.

Of course there are many spheres of uncertainty, many imponderable elements that affect an action's trajectory: an unforeseen denial of permit may derail a march, an eruption of violence in a demonstration can backfire on a movement's peaceful message, cold weather can decrease participation in a sit-in, a last-minute endorsement by a celebrity can boost a cause, an iconic photo can help a protest, international news can divert attention away from an important protest at home, and so on. It does not follow from any of this that practical deliberation is inappropriate in the realm of authentic politics—only that it is limited and fallible. Thus political theorists' use of statistical methods in their study of social movements reflects the uncertainty, but not utter unpredictability of political action.

So while I share Arendt's appreciation for the democratic spirit that suffuses civil disobedience and its power to reorder the world, I disagree with her stress on the boundlessness, spontaneity, and unpredictability of political action. To be sure, acting is very different from making, but it does not mean that the agent has no control over the former. What the uncertainty of political action implies is the need for caution as well as foresight, of a certain set of skills and dispositions such as Aristotelian *phronesis* or Machiavellian *virtù*, of genuine collaborative engagements, to navigate well the fraught terrain of politics. It also calls for courage, the willingness to take risks. None of this, in short, weighs against our political obligations to *act* in the face of injustice or against theoretical efforts to investigate these. On the contrary, it brings us back to the young Freedom Rider's observation that it is "everyone's responsibility."

Resistance in the Age of Trump

I write these lines in the first year of Donald Trump's presidency. The United States under Trump is an exemplary case study, an opportunity to consider how my philosophical arguments apply to actors embedded within nonideal political contexts. What political obligations bind Americans today?

Trump talked about the presidency for a long time before he pursued it seriously. In the years leading up to 2016, he gained traction peddling "birtherism," the racist myth that his predecessor, President Barack Obama, was not a native-born U.S. citizen. He then announced his candidacy with a speech describing Mexican immigrants as "rapists" and soon talked of "rounding . . . up" anyone without papers. "In a very humane way, in a very nice way," of course. He promised to ban Muslims from entering the country and to create a registry for those already in it. He insulted women, veterans, and disabled people, and regularly countenanced violence at his campaign rallies, even offering several times to pay legal fees for fans who might be convicted of assaulting protesters. A month before the election, the *Washington Post* released off-screen footage from the TV program *Access Hollywood* in which Trump brags about groping women and kissing them whenever he feels like it. "When you're a star, they let you do it," Trump says. "You can do anything. . . . Grab them by the pussy. . . . You can do anything." More than twenty women allege that Trump has sexually harassed or assaulted them. He denies any wrongdoing.

The show of misogyny, racism, and demagoguery has continued in office. Trump praised Fox News anchor Bill O'Reilly as "a good person" and publicly declared "I don't think Bill did anything wrong" after the *New York Times* reported that five women who had made harassment claims against him had settled for payouts totaling about $13 million.[1] Trump endorsed Alabama Republican Roy Moore's candidacy for the Senate, despite multiple allegations of sexual misconduct, including molestation of a fourteen-year-old girl. At a Black History Month event, Trump revealed his utter ignorance of Black history, referring to the African American statesman and abolitionist Frederick Douglass as "an example of somebody who's done an amazing job and is getting recognized more and more, I notice."[2] Trump called Massachusetts Senator Elizabeth Warren "Pocahontas" at an event honoring Native American veterans. Having lost the popular vote by nearly three million ballots, a larger margin than any president in history, Trump falsely claimed that he has been a victim of systematic voter fraud, thereby encouraging states to further restrict voting rights and cultivating a conspiratorial narrative that undermines trust in the electoral process. He has questioned the independence of the judiciary by describing appeals courts as "so political."

The president's incendiary and divisive language is realized in policy. Characterizing Muslims and refugees as terrorists, Trump wasted no time issuing executive orders aimed at barring them from the country, drawing judicial rebuke. Following up on campaign promises, he has made deporting immigrants a top priority of his administration, expanding the range of undocumented immigrants

considered criminals and therefore targeted for removal. An executive order aimed at withholding federal funding from sanctuary cities
has been halted by a federal judge.

Whether or not Trump's policies are illegal, many are unjust. And
people have responded in due course with protests and organizing.
The day after the inauguration, millions participated in the Women's
March in Washington, DC, and other places across the country.
When Trump announced his first Muslim ban, protesters and legal-
aid workers gathered spontaneously at airports. The American Civil
Liberties Union (ACLU), which immediately challenged Trump's
travel ban, reported $24.1 million in donations in one weekend. Civil
servants, intelligence officials, government lawyers, police chiefs, city
mayors, corporate CEOs, university presidents and professors, and
scientists have spoken against Trump's policies. Faced by an administration that routinely lies, and a president who has dubbed the press
"the opposition party" and "the enemy of the people," journalists
have redoubled their investigative efforts.

Meanwhile, acclaimed novelist Chimamanda Ngozi Adichie
stresses the rational and dialogical parts of our political responsibilities. "Now is the time to counter lies with facts," she writes.
"Every precious ideal must be reiterated, every obvious argument
made."[3] The Center for Constitutional Rights proclaims on its
website, "Resistance is our civic duty."[4] After Acting Attorney
General Sally Yates was fired for instructing the Justice Department
attorneys not to try to justify the Muslim ban, many civil servants
defended their duty to disobey illegal, unconstitutional, or otherwise unconscionable orders. Scientists have argued that they are
duty-bound to resist Trump's false beliefs that vaccines cause autism
and that global warming is a hoax, and some have proposed acts
of resistance to protect the work of the Environmental Protection
Agency (EPA) from Trump's budget cuts. Claiming a professional
and moral obligation to care for the sick, health and social workers

have been at the front lines of protest against the administration's attempts to undermine laws improving access to health insurance and medical attention.

This is the stuff of resistance—indeed, of *the resistance*, as the opposition movement born in the first days of the Trump presidency has been called. Guides on how to resist Trump abound in the media, from Newsweek's "Twelve Ways to Resist the Trump Presidency" to Politico's "6 Ways Not to Resist Donald Trump."[5] Indivisible, the anti-Trump movement led by former congressional staffers, offers "a practical guide for resisting the Trump agenda" that aims to replicate the Tea Party's success.[6] The despair and anxiety of the election's immediate aftermath turned to energetic activism. The resistance didn't form on the basis of instrumental logic; the issue is not, "If you want to resist Trump, you need to do x and y." The logic is deontological, articulating a duty. Speakers appeal directly to a duty to resist, and indirectly via their grammar. The imperative mood and modal *must* are everywhere.

But what exactly must we do? What does good democratic citizenship demand of us in the age of Trump? American citizens now face the political obligations I have discussed throughout this book, those based on the duty of justice, the principle of fairness, the Samaritan duty, and political membership. After examining those, I'll outline some of the special responsibilities binding civil servants and officials.

CITIZENS' POLITICAL OBLIGATIONS

As we consider a real-life decision-making context, it is important to keep in mind that we need not diagnose complete failure of the duty to obey the law in order to defend obligations to resist injustice. At the same time, even if one believes Trump's presidency is

illegitimate—because of Russian meddling in the election, his pop-
ular-vote loss, or voter disenfranchisement—the rule-governed political institutions preceding him may still generate a moral duty to
obey the law. What we must recognize is that, whether or not the
moral duty to obey the law holds, other political obligations require
us to support just democratic institutions. And these obligations may
demand we disobey the law.

Justice and Democracy

In chapter 3 I developed a typology to help clarify which forms of injustice demand resistance: disrespect (public denial of equal status),
wrongs against nonmembers, deliberative inertia, official misconduct, and public ignorance. The new administration has already
aggravated or caused these five types of injustice. Trump's policies
and rhetoric publicly deny the equal status of Latinos, Muslims, and
Blacks, who are stereotyped as inferior and dangerous. The White
House disrespects all trans people by attempting to bar them from
serving in any capacity in the military. (As of December 2017, a federal judge has temporarily blocked this policy, ruling that it was based
on "disapproval of transgender people generally.")

The administration commits wrongs against nonmembers
through unjust anti-immigration policies. After federal appeals
courts stayed two versions of the Muslim travel ban, the Supreme
Court allowed the third version to take into effect while legal
challenges continue. Most citizens from eight nations, six of them
predominantly inhabited by Muslims, are now barred from entering
the United States. Trump has called for massive Immigration and
Customs Enforcement (ICE) raids to sweep up, detain, and deport undocumented immigrants, including parents of U.S. citizens.
Though he argues that "criminals" among the immigrant population
must be removed, he makes no distinction between criminality and

daily life without proper documents: just being in the country illegally or using a fake social security number to work makes one a priority mark.

The administration commits wrongs against nonmembers through reckless environmental and foreign policies that threaten people all over the world. The White House has formally withdrawn from the 2015 Paris climate accord and instead seeks to repeal fracking regulations, has approved oil drilling in the Gulf of Mexico and the Arctic, and has dramatically shrank national monuments that designated Western lands off-limits to commercial exploitation. These policies endanger animals and the environment, increasing the risk of climate-related harms such as displacement of U.S. persons and people abroad. Trump's face-off with North Korea's leader Kim Jong-Un escalates the risk of nuclear war. The administration seeks symbolic wins at the cost of global instability, as when Trump announced that the U.S. embassy in Israel would move from Tel Aviv to Jerusalem.

Trump's possible breach of the Constitution's emoluments clause, and the many lawsuits against him, speak to official misconduct. And while Trump shares his "unfiltered" thoughts on Twitter, he and his administration keep the public in the dark about what really matters. For instance, by refusing to release his tax returns, Trump maintains public ignorance of his possible conflicts of interest. An ongoing special counsel investigation led by former FBI director Robert Mueller seeks to determine whether Trump's presidential campaign team colluded with the Russian government to interfere with the 2016 elections and to identify links between Trump associates and Russian officials, as well as potential obstruction of justice and financial crimes. To date (February 2018), five people connected to the Trump campaign and thirteen Russian nationals have been charged as part of the Mueller investigation.

Americans face pressing political obligations in response to these injustices and suspicious activities that have provoked investigation.

They have an obligation to protest by joining rallies, spreading the word on social media, and volunteering with or donating to organizations that oppose the administration. They have an obligation to learn about new and prospective policies and how they affect people and the environment, and about how the administration exploits implicit biases and explicit prejudices against ethnic minorities. They have an obligation to educate themselves and each other about how disinformation campaigns work, the better to spot propaganda efforts, such as the administration's attempts to undermine the credibility of the special counsel investigation. Experts and journalists are obligated to inform the public and denounce lies.

Americans may be bound to disobey certain unjust laws, too. In chapter 3, I defended a justice-based political obligation to disobey certain unjustified anti-immigration laws that would make us agents of wrongdoing, such as those that require citizens, civil servants, and government officials to question undocumented immigrants, surveil them, and report their activities to federal authorities. Such disobedience must be covert in order to protect unauthorized immigrants from the harms of detention and deportation.

However, such disobedience could also usefully take a public form. Institutional leaders—in city and university administrations, police departments, corporate environments, and elsewhere—can also take a visible stand by embracing sanctuary status and refusing to report undocumented immigrants. Thus dozens of U.S. cities from Seattle to Miami have declared themselves sanctuaries; and Oakland Mayor Libby Schaaf recently has come under the Justice Department's scrutiny after she publicly warned the immigrant community about an imminent ICE enforcement operation.[7] At a minimum, sanctuary cities' police departments have been ordered to ignore ICE detainer requests, which ask local law enforcement agencies to hold detainees longer than they would otherwise be allowed to, so that ICE can determine whether to take the detainees into federal custody. Some cities have done more, shielding their undocumented population from federal immigration authorities. Oakland, California, has trained school teachers and administrators on what to do if ICE agents approach school grounds. Schools there educate parents on resources such as legal assistance and bail bond funds and provide students with safe spaces to voice their anxieties about the immigration regime. Preventing local complicity in deportations is an important step, though not a sufficient one if we seek to protect undocumented persons' safety.

Since the duty of justice is natural—that is, universal—it doesn't bind only U.S. citizens against their government. It extends to temporary and permanent residents as well as undocumented immigrants (insofar as U.S. institutions apply to them, to use Waldron's criterion[8]). However, the current risks of lawbreaking are so high that we cannot reasonably expect noncitizens to take on the burden of disobedience.[9] Still, noncitizens have been willing to speak out. For instance, undocumented youth known as DREAMers—after the Development, Relief, and Education for Alien Minors Act—have engaged in visible protests.

Cristina Beltrán has analyzed the ways in which DREAMers have "queered" democratic politics, as they defy their forced invisibility and silence using public-facing strategies developed by the gay rights movement.[10] Thus the DREAMers' National Coming Out of the Shadows Day organized in 2010 and held repeatedly since evoked the first LGBTQ community's National Coming Out Day organized in 1988. DREAMers have also used social media to publicize and multiply their narratives, beyond, say, the sanitized, xenophilic story of the valedictorian student eager but unable to join the army. On YouTube one finds hundreds of videos of undocumented youth declaring themselves "unapologetic and unafraid" and recounting their and their parents' stories. Many start with the ominous, "If you're watching this video, I've been arrested." U.S. citizens have a duty to help migrant youth activists by joining their protests, publicizing their cause, protesting their arrests, and donating to organizations such as DreamActivist.org. All of these obligations are that much easier to fulfill when large numbers of people protest and disobey unjust laws.

Fairness

In chapter 4 I showed that, under certain circumstances, benefiting from exploitative and harmful social schemes involves the same kinds of deontic wrongs that make free riding reprehensible, so that fairness prohibits both. We can identify many negative externalities and harms in Trump's America, some currently embryonic and others more fully formed. They must be contested and repaired if fairness is to prevail. Our obligation is to ensure that this is precisely what happens.

Many potential harms are economic. As a staunch capitalist, Trump takes a dim view of welfare protections, which he sees an unfair benefit distributed to those who fail to contribute to society. This is why Trump attempted to eradicate the Obama-era Affordable Care Act, a legislative change that would also have undermined Medicare and Medicaid benefits. Having failed to pass this healthcare reform plan despite holding a congressional majority, the Republican Party devised a tax plan that would slash Medicare and Medicaid programs—adding thirteen million people to the ranks of the uninsured and driving up healthcare premiums—while passing along gains to corporations and the wealthiest Americans, for instance, by eliminating entirely the estate tax. The administration also seeks to weaken labor and financial regulations, further distributing burdens toward workers and away from managers and investors. It is a recipe for aggravating the deficiencies and economic disparities of a social scheme that is already one of the world's most unequal.

Fair play, I have argued, requires the beneficiaries of such schemes to renounce their ill-gotten gains. Per the Negative Argument, benefiting from exploitative and harmful social schemes, under certain circumstances, involves the same kinds of deontic wrongs that make free-riding reprehensible, so that fairness prohibits cooperating with such schemes. Who are the wrongful beneficiaries of Trump's America? His family, his acolytes, big businesses, lobbying organizations, wealthy financiers, and unscrupulous companies seeking federal contracts to implement his agenda. All are required by fair play to cease cooperating with, and seek to reform, a system from which they wrongfully benefit. Ordinary citizens, and especially the worst-off in society, are victims of the unfairness of Trump's America: the Negative Argument does not apply to them in this regard.

However, citizens as a group incur fair-play political obligations of solidarity. Recall the empirical argument for solidarity: successful resistance is possible, but it requires collective action. Chenoweth and Stephan found that sustained participation of just 3.5 percent of the population nearly guarantees movements' success. So if citizens have a general obligation to resist Trump's agenda—say, on the basis of the duty of justice—then we can appeal to fairness to further ground an obligation of solidarity in resistance.

Samaritan Duty

Before Trump, the United States was hardly immune to the Samaritan perils I identified in chapter 5. But his administration exacerbates two in particular: hate crimes and the targeting of undocumented immigrants and prospective migrants seeking asylum. Many U.S. citizens can be viewed as passers-by to these perils.

It is not hard to see how Trump's rhetoric has emboldened extreme-right elements, including White nationalists operating under the "alt-right" label.[11] The Southern Poverty Law Center (SPLC) collected reports of 867 cases of "hateful harassment or intimidation" in just the first ten days after the election.[12] Most involved expressions of anti-immigrant, anti-Black, anti-Muslim, anti-LGBTQ, anti-woman, or anti-Semitic views. The SPLC also observed dramatic growth in U.S. hate groups, with anti-Muslim groups nearly tripling in number between 2015 and 2016. South Asians in the United States have experienced a wave of violence, creating a climate of fear.[13]

A Samaritan intervention designed to reduce the persistent occurrence of hate crimes would thus involve serious cultural change, through everyday resistance. The SPLC counsels ten ways to fight hate: (1) act, because perpetrators will interpret apathy as acceptance; (2) join forces: reach out to allies, open dialogue; (3) support victims; (4) speak up; (5) educate yourself about hatred and implicit bias; (6) create an alternative: fight hatred with love and kindness; (7) press leaders for change; (8) stay engaged; (9) teach acceptance, because bias is learned early; (10) dig deeper: look inside yourself and commit to disrupting hate and intolerance.[14] SPLC's advice aptly combines the short-term intervention tactics of bystanders with the long-term strategies of social movement building.

Undocumented immigrants in particular live in a fearful climate: they may not only be targeted by the public for hate crimes—insofar as they are, overwhelmingly, non-White, accented speakers—but also arrested and deported by official authorities. Noncriminal arrests of undocumented immigrants rose 42 percent in 2017; these immigrants are taken into custody on administrative grounds only. And they increasingly are being rounded up at schools, hospitals, churches, and courthouses, expanding the range of places where it is unsafe to be undocumented. In 2017, ICE courthouse arrests increased by 900 percent in New York City. As César Cuauhtémoc García Hernández has argued, courthouse arrests "don't just derail the lives of the unsuspecting people who are detained, they threaten the very operation of our judicial system."[15] When the government scares people away from the courts, it undermines these people's trust in the judiciary and at the same time the courts' effective operation. In 2017, the number of Latinas reporting rapes in Houston fell more than 40 percent from the previous year. The chief of the Houston Police Department sees in this "the beginnings of people not reporting crime" because they fear that they will be detained and deported. When crime victims and witnesses fear testifying to police and courts, communities are less safe.

Samaritan interventions to protect people's basic freedom from fear would, at a minimum, require ICE to adopt a formal policy of avoiding arrests in sensitive locations such as schools, hospitals, churches, and courthouses. (Under the Obama administration, ICE was committed to avoid churches and schools.) In addition, cities and counties ought to establish sanctuary provisions to prohibit local police from questioning victims and witnesses of crimes about their immigration status. The persistent Samaritan perils undocumented immigrants face cannot be addressed without sweeping immigration reform. The Samaritan duty thus further supports the argument for sanctuary protections and pro-immigration political action articulated on the basis of the duty of justice.

As for the most vulnerable migrants, the United States was only committed to accepting 110,000 refugees per year before Trump took office. But he cut even that number to 50,000. Displaced people—including many children from Syria, Afghanistan, Somalia, and other countries plagued by violence—experience persistent Samaritan perils at home, in refugee camps, and in their journey as they seek asylum.

The Trump administration recognizes that refugees are imperiled and in need of aid but denies that Samaritan assistance can be offered at reasonable cost. The White House claims that taking in refugees not only strains U.S. financial resources but also threatens national security. Some refugees are terrorists in disguise, the administration asserts. During the campaign and in office, Trump and his team decried compassion for refugees as mere "political correctness," at odds with the supposed reality of danger.[16]

It behooves the rest of us to combat such appeals to fear and denials of basic moral duties with informed arguments. One way is through education. Americans should learn about xenophobic and anti-Muslim prejudice and about the domestic origins of most crime, including terrorism. Citizens can also discharge their Samaritan political obligations by pressuring their government to take action, sponsoring resettlement of migrant families, donating money to NGOs working with refugees, and by volunteering with and advocating for sanctuary movements.

Dignitary Political Membership

The Trump administration's treatment of immigrants and trans people; its insulting and divisive language; its slow response to hate crimes; its rollbacks of environmental protections, financial regulations, women's access to healthcare, and reproductive justice; and its contemptuous treatment of the worst-off in society all pose threats to the dignitary political membership grounding my associativist account for political obligation. In response, much of the anti-Trump resistance has cast itself in a dignitary associativist light, stressing demands for dignity and inclusion. For instance, the artist Shepard Fairey produced a set of protest signs featuring Muslim, Latina, and African American women under the banner "Defend Dignity." And faith groups all over the country condemned Trump's Muslim ban while affirming their belief in the inherent dignity of every person.

In solidarity with racially oppressed groups, National Football League (NFL) players have knelt, stayed in their locker rooms, or locked arms during the national anthem. In particular, the players have sought to protest anti-Black racism and police brutality. Some—such as Trump, who called the protesters "sons of bitches," ungrateful, and unpatriotic[17]—view athletes' protests as uncivil and disrespectful. It is illuminating, though, to conceive of the protests precisely in terms of their dignity. They not only denounce injustice but engage in the dignitary political membership Trump and his backers seek to deny through accusations of incivility.

Athletes who take a knee may be silent on the field, yet they also gain a voice. They go on to explain to the media why they engage in such protest. They affirm their epistemic authority—their personal knowledge of racism and police brutality; 70 percent of NFL players are Black. They also affirm their political agency, their determination to "stand for equality and kneel for justice," as the BLM slogan puts it. They not only assert dignity in the face of the president's rebuke, but also, as Dave Zirin has argued, "their humanity in a dehumanizing sport" that exploits Black labor.[18] Zirin analogizes the NFL protests with those of Black sanitation laborers in Memphis, who in 1968 rallied around the slogan "I Am a Man."

Finally the protests offer players a way to confront the United States with its failure to make good on its professed ideals of equality and liberty for all. The players thus redefine patriotism in the process of protest. As a Seattle Seahawks team statement put it:

> We have decided we will not participate in the national anthem. We will not stand for the injustice that has plagued people of color in this country. Out of love for our country and in honor of the sacrifices made on our behalf, we unite to oppose those who would deny our basic freedoms. We remain committed in continuing to work towards equality and justice for all.[19]

The NFL protests may in this sense be conceived through the prism of Dworkin's account. They respond to defective political relationships stained by indignities. In the framework developed in chapter 6, the protesters communicate condemnation of racial injustice to the broader community; they express solidarity among and with the oppressed; and they assert dignity to themselves.

Taking a knee is entirely lawful, but the duty to discharge dignitary associativist political obligations has also inspired civil and even uncivil disobedience. Dozens were arrested for protesting Trump's termination of the Deferred Action for Childhood Arrivals (DACA) program, a decision to place young undocumented immigrants at risk. Protesters illegally obstructed traffic in major U.S. cities in September 2017. Undocumented immigrants detained by ICE have also engaged in hunger strikes to protest their indefinite detention without charges and the denial of access to lawyers—both violations of the right to due process guaranteed in the U.S. Constitution.

The recent mobilization of antifascist groups (antifa for short) in the United States is a clear example of uncivil resistance in the era of Trump. A masked man punched the neo-Nazi Trump supporter Richard Spencer in front of a TV camera on inauguration day in 2017. Antifa activists broke windows, lit fires, and threw fireworks at police on the University of California, Berkeley, campus before a talk by alt-right YouTube personality Milo Yiannopoulos. At another event, activists chased, pepper-sprayed, and beat White-supremacist Trump supporters. Antifa clashed with White nationalists and police in Charlottesville, Virginia, during a large "Unite the Right" rally in August 2017. By the end of the day, dozens were injured and one killed when a White nationalist drove his car in a crowd of counterprotesters.

Cornel West was to give a sermon at St. Paul's Church in Charlottesville on that day. West described the White nationalist demonstrators laying siege to the church:

> The neofascists had their own ammunition. And this is very important to keep in mind, because the police, for the most

part, pulled back. The next day, for example, those twenty of us who were standing, many of them clergy, we would have been crushed like cockroaches if it were not for the anarchists and the anti-fascists who approached, over 300, 350 anti-fascists. We just had twenty. . . . The antifascists, and then, crucial, the anarchists, . . . they saved our lives, actually. We would have been completely crushed, and I'll never forget that.[20]

Given that these antifa activists provided security when the police would not, one may argue that their use of force was justified. But what about the antifa activist who punched Spencer and those who destroyed Berkeley campus property or assaulted White nationalist Trump supporters? Opponents condemn violence categorically and reject antifa as "no better than the fascists," for their attempts to silence fellow citizens.[21] But if we believe that the end sometimes justifies the means, then equating all acts of violence without distinguishing their aims is morally dubious. Many people felt similarly when President Trump blamed both sides for the deadly violence in Charlottesville.[22]

Antifa claim their use of violence is justified as a form of collective self-defense.[23] In their view, fascists (neo-Nazis and White supremacists) seriously threaten the safety of Jews, Blacks, immigrants, Muslims, LGBTQ people, and others held in contempt. This threat is direct, insofar as fascists perpetrate hate crimes. The threat also is indirect, insofar as fascist speeches and writings support and incite violence against despised groups. And fascists' objective is to establish a White-supremacist state that excludes or subjugates despised minorities. To deal with the latter two threats, antifa aim to deprive neo-Nazis of opportunities to speak and be heard and thus to develop the structural conditions for "normalization"—their acceptance in the political mainstream. The strategies are sometimes uncivil and include outing neo-Nazis to their family and employers, disrupting their meetings, preventing speakers from accessing venues through blockades and property destruction, shouting speakers down, and physically confronting them and their supporters.

It might be possible to justify this collective self-defense argument on the basis of the natural duty of justice, the Samaritan duty, or dignitary political membership, depending on how one frames the targeted injustice: as disrespect, per chapter 3; looming danger, per chapter 5; or humiliation, objectification, and violence per chapter 6. However, these justificatory grounds also impose significant constraints on agents, which would exclude a number of antifa tactics. For instance, Dworkinian dignity's requirement to respect other people's dignity in defending one's own and others' cannot justify intimidating and assaulting people. I used dignitary political membership to defend the possible justification of violence as collective self-defense in chapter 6, with the examples of slave uprisings and the ANC's turn to armed resistance in South Africa under Apartheid. In both cases, the threats to persons' lives, freedom, and bodily integrity were grave and immediate. In contrast, antifa use violence as a prophylactic, to prevent fascist hateful speech from being normalized, endorsed, and realized politically. It is thus more difficult to justify their use of violence as an exercise of collective self-defense—except when it plausibly is, as in Charlottesville.

Activists can, and should, avoid violence without abdicating their obligations. Throwing flour and eggs—or, as PETA activists do, tofu cream pie—is preferable to throwing punches, and it can work as well to impose social risks on neo-Nazis and dissuade them from publicly defending their views. Antifa's communicative intent—loud, unwavering condemnation of racist and fascist rhetoric—does not demand violence, and much can be accomplished with nonviolent, if uncivil, activism. The bottom line, though, is that, amid a surge of hate groups, we shouldn't wholesale reject antifa tactics. Instead we need to think carefully about their justifications and whether the combination of justification and action passes the test of political obligation.

OFFICIALS' RESISTANCE FROM WITHIN

Civil servants have debated, and agonized over, whether to serve under Trump. For some, resigning from office or refusing to sign up are the only responsible options. What undergirds this view is the belief that to obey or serve the state is to support it. This position—shared by many classical political thinkers, from Thoreau to Arendt—implies that it is unconscionable to serve seriously unjust governments. Étienne de La Boétie, in his 1553 *Discourse on Voluntary Servitude*, further believed that withdrawing one's cooperation was all it takes, so to speak, to free a people from the reins of illegitimate and abusive authority. Thus, from this perspective, refusal to serve is an act of dissent, disassociation, and resistance, that is especially effective when carried out in large numbers. As of February 2018, there are still hundreds of unfilled positions in Trump's administration, vacancies that may hamper the White House's ability to advance its policies.

However, some argue that these vacancies further the administration's goals of "deconstructing the administrative state," as former White House chief strategist Steve Bannon put it, and centralizing authority among Trump's most loyal inner circle. If the government is staffed only by wholehearted supporters of the president's unethical agenda, the damage will be considerable. In light of these concerns, perhaps civil servants should promote the public good from within the administration. They have a number of strategies at their disposal, such as conscientious refusal of particular orders or covert foot dragging. Gene Sharp outlines various tactics of bureaucratic noncooperation in his *From Dictatorship to Democracy* and *198 Methods of Nonviolent Action*. On this view, whether Trump is a textbook autocrat threatening the demise of American democracy or the legitimate though unfit president of a decent liberal state (or both), civil servants can promote the public good and do damage control from within his administration.

Shortly after Trump took office, Maria Stephan published a short essay in the *Washington Post* entitled "Staying True to Yourself in the Age of Trump: A How-to Guide for Federal Employees."[24] In it she argues that "vigilance and, if necessary, dissent are needed now more than ever to defend American democratic norms, values and institutions." She urges "bureaucratic resistance from below" to challenge unethical or unconstitutional policies and promote the public good. She doesn't discard resignation as a form of resistance, but she considers other methods more responsible and desirable, including foot dragging, leaking internal documents, creating paper trails that enable accountability and may dissuade bad behavior, and suing officials.

A week into Trump's presidency, former State Department adviser Laura Rosenberg offered government lawyers similar advice:

> In many ways, you are the last line of defense against illegal, unethical, or reckless actions—which the first week of this administration confirms will abound. History has shown us that implementation of such policies depends on a compliant bureaucracy of obedient individuals who look the other way and do as they are told. Do what bureaucracy does well: slow-roll, obstruct, and constrain. Resist. Refuse to implement anything illegal, unethical, or unconstitutional.[25]

This pragmatic, lesser-evil view is currently the more popular one, but it too comes with difficulties. David Luban illustrates one such problem using the story of the German lawyer Bernhard Lösener, who persuaded Hitler to choose the more moderate, less sweeping draft of the Nuremberg race laws.[26] Lösener took pride in his tempering influence, even though these laws still sent millions of Jews to their deaths. As Luban notes, this is an odious attempt to rationalize and excuse participation in the Holocaust. Luban thus agrees with Arendt's insightful 1964 essay "Personal Responsibility under Dictatorship," which argues that, under a dictatorship, the only moral course of action is to shun positions of responsibility and refuse to participate.[27]

I find this line of reasoning pursued by Arendt and Luban convincing, but it only purports to apply to dictatorships and authoritarian regimes. As Luban himself recognizes, if there is no "nightmare scenario"—an authoritarian regime intent on crushing opposition and chocking democracy—"then the argument for service becomes compelling." Although Trump's policies are already hurting Americans and eroding democracy, few people think that the current political situation rises to the level of this nightmare scenario, and so many support resistance from within. However, Masha Gessen has warned against this dichotomous thinking, which inflates "small signs of normality" and holds onto the belief that robust institutions will save the day.[28] Confidence that Trump is not dealing a serious blow to American democracy would be misplaced. Vigilance is required.

Upon reflection, the disagreement between the two camps is genuine, not simply a function of the gravity of the political situation. On the one hand, Arendt, Luban, and Gessen stress that bureaucratic participation in small-scale, not-quite disasters habituates civil servants to compromise on their principles and facilitates the advent of full-throated authoritarianism by helping to lubricate the machine of government. For Luban, government lawyers thus ought to refuse to participate not only in large-scale nightmare scenarios but also in "one-off nightmare issues," such as rounding up Mexicans and bringing back torture, which would force them to make "rotten compromises." (Luban concedes that this can be done from within, however.)

For pragmatists, on the other hand, whether the disaster is here or near, much can be done in overt and covert ways to resist the government. Indeed, resistance from within is seen as a critical tool to hinder authoritarianism. I tend toward the pragmatic camp (with some ambivalence, which I'll explain). But my position is stronger than the pragmatic one many authors have advanced. It is one thing to say that civil servants *can* minimize damage and therefore *should* try to do so. It is another to argue, as I do, that they have political *obligation* to do so.

The case for bureaucrats' political obligation to resist rests on two contentions. First, the duty of justice binds civil servants to uphold democratic institutions, including by educating the public, protesting against and/or refusing to follow unethical orders, thwarting wrongdoing, and blowing the whistle on government abuses. Many are following the call of duty. EPA employees have protested Trump's gag orders and archived the agency's climate change research on a publicly accessible website, lest the White House try to hide it from view. Employees of other agencies engaged in environmental protection and scientific research—including the National Parks, NASA, and the Department of Agriculture—have undertaken similar efforts. Trump's White House has been called "the leakiest" of all time.[29] The proliferation of leaks, whose cumulative effect has been to show Trump's unfitness for the office, can be viewed as a swarm-like, collective effort to uphold just democratic institutions.

Second, fulfilling the duty of justice and upholding democratic institutions requires bureaucrats to resist from within *collectively*. And as resistance involves some risks, tends to be costly, and can succeed without everyone's participation, free-riding becomes tempting: that is, individuals might decide not to take on the risks and burdens of the resistance. What are the benefits of a successful resistance movement? One might argue that federal workers have their own material interests at stake (roughly, they get to keep their jobs, in spite of Trump's plan to purge the administrative state). But in my view, the principal benefits are deontic: they consist in the fulfillment of workers' political obligations, including the duty of justice. Here the principle of fairness prohibits bureaucrats and civil servants from riding freely on their colleagues' efforts and demands that each do their fair share of the resistance effort. In this way, civil servants may be bound by a duty of solidarity with each other.

These political obligations are compatible with civil servants' professional code of ethics. Although civil servants are ordinarily supposed to take the orders they receive as preemptive reasons for action (that is, excluding any independent deliberation), they may refuse to comply with a given order that undermines the public good. Indeed, their code of conduct prohibits compliance with un-constitutional and unethical orders and thereby leaves room for the exercise of individual judgment and critique. For instance, a civil servant is not professionally obligated to follow orders to cover up official wrongdoing or obstruct investigations into suspected wrong-doing. Federal and state laws further shield conscientious objectors and whistleblowers from employer retaliation, implying that civil servants do have a right to independent judgment and may choose to resist as a function of their professional responsibility.

Resistance from within, however, should not be considered lightly. It should generate feelings of ambivalence among civil servants. On the one hand, as David Kaye notes, even conscien-tious participation leaves a civil servant at risk of being "roped into complicity."[30] He or she ought not play into the hands of those who seek to de-legitimize democratic government for their own ends. On the other hand, resistance from within could be, and could be perceived as, anti-democratic. This is principled alternative to the White House's sensational, conspiratorial attacks on the "deep state." Setting aside the inappropriateness of the label to the American context, the idea that bureaucratic resistance may be anti-democratic is not unfounded. Bureaucrats, after all, are not representatives of the people. Their job is not to make policy but to carry out those policies designed by elected officials.

The proliferation of leaks at every level of government during Trump's first year in office crystallizes the issue: the leaks justifiably reveal the Trump administration's conflicts of interests and disregard for democratic norms, but they have intensified the administration's paranoia and sown distrust among segments of the public. The leaks look like a threat to democracy even as they seek to expose one. To see why, it is important to distinguish the different kinds of leaks at play and the issues they raise. Among other things, leaks may be indiscretions, breaches of confidentiality, or disclosures of classified information. The persistent leaks from the executive branch have included indiscretions (gossip or "loose lips") and behind-the-scenes glimpses into an impulsive president prone to "tantrums" (a recurrent phrase to describe Trump's moods). Staff have spoken of their dismay at his television and Twitter habits. But not all is palace intrigue. There have also been disclosures of confidential information. For instance an official leaked a memo from National Security Adviser H. R. McMaster urging senior officials to clamp down on leaks. Transcripts of Americans' conversations, intercepted by the NSA, have leaked. And, relying on vetted anonymous sources, Reuters revealed that Trump campaign officials had numerous undisclosed contacts with Russian government agents, before and after the November election.[31]

As of December 2017, the Justice Department is conducting twenty-seven investigations into classified leaks of information. These are the most worrisome kind of leaks, because classified information is necessary to national security. Such leaks are presumptively wrong, as I suggested in chapter 3, insofar as they transgress the boundaries around state secrets. Leakers not only challenge executive decisions to keep certain information out of the public realm but also usurp the power of the state and unilaterally reverse these decisions. This is why, in democratic states, disclosing classified information appears anti-democratic. Leaks of classified information can nonetheless be justified when they contribute to the prevention or cessation of government wrongdoing or strengthen the rule of law. But even when justified, they consist of a problematic, apparently anti-democratic, breach of the executive right to secrecy, with the potential to threaten national security.

Civil servants are thus bound to weigh these issues very seriously in their deliberation. Civil servants should feel ambivalent. The best way to handle this ambivalence, as I argued in chapter 7, is to work together, engage dialogically with fellow civil servants and other relevant professionals, and, as much as possible, be open with the public about one's ambivalence and process. For civil servants, responsibly dispensing duties to resist is not so much a matter of acting on private judgment as it is thinking and acting together.

Other democratic countries face similar challenges as the United States under Trump. Nationalist fervor dragged the United Kingdom out of the European Union, destabilizing the lives of immigrants there and emboldening forces of xenophobia. Poland's Law and Justice government has dismantled the liberal progresses made after the fall of the Soviet Union, seeking to return the country to its past Catholic glory. Extreme-right parties are in power or gaining popularity throughout Europe, from Hungary to France to Scandinavia, threatening the lives, livelihood, and freedom of immigrants and racial and religious minorities.

In all of these places, citizens are expected to obey the law. But they are also bound to resist injustice and uphold just democratic institutions, even, in some cases, if that means breaking the law. Good citizens reflect on their political obligations, in community and on the basis of reliable information. They value public inquiry and speaking out, sometimes uncivilly, on behalf of mutual respect. They take democracy as their responsibility.

NOTES

Introduction

1. *Freedom Riders*, directed by Stanley Nelson (Firelight, 2011), http://www.pbs.
   org/wgbh/americanexperience/freedomriders/watch. Emphasis is apparent
   in tone.
2. A satisfying account would show that the duty to obey the law applies to everyone, covers all laws, and binds citizens to their particular state. See, e.g.,
   Richard Dagger and David Lefkowitz, "Political Obligation," *The Stanford
   Encyclopedia of Philosophy*, ed. Edward N. Zalta (Fall 2014), https://plato.
   stanford.edu/archives/fall2014/entries/political-obligation/; William A.
   Edmundson, "State of the Art: The Duty to Obey the Law," *Legal Theory* 10, 4
   (2004): 215–259. For a recent, qualified defense of the duty to obey the law, see
   Samuel Scheffler, "Membership and Political Obligation," *The Journal of Political
   Philosophy* 26, 1 (2018), 3–23. Scheffler prefaces his associativist argument for
   political obligation by recognizing that "[t]here may be no duty to obey a seriously unjust law, or the laws of an oppressive state, and even when the state and
   its laws are reasonably just, duties of obedience may sometimes be overridden
   by other considerations, and there may be some people who lack any such duty."
3. Henry D. Thoreau, "Resistance to Civil Government," *The Writings of Henry
   David Thoreau: Reform Papers*, ed. Wendell Glick (Princeton, NJ: Princeton
   University Press, 1973), 63–90.
4. Mohandas Ghandi, *Young India*, July 22, 1920.
5. Martin Luther King Jr., "Letter from Birmingham City Jail," 1963.
6. Speech featured in *I Am Not Your Negro*, directed by Raoul Peck (Velvet
   Film, 2016).

7. Stéphane Hessel, *Indignez-vous!* (Montpellier, France: Indigène editions, 2010). The English translation, *Time for Outrage!*, misses the imperative form of the French title—the exhortation to be outraged—and its second-personal address (*vous*).

8. See, e.g., http://ccle.collectifs.net/ and http://www.liguedh.be/images/PDF/documentation/documents_thematiques/delit-solidarite.pdf (accessed August 20, 2016).

9. Adam Nossiter, "A French Underground Railroad, Moving African Immigrants," *New York Times* (October 4, 2016), http://www.nytimes.com/2016/10/05/world/europe/france-italy-migrants-smuggling.html?_r=0 (accessed March 21, 2017).

10. Lizzie Dearden, "Iranian Women Call on Western Tourists to Violate Hijab Law to Fight against Oppression," *The Independent*, April 22, 2016, http://www.independent.co.uk/news/world/middle-east/iranian-women-in-my-stealthy-freedom-campaign-call-on-western-tourists-to-violate-headscarf-law-to-a6996136.html (accessed July 5, 2017). See #NoForcedHijab on Twitter and @StealthyFreedom on Facebook and Twitter.

11. The first YouTube video to go viral and inspire others was Manal al-Sharif's, on May 19, 2011: https://www.youtube.com/watch?v=sowNSH_W2r0 (accessed July 5, 2017). Al-Sharif recently published a memoir: Manal al-Sharif, *Daring to Drive: A Saudi Woman's Awakening* (New York: Simon and Schuster, 2017).

12. Cited in Neil MacFarquhar and Robert Mackey, "Saudi Women Defy Driving Ban," *New York Times* (June 17, 2011), http://thelede.blogs.nytimes.com/2011/06/17/saudi-women-protest-driving-ban (accessed August 20, 2016).

13. Edward Snowden and Laura Poitras, "'Nation' Exclusive: Edward Snowden and Laura Poitras Take on America's Runaway Surveillance State," *The Nation* (May 7, 2014), https://www.thenation.com/article/nation-exclusive-edward-snowden-and-laura-poitras-take-americas-runaway-surveillance/ (accessed July 7, 2017).

14. Cited in Megan Garber, "The Revolutionary Aims of Black Lives Matter," *The Atlantic* (September 30, 2015), http://www.theatlantic.com/politics/archive/2015/09/Black-lives-matter-revolution/408160/.

15. Emmeline Pankhurst to members of The Women's Social and Political Union, "Votes for Women" (January 10, 1913), http://www.nationalarchives.gov.uk/documents/education/suffragettes.pdf.

16. José Bové, Erri de Luca, and Gilles Luneau, *Du sentiment de justice et du devoir de désobéir* (Montpellier, France: Indigène Editions, 2016).

17. See http://www.faucheurs-volontaires.fr/ (accessed July 6, 2017).

18. Exceptions include Michael Walzer, *Obligations: Essays on War, Disobedience, and Citizenship* (Cambridge, MA: Harvard University Press, 1970); Carole Pateman, *The Problem of Political Obligation: A Critique of Liberal Theory* (Berkeley: University of California Press, 1985); Chaim Gans, *Philosophical*

Anarchism and Political Disobedience (Cambridge: Cambridge University Press, 1992); Nancy Hirschmann, *Rethinking Obligation: A Feminist Method for Political Theory* (Ithaca, NY: Cornell University Press, 1992); Kimberley Brownlee, *Conscience and Conviction: The Case for Civil Disobedience* (Oxford: Oxford University Press, 2012); David Lyons, *Confronting Injustice: Moral History and Political Theory* (Oxford: Oxford University Press, 2013); and Tommie Shelby, *Dark Ghettos: Injustice, Dissent, and Reform* (Cambridge, MA: Belknap Press of Harvard University Press, 2016).

19. See A. John Simmons, "The Duty to Obey and Our Natural Moral Duties," in *Is There a Duty to Obey the Law?*, eds. Christopher H. Wellman and A. John Simmons (Cambridge: Cambridge University Press, 2005), 191–193.

20. Gans, *Philosophical Anarchism and Political Disobedience*, 90.

21. Kit Wellman, who champions a Samaritan account of the duty to obey the law, confirmed this in conversation. Ronald Dworkin revised his manuscript of *Justice for Hedgehogs* to acknowledge the possibility that dignity in political association (the basis for his definitive account of the duty to obey the law) could sometimes require civil disobedience and even revolution, rather than legal compliance. See Ronald Dworkin, *Justice for Hedgehogs* (Cambridge, MA: Harvard University Press, 2010), 322–323, responding to Susanne Sreedhar and Candice Delmas, "State Legitimacy and Political Obligation in *Justice for Hedgehogs*: The Radical Potential of Dworkinian Dignity," *Boston University Law Review* 90, 2 (2010): 737–758.

22. See, e.g., Margaret Gilbert, *A Theory of Political Obligation* (Oxford: Oxford University Press, 2006); Philip Soper, *The Ethics of Deference* (Cambridge: Cambridge University Press, 2002).

23. Joseph Raz, *The Authority of Law: Essays on Law and Morality* (Oxford: Oxford University Press, 1979), chaps. 12–13; William E. Scheuerman, "Whistleblowing as Civil Disobedience: The Case of Edward Snowden," *Philosophy and Social Criticism*, 40, 7 (2014): 609–628.

24. Pateman, *The Problem of Political Obligation*; Hirschmann, *Rethinking Obligation*.

25. Carole Pateman, *The Sexual Contract* (Stanford, CA: Stanford University Press, 1988); Iris Marion Young, *Justice and the Politics of Difference* (Princeton, NJ: Princeton University Press, 1990); Lisa Schwartzman, *Challenging Liberalism: Feminism as Political Critique* (University Park: Penn State Press, 2006); Rae Langton, *Sexual Solipsism: Philosophical Essays on Pornography and Objectification* (New York: Oxford University Press, 2009).

26. Iris Marion Young, "Political Responsibility and Structural Injustice," The Lindley Lecture (University of Kansas, 2003), 3–7.

27. Ibid.

28. Marilyn Frye, *The Politics of Reality* (Freedom, CA: Crossing Press, 1983), 4–5.

29. Young, *Justice and the Politics of Difference*, 39–65.

30. Shelby, *Dark Ghettos*, 22.

31. Haslanger, "Culture and Critique," *Proceedings of the Aristotelian Society,* Supplementary Volume XCI (2017): 149–173.
32. Leslie Green, *The Authority of the State* (Oxford: Oxford University Press, 1988); and Christopher H. Wellman, "Liberalism, Samaritanism, and Political Legitimacy," *Philosophy and Public Affairs* 25, 3 (1996): 211–237.
33. A. John Simmons, *Justification and Legitimacy: Essays on Rights and Obligations* (Cambridge: Cambridge University Press, 2001), chap. 7.
34. Amartya Sen, *The Idea of Justice* (Cambridge, MA: Belknap Press of Harvard University Press, 2011), 2.
35. See Tom Ginsburg, Daniel Lansberg-Rodriguez, and Mila Versteeg, "When to Overthrow Your Government: The Right to Resist in the World's Constitutions," *UCLA Law Review* 60 (2013): 1184–1260.
36. Kurt Schock, *Civil Resistance Today* (New York: Polity, 2015), 2.
37. A notable exception is Jennet Kirkpatrick, *Uncivil Disobedience: Studies in Violence and Democratic Politics* (Princeton, NJ: Princeton University Press, 2008). But Kirkpatrick uses the term "uncivil disobedience" to designate violence and terrorism deployed in defense of democratic ideals. She studies four instances of uncivil disobedience in American history, which she uses to highlight the importance of the rule of law to limit popular sovereignty: the contemporary militia movement (chapter 1), frontier vigilantism (chapter 2), Southern lynch mobs (chapter 3), and militant abolitionism (chapter 4).
38. Note that experimental research has recently shown that commonsense morality in fact rejects the "ought implies can" principle, as most people formulate judgments about moral obligation independently of considerations about ability. See Wesley Buckwalter and John Turri, "Inability and Obligation in Moral Judgment," *PLoS ONE* 10, 8 (2015): e0136589.
39. I thank Robin Celikates for pressing me on this issue.
40. Indeed as William Edmundson stresses, a moral requirement entails the permissibility of some enforcement measure, though the social enforcement of morality is itself limited by moral constraints. See William A. Edmundson, "Civility as Political Constraint," *Res Publica* 8, 3 (2002): 217–229.

Chapter 1

1. See, e.g., Linda Ford, "Alice Paul and the Politics of Nonviolent Protest," in *Votes for Women: The Struggle for Suffrage Revisited,* ed. Jean H. Baker (New York: Oxford University Press, 2002), 176; Daniel Schwartz, "Searching for a New Sanctuary Movement," *Dissent Magazine* (June 25, 2010); Tom Watson, "Why #PussyRiot Is the Future of Civil Disobedience (and Not Just in Putin's Russia)," *Forbes.com* (August 17, 2012); Jennifer Welchman on ELF in "Is Ecosabotage Civil Disobedience?," *Philosophy & Geography* 4, 1 (2001): 97–107; William A. Scheuerman, "Whistleblowing as Civil

Disobedience: The Case of Edward Snowden," *Philosophy and Social Criticism* 40, 7 (2014): 609–628; Peter Ludlow, "Hacktivists on Trial," *The Nation* (December 4, 2013).

2. I thank Liam Murphy for pushing me to clarify the stakes of the conceptual inquiry.

3. See, e.g., Patrick J. Buchanan, "Kim Davis and the Rise of Right-Wing Civil Disobedience," *The American Conservative* (September 11, 2015), http://www.theamericanconservative.com/buchanan/kim-davis-and-the-rise-of-conservative-civil-disobedience/ (accessed January 25, 2017).

4. Haslanger distinguishes three approaches to questions about "What is x?" In the first, "conceptual" approach, we investigate our ordinary concept of x using traditional a priori methods. In the second, "descriptive" or "naturalistic" approach, we investigate x's extension, i.e., what people refer to when they use x. In the third, "ameliorative" or "analytic" approach, we inquire into the purpose of having x and see if we can put the concept of x to good use in a liberatory project. Sally Haslanger, *Resisting Reality: Social Construction and Social Critique* (Oxford: Oxford University Press, 2012), chap. 13.

5. Erin Pineda, *The Awful Roar: Civil Disobedience in the Wake of the Civil Rights Movement* (manuscript in progress), chap. 1.

6. John Rawls, *A Theory of Justice*, rev. ed. (Cambridge, MA: Harvard University Press, 1999), 320.

7. Brownlee notes this in Brownlee, "Civil Disobedience," *The Stanford Encyclopedia of Philosophy*, ed. Edward N. Zalta (Fall 2017 Edition), https://plato.stanford.edu/archives/fall2017/entries/civil-disobedience/

8. David Lyons, "Moral Judgment, Historical Reality, and Civil Disobedience," *Philosophy and Public Affairs* 27, 1 (1998): 31–49. My thinking in this chapter is very much indebted to David Lyons's work.

9. It is worth noting that the Good Friday march is the only campaign in this list that King organized, although he is often credited for these other iconic campaigns. The Congress for Racial Equality (CORE) organized the Freedom Rides and the Student Nonviolent Coordinating Committee (SNCC) organized most lunch counter sit-ins. This is part of the misrepresentation of the Black freedom struggle detailed below. King's most famous civil rights campaign, the 1955–1956 Birmingham Bus Boycott, did not involve any lawbreaking.

10. Again, I am following: Lyons, "Moral Judgment, Historical Reality, and Civil Disobedience."

11. Martin Luther King Jr., *Testament of Hope: The Essential Writings and Speeches of Martin Luther King, Jr.*, ed. James M. Washington (New York: HarperCollins, 2003 [1986]), 47.

12. Ibid., 47, 360, 429.

13. See, e.g., Martha Nussbaum, *Anger and Forgiveness: Resentment, Generosity, Justice* (New York: Oxford University Press, 2016), chap. 7; and Brandon M.

Terry, "MLK Now," in *Fifty Years Since MLK*, ed. Brandon M. Terry (Boston Review Forum 5, 43.1, 2017).

14. King, *Testament of Hope*, 291. Rawls understands coercion as basically synonymous with use of force: coercion is what the state does, and has monopoly over. But if one defines coercion as the use of cost-levying tactics to exert pressure, it can be compatible with civil disobedience.

15. King, *Testament of Hope*, 348.

16. I am grateful to William Smith for pointing me to Rawls's comments that invite a more charitable (and perhaps radical) understanding of Rawls's view on this issue, and to Robert Jubb for illuminating the problematic implications of Rawls's narrow approach.

17. Rawls, *Theory*, 8.

18. John Rawls, "Legal Obligation and the Duty of Fair Play," in *John Rawls: Collected Papers*, ed. Samuel Freeman (Cambridge, MA: Harvard University Press, 2001), 117–129. Drawing from Rawls's personal correspondence, Erin Pineda provides further support that this was his belief and underscores how mainstream this view was among philosophers (as among other privileged White men). See Pineda, *The Awful Roar*.

19. Rawls, *Theory*, 310.

20. Rawls, *Theory*, 321–322.

21. John Rawls, *Justice as Fairness: A Restatement*, ed. Erin Kelly (Cambridge, MA: Belknap Press of Harvard University Press, 2001), 128.

22. Social scientists refer to it as the "positive radical flank effect." Radical flank effects can be negative too. See, e.g., Herbert H. Haines, "Radical Flank Effects," *The Wiley-Blackwell Encyclopedia of Social and Political Movements* (Blackwell, 2013); and Kurt Schock, *Civil Resistance Today*, chap. 1: esp. 27–29.

23. King, "Letter from Birmingham City Jail."

24. Ta-Nehisi Coates, *Between the World and Me* (New York: Spiegel and Grau, 2015), 30–32. Emphasis in text.

25. Ta-Nehisi Coates, "Nonviolence as Compliance," *The Atlantic* (April 27, 2015), http://www.theatlantic.com/politics/archive/2015/04/nonviolence-as-compliance/391640/ (accessed September 23, 2016).

26. Interview featured in *The Black Power Mixtape 1967–1975*, directed by Göran Olsson (IFC Films, 2011).

27. Bernard Harcourt, "The Politics of Incivility," *Arizona Law Review* 54, 2 (2012): 345–373.

28. 388 U.S. 307 (1967). Austin Sarat, "Keeping Civility in Its Place: Dissent, Injustice, and the Lessons of History," in *Law, Society, and Community: Socio-Legal Essays in Honour of Roger Cotterrell*, eds. Richard Nobes and David Schiff (New York: Routledge, 2016), 293–308, 294.

29. Sarat, "Keeping Civility in Its Place," 304.

30. Harcourt, "Politics of Incivility," 348.

31. See, in particular, Miranda Fricker, *Epistemic Injustice: Power and the Ethics of Knowing* (Oxford: Oxford University Press, 2007).

32. Brownlee, *Conscience and Conviction*, chap. 1.

33. Brownlee, "Civil Disobedience"; Brownlee, "The Civil Disobedience of Edward Snowden: A Reply to William Scheuerman," *Philosophy and Social Criticism* 42, 10 (2016): 965–970.

34. His objection assumes, problematically in some ways, an equation between conscientiousness and selflessness. See Robin Celikates, "Civil Disobedience as Practice of Civic Freedom," in *On Global Citizenship James Tully in Dialogue*, ed. David Owen (London: Bloomsbury Press, 2014), 207–228.

35. Robin Celikates, "Democratizing Civil Disobedience," *Philosophy and Social Criticism* 42, 10 (2016): 982–994, esp. 985.

36. Robin Celikates, "La désobéissance civile: entre nonviolence et violence," *Rue Descartes* 77, 1 (2013): 35–51.

37. Brownlee, *Conscience and Conviction*; Celikates, "Democratizing Civil Disobedience."

38. Brownlee, *Conscience and Conviction*, 20.

39. Robin Celikates and Daniel De Zeeuw, "Botnet Politics, Algorithmic Resistance and Hacking Society," *Hacking Habitat* (Rotterdam: nai010, 2016): 209–217, 213. I examine some other arguments for conceiving of DDoS actions and related hacktivist acts as electronic civil disobedience in "Is Hacktivism the New Civil Disobedience?" *Raisons Politiques* 69, 1 (2018): 63–81.

40. Femen, "About Us," *Femen* blog, http://femen.org/about-us (accessed December 10, 2016).

41. Mark Dery, "Culture Jamming: Hacking, Slashing and Sniping in the Empire of Signs," *Open Magazine Pamphlet Series* (Unknown, 1993).

42. Tony Milligan discusses various more or less radical movements that refuse to describe their methods as "civil disobedience" because of their deliberate departure from the standard conception. See Tony Milligan, *Civil Disobedience: Protest, Justification and the Law* (New York: Bloomsbury 2013).

43. Shelby, *Dark Ghettos*, 223.

44. Avia Pasternak, "Political Rioting: A Moral Assessment" (unpublished manuscript)

45. See, e.g., Young, *Justice and the Politics of Difference*; Jean Harvey, *Civilized Oppression* (Lanham, MD: Rowman and Littlefield, 1999); Ann Cudd, *Analyzing Oppression* (Oxford: Oxford University Press, 2006); Carol Hay, *Kantian, Liberalism, and Feminism: Resisting Oppression* (New York: Palgrave Macmillan, 2013).

46. See, e.g., Edward E. Baptist, *The Half Has Never Been Told: Slavery and the Making of American Capitalism* (New York: Basic Books, 2014).

47. See *O.J. Simpson: Made in America*, directed by Ezra Edelman (ESPN, 2016).

48. In case the retaliatory motive is not clear enough, "Operation: Avenge Assange" was one of a series of DDoS attacks called "Operation: Payback." See Gabriella Coleman, *Hacker, Hoaxer, Whistleblower, Spy: The Many Faces of Anonymous* (London: Verso, 2014).

49. Shelby, Dark Ghettos, chap. 9.

50. See Jessica Bulman-Pozen and David Pozen, "Uncivil Obedience," *Columbia Law Review* 115 (2015): 809–872. For a critique of the category of "uncivil obedience," see Daniel Markovits, "Civility, Rule-Following, and the Authority of Law," *Columbia Law Review* 116 (2016): 32–43.

51. I take terrorism to lie at the outer edge of uncivil (as well as of principled) disobedience. Other categories of unlawful resistance besides principled disobedience include revolution and criminal disobedience (among others). For instance, Shelby argues that criminal activity under conditions of material deprivation and institutional racism constitutes an intelligible response to the ghetto plight—a kind of defiance that does not necessarily express flawed character or disregard for the authority of morality. See Shelby, *Dark Ghettos*, chap. 7. On revolution in colonial contexts, see, e.g., Frantz Fanon, *The Wretched of the Earth*, trans. Richard Philcox (New York: Grove Press, 2004 [1963]). I thank Alex Gourevitch for drawing my attention to this space within resistance and besides principled disobedience.

52. John Rawls, *Political Liberalism* (New York: Columbia University Press, 1993), 217. Linda Zerilli dubs the liberal conception of civility "the method of avoidance": I prefer to call it "decorum" to emphasize the way some of its demands boil down to a matter of manners. See Linda M. G. Zerilli, "Against Civility: A Feminist Perspective," *Civility, Legality, and Justice in America*, ed. Austin Sarat (Cambridge: Cambridge University Press, 2014), 107–131.

53. See, e.g., "Colin Kaepernick Branded a 'Traitor' by NFL Executives over Anthem Protest," *The Guardian* (August 31, 2016), https://www.theguardian.com/sport/2016/aug/31/colin-kaepernick-traitor-national-anthem-protest-nfl (accessed October 6, 2017).

Chapter 2

1. See Alex Gourevitch, "The Right to Strike: A Radical View" (unpublished manuscript). Elizabeth Anderson's work on the tyrannical aspects of many workplaces is especially relevant here. See Elizabeth Anderson, *Private Government: How Employers Rule Our Lives (and Why We Don't Talk about It)* (Princeton, NJ: Princeton University Press, 2017).

2. David Lefkowitz, "On a Moral Right to Civil Disobedience," *Ethics* 117, 2 (2007): 202–233.

3. See, e.g., Daniel Weinstock, "How Democratic Is Civil Disobedience?," *Criminal Law and Philosophy* 10, 4 (2016): 707–720.

4. See, e.g., Carl Cohen, *Civil Disobedience: Conscience, Tactics, and the Law* (New York: Columbia University, 1971), chap. 6.

5. See Jeremy Waldron, *The Dignity of Legislation* (Cambridge: Cambridge University Press, 1999), 59–62.

6. Hannah Arendt, "Reflections on Civil Disobedience," *The New Yorker* (September 12, 1970), 70–105.

7. Ronald Dworkin, "On Not Prosecuting Civil Disobedience," *The New York Review of Books* (June 6, 1968).

8. William E. Scheuerman, "Recent Theories of Civil disobedience: An Anti-Legalistic Turn?," *The Journal of Political Philosophy* 23, 4 (2015): 427–449, 431.

9. See Daniel Markovits, "Democratic Disobedience," *The Yale Law Review* 114, 8 (2005): 1897–1952; Celikates, "Civil Disobedience as Practice of Civic Freedom"; William Smith, *Civil Disobedience and Deliberative Democracy* (Abingdon, UK: Routledge, 2013), chap. 3.

10. Cornell Clayton, "Incivility Crisis of Politics Is Just a Symptom of Division," *The Seattle Times* (October 27, 2012), http://old.seattletimes.com/html/opinion/2019534569_cornellclaytonopedxml.html.

11. Erica Chenoweth and Maria Stephan, *Why Civil Resistance Works: The Strategic Logic of Nonviolent Conflict* (New York: Columbia University Press, 2011).

12. Erica Chenoweth, "Violence Will Only Hurt the Trump Resistance," *New Republic* (February 7, 2017); Erica Chenoweth and Kurt Schock, "Do Contemporaneous Armed Challenges Affect the Outcomes of Mass Nonviolent Campaigns?," *Mobilization: An International Quarterly* 2, 4 (2015): 427–451.

13. Chenoweth and Stephan, *Why Civil Resistance Works*, 42–46.

14. Quoted in K. J. Kenafick's 1950 "Foreword" to Mikhail Bakunin, *Marxism, Freedom, and The State* (Whitefish, MT: Kessinger, 2010), 4.

15. Sabl conceives of the piecewise-just society as the best way to understand Rawls's "nearly just" society. Andrew Sabl, "Looking Forward to Justice: Rawlsian Civil Disobedience and Its Non-Rawlsian Lessons," *The Journal of Political Philosophy* 9, 3 (2001): 307–330, 311.

16. Ibid., 310.

17. Ibid. I freely substituted King's civil rights movement to Sabl's talk of American Blacks in general in my reconstruction of his argument, since many Black activists in fact favored revolution.

18. Norman Geras, "Our Morals: The Ethics of Revolution," *The Socialist Register* 25 (1989): 185–211, 188.

19. Lisa Tessman, *Burdened Virtues: Virtue Ethics for Liberatory Struggles* (New York: Oxford University Press, 2005).

NOTES

20. Aristotle, *Nicomachean Ethics*, Terence Irwin (trans.), second edition, Indianapolis, IN: Hackett Publishing, 1999.
21. Rawls, *Theory of Justice*, 5, and *Political Liberalism* (New York: Columbia University Press, 1993), xlix and 253.
22. Rawls, *Theory of Justice*, 337.
23. Pasternak, "Political Rioting."
24. Susan Bickford, "Emotion Talk and Political Judgment," *Journal of Politics* 73, 4 (2011): 1025–1037, 1032.
25. See National Poll, July 2017, available at: http://harvardharrispoll.com/ (accessed September 5, 2017). For comparison, note that in a 1966 Gallup survey, 63 percent of Americans gave Martin Luther King Jr. a negative rating.
26. I am grateful to Juliet Hooker for pushing this objection. Charles Mills, "White Ignorance," in *Race and Epistemologies of Ignorance*, eds. N. Tuana and S. Sullivan (Albany: State University of New York Press, 2007), 21.
27. Amna A. Akbar, "On the Memory, Mechanics, and Imagination of Protest," (presentation at the APSA meeting, San Francisco, August 2017).
28. Lefkowitz, "On a Moral Right to Civil Disobedience."
29. Smith, *Civil Disobedience and Deliberative Democracy*, 85.
30. Brownlee, *Conscience and Conviction*, chaps. 5–6.
31. See Miranda Fricker, *Epistemic Injustice: Power and the Ethics of Knowing* (Oxford: Oxford University Press, 2007), 23–29 (illustrating testimonial injustice with the trial of Tom Robinson, the Black defendant in Harper Lee's *To Kill a Mockingbird*). In Fricker's view, testimonial injustice occurs when prejudice causes a hearer to give a deflated level of credibility to a speaker's word.

Chapter 3

1. The International Consortium of Investigative Journalists (ICCJ), *The Panama Papers* (April 3, 2016), https://panamapapers.icij.org/20160403-panama-papers-global-overview.html.
2. Le Monde, "'Paradise Papers': paradis fiscal, enfer démocratique" (November 10, 2017), http://www.lemonde.fr/evasion-fiscale/article/2017/11/10/paradise-papers-l-egalite-devant-l-impot-pilier-essentiel-du-contrat-democratique_5213081_4862750.html#u74WBQjMkzh91mJT.99.
3. Rawls, *Theory of Justice*, 308.
4. Jeremy Waldron, "Special Ties and Natural Duties," *Philosophy and Public Affairs* 22 (1993): 3–30; Smith, *Civil Disobedience and Deliberative Democracy*, chap. 1; Thomas Christiano, *The Constitution of Equality:Democratic Authority and Its Limits* (Oxford: Oxford University Press, 2008); Anna Stilz, *Liberal Loyalty: Freedom, Obligation, and the State* (Princeton, NJ: Princeton University Press, 2009); Anna Stilz, "Why Does the State Matter Morally? Political Obligation and Particularity," in *Varieties of Sovereignty and Citizenship*, eds.

S. R. Ben-Porath and R. M. Smith (Philadelphia: University of Pennsylvania Press, 2013), 244–264; Daniel Viehoff, "Democratic Equality and Political Authority," *Philosophy and Public Affairs* 42, 4 (2014): 337–375.

5. Stilz, "Why Does the State Matter Morally?," 257.
6. Smith, *Civil Disobedience and Deliberative Democracy*, 29.
7. Ibid., chap. 2.
8. Ibid., 39–41.
9. Ibid., 41–43.
10. *Obergefell v. Hodges*, 135 S. Ct. 2071 (2015).
11. The Council of State, France's highest administrative court soon struck down these municipal bans as unconstitutional, though they remained in effect through the summer. See Conseil d'Etat statuant au contentieux, ordonnance du 26 août 2016, Ligue des droits de l'homme et autres—association de défense des droits de l'homme collectif contre l'islamophobie en France, Nos 402742, 402777.
12. One could make an indirect case against immigration policies by showing that it violates the rights of citizens, for instance, when parents, children, and spouses are broken up by deportation orders. But the point is that immigration policies involve serious wrongs even where they do not concern citizens.
13. See Serena Parekh, *Refugees and the Ethics of Forced Displacement* (New York: Routledge, 2016).
14. Smith, *Civil Disobedience and Deliberative Democracy*, 68–70. This target of civil disobedience was previously conceptualized in Markovits, "Democratic Disobedience."
15. See Sheheryar T. Sardar and Benish A. Shah, "Social Media, Censorship, and Control: Beyond SOPA, PIPA, and the Arab Spring," *University of Pennsylvania Journal of Law and Social Change* 15, 4 (2012): 577–585. Available at http://scholarship.law.upenn.edu/jlasc/vol15/iss4/10.
16. Lawrence Lessig, *Code and Other Laws of Cyberspace* (New York: Basic Books, 1999).
17. Bernard Harcourt, *Exposed: Desire and Disobedience in the Digital Age* (Cambridge, MA: Harvard University Press, 2015).
18. Ethan Zuckerman, "Intermediary Censorship," in *Access Controlled: The Shaping of Power, Rights, and Rule in Cyberspace*, eds. R. J. Deibert, J. G. Palfrey, R. Rohozinski, and J. Zittrain (Cambridge, MA: MIT Press, 2009), 71–85.
19. Rebecca MacKinnon, *Consent of the Networked: The Worldwide Struggle for Internet Freedom* (New York: Basic Books, 2009).
20. *U.S. v. Cruikshank* (92 U.S. 542, 1875) is a case in point. The *Cruikshank* Court overturned the convictions of two White defendants in the 1873 Colfax massacre (around 105 Blacks were killed), and put an end to the Ku Klux Klan prosecutions. Legal scholars have argued that this decision judicially constrained the Fourteenth Amendment's equal protection principle in a manner that has not been undone. See Charles Lane, *The Day Freedom*

Died: The Colfax Massacre, the Supreme Court, and the Betrayal of Reconstruction (New York: Henry Holt, 2008); William J. Stuntz, *The Collapse of American Criminal Justice* (Cambridge, MA: Belknap Press of Harvard University Press, 2011).

21. David Lyons, "The Legal Entrenchment of Illegality," in *The Legacy of H. L. A. Hart: Legal, Political, and Moral Philosophy*, eds. Matthew H. Kramer, Claire Grant, Ben Colburn, and Antony Hatzistavrou (Oxford: Oxford University Press, 2008), 29–43.

22. Bureau of Justice Statistics, *Arrest-Related Deaths Program Redesign Study, 2015–16: Preliminary Findings* (December 15, 2016), NCJ 250112: https://www.bjs.gov/index.cfm?ty=pbdetail&iid=5864.

23. Mapping Police Violence, https://mappingpoliceviolence.org/aboutthedata/ (accessed November 21, 2017).

24. *Graham v. Connor*, 490 U.S. 386 (1989).

25. See, e.g., John Yoo, "Memorandum for Department of Defense Re: Application of Treaties and Laws to al Qaeda and Taliban Detainees" (January 9, 2002). Draft available at http://nsarchive.gwu.edu/NSAEBB/NSAEBB127/02.01.09.pdf.

26. Joseph Nye, "Corruption and Political Development: A Cost-Benefit Analysis," *American Political Science Review* 61, 2 (1967): 417–427.

27. See Transparency International's Corruption Perceptions Index at http://www.transparency.org/cpi2015.

28. Indeed I do not mean to champion transparency in all domains of government and at all costs. For a nuanced, empirically informed discussion of the issues of secrecy, transparency, and democratic accountability, see Rahul Sagar, *Secrets and Leaks: The Dilemma of State Secrecy* (Princeton, NJ: Princeton University Press, 2013); and Michael P. Colaresi, *Democracy Declassified: The Secrecy Dilemma in National Security* (Oxford: Oxford University Press, 2014).

29. Jon Swaine and Luke Harding, "Trump Commerce Secretary's Business Links with Putin Family Laid Out in Leaked Files," *The Guardian* (November 5, 2017), https://www.theguardian.com/news/2017/nov/05/trump-commerce-secretary-wilbur-ross-business-links-putin-family-paradise-papers (accessed November 24, 2017).

30. Liam Murphy, "The Case of Required Rescue: Beneficence, Law and Liberty," *Georgetown Law Review* (2001): 647.

31. Viehoff, "Democratic Equality and Political Authority." The article first shows why common duty of justice-based arguments for the duty to obey democratically made law fail.

32. Ibid., 352–359.

33. He proposes the following test: "To determine whether disobedience is justifiable, we must, in the first instance, ask not how disobeying in any particular instance will advance justice, but rather whether a general moral rule of

disobeying under certain circumstances will advance justice sufficiently to make up for the threat this poses to relational equality." Ibid., 374.

34. Ibid. 352.

35. See, e.g., Eli Pariser, *The Filter Bubble: What the Internet Is Hiding from You* (New York: Penguin, 2011); and Jessica Clark and Tracy Van Slyke, *Beyond the Echo Chamber: Reshaping Politics through Networked Progressive Media* (New York: The New Press, 2010).

36. Wikipedia contributors, "Protests against SOPA and PIPA," *Wikipedia, The Free Encyclopedia*,https://en.wikipedia.org/w/index.php?title=Protests_against_SOPA_and_PIPA&oldid=760306719 (accessed February 12, 2017).

37. Robin Celikates, "Digital Publics, Digital Contestations," in *Transformations of Democracy*, eds. R. Celikates, R. Kreide, and T. Wesche (Lanham, MD: Rowman and Littlefield, 2015), chap. 8.

38. As a caveat, note that Swartz's lawyers, MIT itself, and prominent intellectuals like Lawrence Lessig, have argued that Swartz did not in fact violate any law. See, e.g., Lawrence Lessig, "Aaron's Laws—Law and Justice in a Digital Age," public talk (2013), available at http://www.youtube.com/watch?v=9HAw1i4gOU4.

39. Jose Antonio Vargas, "My Life as an Undocumented Immigrant," *New York Times* online (June 22, 2011), http://www.nytimes.com/2011/06/26/magazine/my-life-as-an-undocumented-immigrant.html?ref=magazine. A version of this article appeared in print in the *Sunday Times Magazine* on June 26, 2011.

40. See, e.g., Carmen Fishwick, "Why We Wear the Burkini: Five Women on Dressing Modestly at the Beach," *The Guardian* (August 31, 2016); Margaux Mazellier, "Interdiction du burkini: paroles de musulmanes" *RFI* (August 19, 2016, last modified August 24, 2016); Asma Fares, "Touche pas à mon burkini!" (August 5, 2016), available at https://www.youtube.com/watch?v=lpjSZJDY8Pw (accessed February 13, 2017).

41. See economic effects on small businesses, including LGBTQ shops, in Asheville, North Carolina: https://www.washingtonpost.com/lifestyle/style/how-north-carolinas-idyllic-hipster-haven-is-being-hurt-by-the-bathroom-bill-boycott/2016/06/28/28fc707a-33d4-11e6-8758-d58e76e11b12_story.html.

42. On the movement, see Susan Bibler Coutin, *The Culture of Protest: Religious Activism and the U.S. Sanctuary Movement* (Boulder, CO: Westview Press, 1993).

43. See especially Arizona SB 1070 (2010) and Alabama's HB 56 (AL Act 2011-535). The Department of Justice and a coalition of groups including the American Civil Liberties Union filed successful legal challenges to the most pernicious provisions of these laws, such as the criminalization of assisting, caring for, or renting to undocumented people. However, the laws have remained on the books, with key provisions still in effect. For instance, the "Papers, Please" provision makes it a crime to fail to carry registration papers

and compels officers to question the immigration status of, and arrest without a warrant, those they suspect are in the country illegally. HB 56 even includes a provision empowering citizens to sue individual officers shirking their enforcement duties.

44. Javier Hidalgo, who has recently propounded an argument of this form, though without appealing to the duty of justice, greatly influenced my thinking here. Javier S. Hidalgo, "The Duty to Disobey Immigration Law," *Moral Philosophy & Politics* 3, 2 (2016): 165–186.

45. See Prentice Earl Sanders and Ben Cohen, *The Zebra Murders: A Season of Killing, Racial Madness and Civil Rights* (New York: Arcade Publishing, 2011).

46. On the movement, see Lance Hill, *The Deacons for Defense: Armed Resistance and the Civil Rights Movement* (Chapel Hill: University of North Carolina Press, 2006).

47. Malcolm X, "The Ballot or the Bullet," speech delivered on April 3, 1964, at Cory Methodist Church in Cleveland, Ohio. Part of Malcolm X's point here is also to defend Blacks' access to guns under the Second Amendment of the U.S. Constitution.

48. One participant boasted on an internet relay chat, "We have probably done some million pound of dmg (damage) to mc (MasterCard)." PayPal alleged that the attack cost the company £3.5 million. The Ministry of Sound estimated the cost of the attack on the four sites they operate that were targeted as being £9,000, while the IFPI's costs were more than £20,000 and the BPI's more than £4,000. MasterCard and Visa did not disclose the financial impact. Lauren Turner, "Anonymous Hackers Jailed for DDoS Attacks on Visa, MasterCard, and Paypal," *The Independent* (January 24, 2013), http://www.independent.co.uk/news/uk/crime/anonymous-hackers-jailed-for-ddos-attacks-on-visa-mastercard-and-paypal-8465791.html.

49. I articulate an account of the presumptive wrongfulness of government whistleblowing and the conditions under which it can be justified in: Candice Delmas, "The Ethics of Government Whistleblowing," *Social Theory and Practice* 41, 1 (2015): 77–105.

50. Hillary Clinton, among many other politicians and pundits, suggested Snowden was disloyal. See https://www.theatlantic.com/politics/archive/2014/04/hillary-clinton-edward-snowdens-leaks-helped-terrorists/455586/. American investigative journalist Edward Jay Epstein lays out the case that Snowden was a spy for Russia in his *How America Lost Its Secrets: Edward Snowden, the Man and the Theft* (New York: Alfred A. Knopf, 2017).

51. In fact, Buchanan even shows that promoting the cause of justice does not require giving priority to domestic law. Allen Buchanan, *Justice, Legitimacy, and Self-Determination: Moral Foundations for International Law* (Oxford: Oxford University Press, 2004), 85–98.

52. See, e.g., Kevin Davis and Stephen Choi, "Foreign Affairs and Enforcement of the Foreign Corrupt Practices Act," *Journal of Empirical Legal Studies* 11, 3 (2014) 409–445

53. Jeremy Waldron, in conversation with Kevin Davis, New York University Colloquium in Social, Legal, and Political Philosophy, October 8, 2016.

Chapter 4

1. H. L. A. Hart, "Are There Any Natural Rights?," *Philosophical Review* 64, 2 (1955): 175–191; George Klosko, *The Principle of Fairness and Political Obligation* (Lanham, MD: Rowman and Littlefield, 1992); and John Rawls, "Legal Obligation and the Duty of Fair Play," in *John Rawls: Collected Papers*, ed. Samuel Freeman (Cambridge, MA: Harvard University Press, 2001): 117–129. The fair play defense of political obligations also appears in Garrett Cullity, "Moral Free Riding," *Philosophy and Public Affairs* 24, 1 (1995): 3–34; Richard Dagger, "Membership, Fair Play and Political Obligation," *Political Studies* 48, 1 (2000): 104–117; Norman Davis, "Nozick's Argument for the Legitimacy of the Welfare State," *Ethics* 97, 3 (1987): 576–594; David Lefkowitz, "The Nature of Fairness and Political Obligation: A Response to Carr," *Social Theory and Practice* 30, 1 (2004): 1–31; and Massimo Renzo, "Fairness, Self-Deception and Political Obligation," *Philosophical Studies* 169, 3 (2013): 467–488.

2. Young, *Justice and the Politics of Difference*, 49.

3. For an analysis of these dual facets, see G. A. Cohen, "The Structure of Proletarian Unfreedom," *Philosophy and Public Affairs* 12, 1 (1983): 3–33.

4. Ann E. Cudd, "Wanting Freedom," *Journal of Social Philosophy* 43, 4 (2012): 367–385.

5. Robert Dahl, *Polyarchy* (New Haven, CT: Yale University Press, 1971), 28–29, 93–94.

6. Cullity, "Moral Free Riding," 28.

7. Ibid., 22.

8. See, e.g., Marc Fleurbaey, "The Facets of Exploitation," *Journal of Theoretical Politics* 26, 4 (2014): 653–676.

9. Robert Mayer, "What's Wrong with Exploitation?," *Journal of Applied Philosophy* 24, 2 (2007): 137–150.

10. Avia Pasternak, "Voluntary Benefits from Wrongdoing," *Journal of Applied Philosophy* 31, 4 (2014): 377–391, 379.

11. Axel Gosseries characterizes beneficiaries of wrongdoing as "morally objectionable free riders": they enjoy the fruits of an activity that imposed costs on others, without themselves sharing in these costs. See Axel Gosseries, "Historical Emissions," *Ethical Perspectives* 11, 1 (2004): 36–60, 43. I think it is more apt to characterize beneficiaries of injustice as *morally analogous*

to free-riders, than as free-riders simpliciter, though nothing hinges on the distinction.

12. Simone de Beauvoir, *The Second Sex*, trans. H. M. Parshley (New York: Random House, [1952] 1972), xxx.

13. See, e.g., Mab Segrest, *Memoir of a Race Traitor* (Cambridge, MA: South End Press, 1999).

14. King, "Letter."

15. See Isabel Wilkerson, *The Warmth of Other Suns* (New York: Random House, 2010); and James N. Gregory, *The Southern Diaspora: How the Great Migrations of Black and White Southerners Transformed America* (Chapel Hill: University of North Carolina Press, 2005). Whites' motives for emigrating were mainly economic and not related to the injustice of Jim Crow.

16. See John Locke, *Second Treatise of Government*, ed. C. B. Macpherson (Indianapolis, IN: Hackett, 1980 [1690]), § 119; David Hume, "Of the Original Contract," in *Essays: Moral Political, and Literary*, Vol. 1, ed. E. F. Miller (Indianapolis, IN: Liberty Classics: 1985 [1752]), 443–460.

17. Robert Goodin, "Disgorging the Fruits of Historical Wrongdoing," *American Political Science Review* 107, 3 (2013): 478–491.

18. See Karl Marx and Friederich Engels, "Manifesto of the Communist Party," in *The Marx-Engels Reader*, ed. Robert C. Tucker (New York: W. W. Norton, 1978 [1848]), 473–500. For a recent, liberal version of this argument, see Liam D. Murphy and Thomas Nagel, *The Myth of Ownership: Taxes and Justice* (New York: Oxford University Press, 2002).

19. Thomas Hill Jr., "The Message of Affirmative Action," *Social Philosophy and Policy* 8, 2 (1991): 108–129.

20. Ibid., 108.

21. See Jean Harvey, "Victims, Resistance, and Civilized Oppression," *Journal of Social Philosophy* 41, 1 (2010): 13–27, 15–16.

22. See especially Chenoweth and Stephan, *Why Civil Resistance Works*; Daniel Q. Gillion. *The Political Power of Protest: Minority Activism and Shifts in Public Policy* (Cambridge: Cambridge University Press, 2013).

23. Alex Gourevitch, "Strikes, Force, and Resistance to Oppression" (unpublished ms.).

24. Avery Kolers, "The Priority of Solidarity to Justice," *Journal of Applied Philosophy* 31, 4 (2014): 420–433, 426–427.

25. Mia McKenzie, "8 Ways Not to Be an 'Ally': A Non-Comprehensive List," *BGD* blog (June 17, 2013), http://www.Blackgirldangerous.org/2013/06/20136178-ways-not-to-be-an-ally/ (accessed January 15, 2017).

26. Kolers, "The Priority of Solidarity to Justice," 429.

27. These estimates are from the Tuskegee Institute and err on the conservative side. See "1959 Tuskegee Institute Lynch Report," *Montgomery Advertiser* (April 26, 1959).

Chapter 5

1. https://www.facebook.com/events/1640071269598406 (accessed December 5, 2017).
2. See, e.g., Human Rights Watch Report, *"Everyone Blames Me": Barriers to Justice and Support Services for Sexual Assault Survivors in India* (November 8, 2017), available at https://www.hrw.org/report/2017/11/08/everyone-blames-me/barriers-justice-and-support-services-sexual-assault-survivors (accessed December 5, 2017).
3. BuzzFeed, https://www.buzzfeed.com/andreborges/hundreds-of-women-around-india-are-sleeping-in-parks-to-recl?utm_term=.tgLdRgXdr#.tf1B1l4BL (accessed December 5, 2017).
4. We can distinguish two Samaritan duties: the duty to rescue and the duty to aid people in dire need. The distinction is a matter of degree: it is the difference between being caught in a house on fire and being left without a home after the fire has been put down. I refer to *the* Samaritan duty throughout the chapter.
5. For the issue of legal enforcement, which I will not address, see Ernest J. Weinrib, "The Case for a Duty of Rescue," *The Yale Law Journal* 90, 2 (1980): 247–293; Robert J. Lipkin, "Beyond Good Samaritans and Moral Monsters: An Individualistic Justification of the General Legal Duty to Rescue," *UCLA Law Review* 31 (1983): 252–290; Liam Murphy, "Beneficence, Law, and Liberty: The Case of Required Rescue," *Georgetown Law Journal* 89, 3 (2001): 605–665.
6. Joel Feinberg, *Harm to Others* (New York: Oxford University Press, 1984), 171.
7. Peter Unger, *Living High and Letting Die: Our Illusion of Innocence* (Oxford: Oxford University Press, 1996), chap. 2. Feinberg thinks that, cast as a duty of beneficence, the case for the legal enforcement of the duty of rescue would be harder to make. Murphy shows that this assumption is misguided. See Murphy, "Beneficence, Law, and Liberty." I do not need to take a side in the debate, since I do not defend the enforceability of Samaritan political obligations in the face of injustice.
8. This basic account synthesizes the following sources: Maimonides, *Mishneh torah—The book of torts*, ed. H. Klein (New Haven, CT: Yale University Press, 1954 [1180]), 1:14; Luke 10:30–37; Christopher Heath Wellman and A. John Simmons, eds., *Is There a Duty to Obey the Law?* Joel Feinberg, "Offense to Others: The Moral Limits of the Criminal Law," *Philosophical Review* 98, 2 (1989): 239–242; Cécile Fabre, "Mandatory Rescue Killings," *Journal of Political Philosophy* 15, 4 (2007): 363–384.
9. Cécile Fabre, "Good Samaritanism: A Matter of Justice," *Critical Review of International Social and Political Philosophy* 5, 4 (2002): 128–144.
10. See Christopher H. Wellman, "Liberalism, Samaritanism, and Political Legitimacy," *Philosophy and Public Affairs* 25, 3 (1996): 211–237; "Toward a Liberal Theory of Political Obligation," *Ethics* 111, 4 (2001): 735–759;

Christopher H. Wellman, "Samaritanism and the Duty to Obey the Law," in *Is There a Duty to Obey the Law?*, 3–90. Other champions include Dudley Knowles, "Good Samaritans and Good Government," *Proceedings of the Aristotelian Society* 112, 2 (2012): 161–178.

11. Wellman, *Is There a Duty to Obey the Law?*, 19, emphases in the original. Wellman denies the paternalistic claim that the state is justified in coercing its constituents because it ultimately benefits each of them.

12. Ibid., 33.

13. Ibid., 86.

14. The defense is recognized in the United States as part of common law and most states' statutory law. For an overview of the necessity defense, see, e.g., Laurie Levenson, "Criminal Law: The Necessity Defense," *National Law Journal* (1999). For a discussion of the rationales behind the necessity defense, see Brownlee, *Conscience and Conviction*, 181–184.

15. Douglass adds that the law "bribes the judge who tries them," since judges would get $10 for every victim they consigned to slavery and $5 for those they set free. Frederick Douglass, "What to the Slave Is the Fourth of July?," in *Frederick Douglass: Selected Speeches and Writings*, ed. Philip S. Foner (Chicago: Lawrence Hill, 1999), 188–206.

16. Groupe d'Information et de soutien des immigré·e·s, "Si la solidarité devient un délit, nous demandons à être poursuivis pour ce délit!," http://www.gisti. org/spip.php?article1404 (accessed November 20, 2016).

17. Michelle Alexander has famously dubbed it the "new Jim Crow." She attributes increased incarceration rates, and its adverse impact on Black and Brown people, to the failed War on Drugs, draconian sentencing laws, racist profiling, and increasing reliance on private prisons. See Michelle Alexander, *The New Jim Crow: Mass Incarceration in the Age of Color Blindness* (New York: The New Press, 2010). Theorists have recently pushed back against Alexander's account. According to Marie Gottschalk, drug laws and law enforcement practices by themselves are insufficient to explain mass incarceration, since drug offenders comprise only 20 percent of offenders in state prisons, while violent offenders comprise about half. See Marie Gottschalk, *Caught: The Prison State and the Lockdown of American Politics* (Princeton, NJ: Princeton University Press, 2015). According to John Pfaff, the single most important factor that explains mass incarceration is the major shift in prosecutor behavior that occurred in the mid-1990s, when prosecutors began bringing felony charges against arrestees about twice as often as they had before. See John Pfaff, *Locked In: The True Causes of Mass Incarceration—and How to Achieve Real Reform* (New York: Basic Books, 2017).

18. Peter Wagner and Bernadette Rabuy, "Mass Incarceration: The Whole Pie 2017," Prison Policy Initiative, March 14, 2017, https://www.prisonpolicy. org/reports/pie2017.html (accessed September 14, 2017).

19. *Brown v. Plata* 131 S. Ct. 1910 (2011). See also William J. Newman and Charles L. Scott, "*Brown v. Plata*: Prison Overcrowding in California," *Journal of the American Academy of Psychiatry and the Law* 40, 4 (2012): 547–552.

20. See David Kaiser and Lovisa Stannow, "Prison Rape and the Government," *The New York Review of Books* (March 24, 2011).

21. See Bruce Arrigo and Jennifer Bullock, "The Psychological Effects of Confinement on Prisoners in Supermax Units: Reviewing What We Know and Recommending What Should Change," *International Journal of Offender Therapy and Comparative Criminology* 52, 6 (2008): 622–640.

22. Geoffrey Canada, *Fist Stick Knife Gun: A Personal History of Violence* (Boston: Beacon Press, 1995); Coates, *Between the World and Me*; see also Carolyn E. Cutrona, Gail Wallace, and Kristin A. Wesner, "Neighborhood Characteristics and Depression: An Examination of Stress Processes," *Current Directions in Psychological Science* 15, 4 (2006): 188–192.

23. See Kimberlé Williams Crenshaw and Andrea J. Ritchie, "Say Her Name: Resisting Police Brutality against Black Women" (July 2015). An interactive website, Mapping Police Violence, displays the photographs, stories, and legal disposition of the Black people killed by police since 2015: https://mappingpoliceviolence.org/. Another site, The Counted, maintained by *The Guardian*, counts the number of people killed by police and other law enforcement agencies in the United States throughout 2015 and 2016, monitors their demographics, and tells the stories of how they died. See https://www.theguardian.com/us-news/ng-interactive/2015/jun/01/the-counted-police-killings-us-database (last accessed February 14, 2017).

24. Report of the U.S. Department of Justice Civil Rights Division, "Investigation of the Baltimore City Police Department" (August 10, 2016), available at https://www.justice.gov/opa/file/883366/download.

25. This is a conservative estimate, cited in https://www.rainn.org/statistics/scope-problem. Others find that a rape occurs every two minutes: http://www.wcsap.org/how-often-does-it-happen.

26. See http://www.whitehouse.gov/the-press-office/remarks-president-signing-tribal-law-and-order-act.

27. That figure is probably underestimated given the low rates of report. See Amnesty International's report "Maze of Injustice: The Failure to Protect Indigenous Women from Violence," available at http://www.amnesty.org/en/library/asset/AMR51/035/2007/en/ce2336a3-d3ad-11dd-a329-2f46302a8cc6/amr510352007en.html.

28. See, e.g., Tuesday Reitano, Laura Adal, and Mark Shaw, "Smuggled Futures: The Dangerous Path of the Migrant from Africa to Europe," *The Global Initiative Against Transnational Organized Crime*, Geneva, last modified May 7, 2014, http://globalinitiative.net/smuggled-futures/ (accessed June 22, 2016).

29. See, e.g., Paul Dourgnon and Kassene Kassar,"Refugees In and Out of North Africa: A Study of the Choucha Refugee Camp in Tunisia," *European Journal*

of Public Health 24, Supplement 1 (2014): 6–10; Thomas M. Crea, Rocio Calvo, and Maryanne Loughry, "Refugee Health and Wellbeing: Differences between Urban and Camp-Based Environments in Sub-Saharan Africa," *Journal of Refugee Studies* 28, 3 (2015): 319–330. See also Phoebe Weston, "Inside Zaatari Refugee Camp: The Fourth Largest City in Jordan," *The Telegraph* (August 5, 2015), http://www.telegraph.co.uk/news/worldnews/middleeast/jordan/11782770/What-is-life-like-inside-the-largest-Syrian-refugee-camp-Zaatari-in-Jordan.html (accessed January 5, 2017); and Abu Amar, "Our Life in the Zaatari Refugee Camp: No Electricity, No Space to Sleep, No Escape," *The Guardian* (September 14, 2015), https://www.theguardian.com/commentisfree/2015/sep/14/life-refugee-camp-syrian-family-jordan-escape (accessed January 5, 2017).

30. See, e.g., Amnesty International's reports on Uganda: https://www.amnesty.org/en/latest/news/2016/08/uganda-minister-remarks-against-lgbti-people-amount-to-advocacy-of-hatred/, and Jamaica: https://www.amnesty.org/en/countries/americas/jamaica/report-jamaica/ (accessed December 15, 2016).

31. Kidnapping statistics are unreliable, with an estimated 80 percent of cases never officially reported, due to police corruption. However, it is estimated that, in absolute numbers, Mexico has been the world's kidnapping capital since 2005, followed closely by Nigeria and Colombia. See Simeon Tegel, "Wealthy Mexicans Turn to Tracking Devices as Kidnap Rate Soars," *The Independent* (August 22, 2011), http://www.independent.co.uk/news/world/americas/wealthy-mexicans-turn-to-tracking-devices-as-kidnap-rate-soars-2342174.html (accessed November 1, 2016). One may object to my characterization that their vulnerability results from an unjust war on drugs, and so that they are in fact in persistent Samaritan peril.

32. See, e.g., http://www.interventionanddeescalation.com/resources.html; https://watt.cashmusic.org/writing/deescalation; and Alyssa Hernandez, "Bystander Intervention," online video, https://www.youtube.com/channel/UC69feU1j6NL5eTXyxRV0v8w (accessed February 5, 2017).

33. Feinberg, *Harm to Others*, 171.

34. Charles Mills, *The Racial Contract* (Ithaca, NY: Cornell University Press, 1997).

35. Elizabeth Anderson, *The Imperative of Integration* (Princeton, NJ: Princeton University Press, 2010).

36. Simmons, "The Duty to Obey and Our Natural Moral Duties," 184.

37. Peter Singer, "Famine, Affluence, and Morality," *Philosophy & Public Affairs* 1, 1 (1972): 229–243.

38. Equal Justice Initiative, "Lynching in America: Confronting the Legacy of Racial Terror," 2nd ed., (2015), http://eji.org/sites/default/files/lynching-in-america-second-edition-summary.pdf (accessed November 15, 2016).

39. See http://www.alslegal.org and http://www.indianlaw.org.

40. See Amnesty, "Maze of Injustice."

41. Louise Erdrich, *The Round House* (New York: HarperCollins, 2012).

42. See http://www.whitehouse.gov/the-press-office/remarks-president-signing-tribal-law-and-order-act.

43. For a discussion of the negative and dehumanizing stereotypes of Native Americans in general, and indigenous women in particular, see Amnesty, "Maze of Injustice."

44. Peter A. Leavitt, Rebecca Covarrubias, Yvonne A. Perez, and Stephanie A. Fryberg, "'Frozen in Time': The Impact of Native American Media Representations on Identity and Self-Understanding," *Journal of Social Issues* 71, 1 (2015): 39–53.

45. See Human Rights Watch Report, "Everyone Blames Me."

46. See Lolly Bowean, "Protesters Chain Themselves Together in Front of Chicago Police Station," *Chicago Tribune* (July 21, 2016): http://www.chicagotribune.com/news/local/breaking/ct-Black-lives-matter-march-lawndale-police-strategies-20160720-story.html (accessed February 15, 2017).

47. See, e.g., *United States v. Hill*, 893 F Supp 1044, 1048 (ND Fla 1994), *Zal v. Steppe*, 968 F2d 924, 929 (9th Cir. 1992), and *Northeast Women's Center v. McMonagle*, 868 F2d 1342, 1350–52 (3d Cir. 1989). Courts generally emphasize the legal alternatives available to abortion protesters. 971 F.2d 193 (9th Cir.) *cert. denied*, 112 S. Ct. 2980 (1992).

48. See Jennifer Jefferis, *Armed for Life: The Army of God and Anti-Abortion Terror in the United States* (Westport, CT: Praeger, 2011).

49. Judith Jarvis Thomson, "A Defense of Abortion," *Philosophy and Public Affairs* 1, 1 (1971): 47–66.

50. Knowles, "Good Samaritans and Good Government."

51. See "Lives in Peril: How Ineffective Inspections Make ICE Complicit in Detention Center Abuse," *Immigration Detention Transparency and Human Rights Project*, http://immigrantjustice.org/lives-peril-how-ineffective-inspections-make-ice-complicit-detention-center-abuse-0 Proceedings of the Aristotelian Society 112, 2 (2012): 161– 178. (accessed September 25, 2016).

52. Ibid.; Sibylla Brodzinsky and Ed Pilkington, "US Government Deporting Central American Migrants to Their Deaths," *The Guardian* (October 12, 2015), https://www.theguardian.com/us-news/2015/oct/12/obama-immigration-deportations-central-america (accessed September 18, 2017); and Amnesty International, "Home Sweet Home? Honduras, Guatemala, and El Salvador's Role in a Deepening Refugee Crisis" (2016), https://www.amnestyusa.org/files/central_american_refugees_-_report_eng_1-min.pdf (accessed September 18, 2017).

53. Colson Whitehead, *The Underground Railroad* (New York: Random House, 2016).

54. Samuel P. Oliner and Pearl M. Oliner, *The Altruistic Personality: Rescuers of Jews in Nazi Europe* (New York: Macmillan, 1988).

55. See Julia Nefsky, "How You Can Help, without Making a Difference," *Philosophical Studies* 174, 11 (2016): 2743–2767.

56. Simmons, "The Duty to Obey and Our Natural Moral Duties," 184.

57. Knowles, "Good Samaritans and Good Government," 168.

58. Fabre, "Good Samaritanism: A Matter of Justice."

59. Deborah Small and George Loewenstein, "Helping *a* Victim or Helping *the* Victim: Altruism and Identifiability," *Journal of Risk and Uncertainty* 26, 1 (2003): 5–16.

60. See, e.g., Norman Daniels, "Reasonable Disagreement about Identified vs. Statistical Victims," *Hastings Center Report* 42 (2012): 35–45.

61. See, e.g., Jan Narveson, "Intentional Behavior and Social Science," *Journal for the Theory of Social Behavior* 6 (1976): 267–270; John Broome, *Ethics Out of Economics* (Cambridge: Cambridge University Press, 1999).

62. Caspar Hare, "Voices from Another World: Must We Respect the Interests of People Who Do Not, and Will Never, Exist?," *Ethics* 117, 3 (2007): 498–523.

63. Caspar Hare, "Obligations to Merely Statistical People," *Journal of Philosophy* 109, 5/6 (2012): 378–390, p. 379.

64. See Hasan Suroor, "From 'incredible India' to 'area of darkness'," *The Hindu* (January 12, 2013), http://www.thehindu.com/todays-paper/tp-opinion/from-incredible-india-to-area-of-darkness/article4300421.ece Amrit Wilson, "India's anti-rape movement: redefining solidarity outside the colonial frame" Open Democracy (April 8, 2013), https://www.opendemocracy.net/5050/amrit-wilson/indias-anti-rape-movement-redefining-solidarity-outside-colonial-frame

Chapter 6

1. *Hunger*, directed by Steve McQueen (Film4, 2008).

2. Margaret Gilbert, "Group Membership and Political obligation," *Monist* 76, 1 (1993): 119–131, 128.

3. Andrew Mason, "Special Obligations to Compatriots," *Ethics* 107, 3 (1997): 427–447.

4. See Thomas McPherson, *Political Obligation* (London: Routledge and Kegan Paul, 1967); Hans Kelsen, "Why Should the Law Be Obeyed?," in *What is Justice?* (Berkeley and Los Angeles: University of California Press, 1960), 262; Hanna Pitkin, "Obligation and Consent—I," *American Political Science Review* 59 (1965): 990–999, esp. 990–991; Margaret Macdonald, "The Language of Political Theory," in *Logic and Language*, ed. A. G. N. Flew (Garden City, NY: Doubleday, 1965). For a brief and illuminating discussion of the institutional model, see Richard Dagger, "What Is Political Obligation?," *American*

Political Science Review 71, 1 (1977): 86–94, esp. 86, 90–92. The most prominent contemporary champion of such accounts is Margaret Gilbert, *On Social Facts* (Princeton, NJ: Princeton University Press, 1992 [1989]). Gilbert calls hers a conceptual account of "analytical membership."

5. See, e.g., Alasdair MacIntyre, *After Virtue*, 2d ed. (Notre Dame: University of Notre Dame Press, 1984); Yael Tamir, *Liberal Nationalism* (Princeton, NJ: Princeton University Press, 1993).

6. See, e.g., John Horton, "In Defense of Associative Political Obligations. Part Two," *Political Studies* 55 (2007): 1–19; William Kymlicka, *Multicultural Citizenship* (Oxford: Oxford University Press, 1995); Michael Walzer, *Spheres of Justice: A Defense of Pluralism and Equality* (New York: Basic Books, 1983).

7. Dworkin, *Justice for Hedgehogs*, 204.

8. Ibid., 321–322.

9. Ibid.

10. See Avishai Margalit, *The Decent Society*, trans. N. Goldblum (Cambridge, MA: Harvard University Press, 1996).

11. See Martha Nussbaum, "Objectification," *Philosophy and Public Affairs* 24 (1995): 249–291.

12. See Andrew Altman, "Discrimination," *The Stanford Encyclopedia of Philosophy*, ed. Edward N. Zalta (Winter 2016 Edition), https://plato.stanford.edu/archives/win2016/entries/discrimination/.

13. See Allen Wood, "Exploitation," *Social Philosophy and Policy* 12 (1995): 150–151.

14. See Young, *Politics of Difference*, 53–58.

15. Ibid., 61–63.

16. Frederick Douglass, *Narrative of the Life of Frederick Douglass: An American Slave, Written by Himself* (Minneapolis, MN: Filiquarian Publishing, 2007), 85.

17. Frantz Fanon, *The Wretched of the Earth*, trans. Richard Philcox (New York: Grove Press, 2004 [1963]), 147.

18. I am here following Nelson Mandela's political narrative as set out in his autobiography, *Long Walk to Freedom: The Autobiography of Nelson Mandela* (New York: Little, Brown, 2008). But the point is a matter of controversy. David Dyzenhaus and others argue that the turn to the armed struggle was not a popular decision in the ANC and actually set back the cause. See David Dyzenhaus, "'With the Benefit of Hindsight': Dilemmas of Legality," in *Lethe's Law: Justice, Law, and Ethics in Reconciliation*, ed. Emilios Christodoulidis and Scott Veitch (Oxford: Hart, 2001), 65.

19. Available at http://www.anc.org.za/show.php?id=77.

20. Heather Ann Thompson, *Blood in the Water: The Attica Prison Uprising of 1971 and Its Legacy* (New York: Pantheon, 2016).

21. Jean Casella, James Ridgeway, and Sarah Shourd, eds., *Hell Is a Very Small Place: Voices from Solitary Confinement* (New York: The New Press, 2016).

22. Martin Garbus, "America's Invisible Inferno," *The New York Review of Books* (December 8, 2016).

23. Victoria Law, "We Are Not the Worst of the Worst," *Solitary Watch* (July 7, 2014), http://solitarywatch.com/2014/07/07/worst-worst-one-year-later-whats-changed-pelican-bays-hunger-strikers/.

24. See Incarcerated Workers Coalition, https://iwoc.noblogs.org/about/ (accessed January 17, 2017).

25. It seems to me that stressing these methods' nonviolence, as Keramet Reiter and Lisa Guenther do, hides from view their distinctive coerciveness, especially in the prison context (I further think that prisoners' hunger strikes and civilians' political fasts invite different normative analyses). See Keramet Reiter, "The Pelican Bay Hunger Strike: Resistance within the Structural Constraints of a US Supermax Prison," *The South Atlantic Quarterly* 113, 3 (2014): 579–611; Lisa Guenther, "Political Action at the End of the World: Hannah Arendt and the California Prison Hunger Strikes," *Canadian Journal of Human Rights* 4, 1 (2015): 33–56.

26. Padraig O'Malley, *Biting at the Grave: The Irish Hunger Strikes and the Politics of Despair* (Boston: Beacon, 1990).

27. Bernard Boxill, "Self-Respect and Protest," *Philosophy and Public Affairs* 6, 1 (1976): 58–69.

28. Ibid., 67.

29. Hay, *Kantian, Liberalism, and Feminism*, 141.

30. Letter to the members of the Women's Social and Political Union dated January 10, 1913. Available online at http://www.nationalarchives.gov.uk/documents/education/suffragettes.pdf.

31. Kendrick T. Brown and Joan M. Ostrove, "What Does It Mean to Be an Ally?: The Perception of Allies from the Perspective of People of Color," *Journal of Applied Social Psychology* 43 (2013): 2211–2222, esp. 2211.

32. Princess Harmony Rodriguez, "Caitlyn Jenner, Social Media and Violent 'Solidarity': Why Calling Out Abusive Material by Sharing It Is Harmful," *BDG* blog (June 8, 2015), http://www.Blackgirldangerous.org/2015/06/caitlyn-jenner-social-media-and-violent-solidarity-calling-out-abusive-material-sharing-it/ (accessed February 1, 2017).

33. Rachel McKinnon, "Allies Behaving Badly: Gaslighting as Epistemic Injustice," in *Routledge Handbook to Epistemic Injustice*, ed. Gaile PolhausJr., Ian James Kidd, and José Medina (New York: Routledge, 2017), 167–174.

34. Ibid., 172.

35. Nicolas Bommarito, "Private Solidarity," *Ethical Theory and Moral Practice* 19, 2 (2016): 445–455.

36. Daniel Silvermint, "Resistance and Well-Being," *Journal of Political Philosophy* 21 (2013): 405–425.

37. Marilyn Frye, "History and Responsibility," *Hypatia* 8, 3 (1985): 215–217.

38. W. E. B. Du Bois, *Darkwater: Voices from within the Veil* (Mineola, NY: Dover, 1999), chap. 6.
39. Stokely Carmichael, *The Basis of Black Power* (USA History Archive: marxists. org, 2001).
40. Ibid.

Chapter 7

1. Haslanger, *Resisting Reality*, 312–317.
2. Robert Gellately, "Denunciations in Twentieth-Century Germany: Aspects of Self-Policing in the Third Reich and the German Democratic Republic," in *Accusatory Practices: Denunciation in Modern European History, 1789–1989,* eds. Sheila Fitzpatrick and Robert Gellately (Chicago: University of Chicago Press, 1997), 185–221; Robert Gellately, *Backing Hitler. Consent and Coercion in Nazi Germany* (Oxford: Oxford University Press, 2001).
3. See Angelina Grimké, *Walking by Faith: The Diary of Angelina Grimké 1828–1835,* ed. Charles Wilbanks (Columbia: University of South Carolina, 2003).
4. Stanley Cohen, *States of Denial: Knowing about Atrocities and Suffering* (Cambridge, MA: Polity, 2001), 82.
5. This follows Cohen, *States of Denial*, 7–9.
6. Gitta Sereny, *Albert Speer: His Battle with Truth* (London: Picador, 1996), 200.
7. Bob Dylan, "Blowin' in the Wind" (1963).
8. *Shoah*, directed by Claude Lanzmann (BBC, 1985).
9. Alison Bailey, "Privilege: Expanding on Marilyn Frye's Oppression," *Journal of Social Philosophy* 29, 3 (1998): 104–119, 110. Bailey's definition is stipulative, distinct from the legal concept of privilege as "legal benefit that is not a right." The advantages she is interested in are the flipside of the harms of structural injustice (which are also systemic and unjustified). I use the term "privilege" in Bailey's sense.
10. Bailey, "Privilege," 112.
11. Ibid.
12. See Alexander, *The New Jim Crow*.
13. Tommie Shelby, "Ideology, Racism, and Critical Social Theory," *The Philosophical Forum* 34, 2 (2003): 153–188, 170. Shelby notes that both true and false beliefs can be held with a false consciousness, so that detecting false consciousness is not sufficient for rejecting a form of social consciousness, but further requires showing the illusory content of that form of consciousness.
14. Ibid., 171.
15. Hay, *Kantianism, Liberalism, and Feminism*, chap. 2.
16. Brownlee, *Conscience and Conviction*, 66–70.
17. Mark Twain, *The Adventures of Huckleberry Finn* (New York: Bantam Classic, 2003 [1884]).

18. Douglass, *Frederick Douglass: Selected Speeches and Writings*, 188–206.

19. Kwame Anthony Appiah, *The Honor Code: How Moral Revolutions Happen* (New York: W. W. Norton, 2010).

20. Ibid., 161.

21. Irish Murdoch, *The Sovereignty of the Good* (London: Routledge and Kegan Paul, 1985), 91.

22. Daniel Kahneman and Amos Tversky, "Judgment under Uncertainty: Heuristics and Biases," *Science* (September 1974): 1124–1131, explores three heuristics and biases. More recently, Daniel Kahneman, *Thinking Fast and Slow* (New York: Farrar, Strauss and Giroux, 2011) analyzes dozens of these. Wikipedia lists and illustrates over a hundred cognitive biases. See https://en.wikipedia.org/wiki/List_of_cognitive_biases (accessed December 20, 2016).

23. For a review of the research conducted by psychologists and cognitive scientists, see Cheryl Staats, Kelly Capatosto, Robin A. Wright, and Danya Contractor, *State of the Science: Implicit Bias Review 2015*, Kirwan Institute for the Study of Race and Science, available at http://kirwaninstitute.osu.edu/wp-content/uploads/2015/05/2015-kirwan-implicit-bias.pdf. For philosophical work on implicit bias, see *Implicit Bias and Philosophy, Volume 2: Moral Responsibility, Structural Injustice, and Ethics*, eds. Michael Brownstein and Jennifer Saul (Oxford: Oxford University Press, 2016).

24. Jean-Jacques Rousseau, *The Social Contract* in *The Social Contract and Other Later Political Writings*, ed. Victor Gourevitch (Cambridge: Cambridge University Press, 1997), 41.

25. Rush Limbaugh, *The Rush Limbaugh Show*, September 12, 2008. Transcript available at http://www.rushlimbaugh.com/daily/2008/09/12/media_and_democrats_will_try_everything_to_destroy_sarah_palin (accessed December 21, 2016).

26. See *Rachel Maddow Show* (December 13, 2016), http://www.msnbc.com/rachel-maddow/watch/attorney-general-lynch-calls-for-vigilance-on-abuse-of-power-832507459842 (accessed December 21, 2016).

27. *Last Week Tonight with John Oliver* (November 13, 2016), http://www.hbo.com/last-week-tonight-with-john-oliver (accessed December 16, 2016).

28. Julie L. Rose defends citizens' entitlement to free time on the basis of widely held liberal egalitarian principles in Julie L. Rose, *Free Time* (Princeton, NJ: Princeton University Press, 2017).

29. Melissa Schwartzberg, *Counting the Many: The Origins and Limits of Supermajority Rule* (Cambridge: Cambridge University Press, 2013).

30. I thank Amélie Rorty for alerting me to civic virtues' complex make-up and paired contraries.

31. Elizabeth Spelman, *Inessential Woman: Problems of Exclusion in Feminist Thought* (Boston: Beacon, 1988), 179.

32. See Carol Gilligan, *In a Different Voice: Psychological Theory and Women's Development* (Cambridge, MA: Harvard University Press, 1982). In psychology and neuroscience, see also Jean Decety and William Ickes, eds., *The Social Neuroscience of Empathy* (Cambridge, MA: MIT Press, 2009); David Howe, *Empathy: What It Is and Why It Matters* (New York: Palgrave Macmillan, 2012). In feminist philosophy, see, e.g., Jean Harvey, *Civilized Oppression* (Lanham, MD: Rowman and Littlefield, 1999); Michael Slote, *The Ethics of Care and Empathy* (New York: Routledge, 2007).

33. Laurence Thomas, "Moral Deference," in *Theorizing Multiculturalism: A Guide to the Current Debate*, ed. Cynthia Willet (Oxford: Blackwell Publishers, 1998), 359–381.

34. See, e.g., The National SEED Project on Inclusive Curriculum[SM], http://www.nationalseedproject.org/about-us. SEED (Seeking Educational Equity & Diversity) aims to create "gender fair, multiculturally equitable, socioeconomically aware, and globally informed education" by engaging educators, parents, and community leaders. It is the nation's largest peer-led leadership development project.

35. See Cass Sunstein, *Why Societies Need Dissent* (Cambridge, MA: Harvard University Press, 2003).

36. For a review of this literature and philosophical analysis of integration, see Anderson, *The Imperative of Integration*.

37. Amélie Oksenberg Rorty, "The Ethics of Collaborative Ambivalence," *Journal of Ethics* 18, 4 (2014): 391–403, 394.

38. Ibid.

39. Ibid.

40. Ibid., 395.

41. Ibid., 396–397.

42. Ibid., 399.

43. Ibid., 392.

44. Ibid.

45. Arendt, "Reflections on Civil Disobedience," 104.

46. Walzer, *Obligations*, 22.

47. *Snowden*, directed by Oliver Stone (Wild Bunch, 2016); *Serpico*, directed by Sidney Lumet (Artists Entertainment Complex, 1973).

48. Emanuela Ceva, "Political Justification through Democratic Participation: The Case for Conscientious Objection," *Social Theory and Practice* 41, 1 (2015): 26–50.

49. David Kaye, "Anticipating Trump: Should Government Lawyers Stay or Go?," *JustSecurity.org*, https://www.justsecurity.org/34373/anticipating-trump-government-lawyers-stay-go/ (accessed November 20, 2016).

50. The Polish legislature is currently considering curriculum changes that would add hours of patriotic history lessons. See Anthony Faiola, "In Poland, a

Window on What Happens When Populists Take Over," *Washington Post* (December 18, 2016). For philosophical defenses of patriotism, see Alasdair MacIntyre, "Is Patriotism a Virtue?," E. H. Lindley Lecture (University of Kansas, 1984), reprinted in *Patriotism*, ed. Igor Primoratz (Amherst, NY: Humanity Books, 2002), 43–58; Andrew Oldenquist, "Loyalties," *Journal of Philosophy* 79, 4 (1982): 173–193.

51. Abby Phillip, "Trump Names His Inauguration Day a 'National Day of Patriotic Devotion,'" *Washington Post* (January 23, 2017).

52. Simon Keller, "Patriotism as Bad Faith," *Ethics* 115, 3 (2005): 563–592.

53. Simon Keller, "Worldly Citizens: Civic Virtue without Patriotism," in *Cosmopolitanism versus Non-Cosmopolitanism: Critiques, Defenses, Reconceptualizations*, ed. Gillian Brock (Oxford: Oxford University Press, 2013).

54. Ta-Nehisi Coates, *We Were Eight Years in Power: An American Tragedy* (New York: One World, Random House, 2017), 200.

55. William A. Edmundson, "The Virtue of Law-Abidance," *Philosophers' Imprint* 6, 4 (2006): 1–21.

Conclusion

1. Arendt, "Reflections on Civil Disobedience."

2. See George Kateb, "Political Action," in *The Cambridge Companion to Hannah Arendt*, ed. D. Villa (Cambridge: Cambridge University Press, 2000), 130–148.

Postscript

1. Michael Grynbaum and Jim Rutenberg, "Trump, Asked about Accusations against Bill O'Reilly, Calls Him a 'Good Person,'" *New York Times* (April 5, 2017), https://www.nytimes.com/2017/04/05/business/media/trump-oreilly-fox-murdochs.html. Fox News ousted O'Reilly shortly after the sexual harassment claims became public in April 2017.

2. "Remarks by President Trump in African American History Month Listening Session" (February 1, 2017), https://www.whitehouse.gov/the-press-office/2017/02/01/remarks-president-trump-african-american-history-month-listening-session.

3. Chimamanda Ngozi Adichie, "Now *Is* the Time to Talk about What We Are Actually Talking about," *New Yorker* (December 2, 2016), http://www.newyorker.com/culture/cultural-comment/now-is-the-time-to-talk-about-what-we-are-actually-talking-about.

4. Center for Constitutional Rights, "Resistance Is Our Civic Duty," https://ccrjustice.org/home/press-center/press-releases/resistance-our-civic-duty-ccr-responds-trump-election (last accessed September 22, 2017).

5. Robert Reich, "Twelve Ways to Resist the Trump Presidency," *Newsweek* (January 6, 2017), http://www.newsweek.com/robert-reich-twelve-ways-resist-trump-presidency-539411; Bill Scher, "6 Ways Not to Resist Donald Trump," *Politico Magazine* (January 25, 2017), http://www.politico.com/magazine/story/2017/01/6-ways-not-to-resist-donald-trump-214689.

6. *Indivisible: A Practical Guide for Resisting the Trump Agenda* is licensed under the Creative Commons Attribution-NonCommercial- ShareAlike 4.0 International License. Available at https://www.indivisibleguide.com/guide/.

7. Meagan Flynn, "Oakland mayor who tipped off immigrants to ICE raid draws Justice Department scrutiny," *Washington Post* (March 2, 2018), https://www.washingtonpost.com/news/morning-mix/wp/2018/03/02/justice-department-reviewing-actions-of-oakland-mayor-who-tipped-off-immigrants-of-ice-raid-white-house-says/?utm_term=.36f57c49ff76.

8. Jeremy Waldron, "Special Ties and Natural Duties," *Philosophy and Public Affairs* 22 (1993): 3–30.

9. See Juliet Stumpf, "The Crimmigration Crisis: Immigrants, Crime, and Sovereign Power," *American University Law Review* 56, 2 (2006): 367–419; César Cuauhtémoc García Hernández, *Crimmigration Law* (Chicago, Illinois: American Bar Association, 2017).

10. Cristina Beltrán, "'Undocumented, Unafraid and Unapologetic': DREAM Activists, Immigrant Politics, and the Queering of Democracy," in *From Voice to Influence: Understanding Citizenship in a Digital Age*, eds. Danielle Allen and Jennifer S. Light (Chicago: University of Chicago Press, 2015), 80–104.

11. Southern Poverty Law Center, "Hate Groups Increase for Second Consecutive Year as Trump Electrifies Radical Right" (February 15, 2017), https://www.splcenter.org/news/2017/02/15/hate-groups-increase-second-consecutive-year-trump-electrifies-radical-right.

12. SPLC Hate Watch, https://www.splcenter.org/hatewatch/2016/12/16/update-1094-bias-related-incidents-month-following-election, last update December 16, 2016. In my view, hate crimes, like hate speech, stem from prejudice without necessarily being motivated by emotions, feelings, or attitudes of hatred per se. See Alexander Brown, "What Is Hate Speech? Part 1: The Myth of Hate," *Law and Philosophy* 36, 4 (2017): 419–468.

13. Anna North, "After Kansas Shooting, a Community in Fear," New York Times (March 3, 2017), https://www.nytimes.com/2017/03/03/opinion/after-kansas-shooting-a-community-in-fear.html.

14. SPLC, "Ten Ways to Fight Hate: A Community Response Guide" (August 14, 2017), https://www.splcenter.org/20170814/ten-ways-fight-hate-community-response-guide.

15. César Cuauhtémoc García Hernández, "ICE's Courthouse Arrests Undercut Democracy," *New York Times* (November 26, 2017).

16. For instance, Donald Trump, Jr., alleged that terrorists effectively poisoned the crop of refugees and that failing to recognize this constituted a "politically

correct agenda." See Leo Kelion, "Trump Jr's Skittles Graphic Deleted From Twitter," *BBC* (September 28, 2016), http://www.bbc.com/news/technology-37495094.

17. Bryan Armen Graham, "Donald Trump blasts NFL anthem protesters: 'Get that son of a bitch off the field'," *The Guardian* (September 23, 2017), https://www.theguardian.com/sport/2017/sep/22/donald-trump-nfl-national-anthem-protests.

18. Dave Zirin, "The Houston Texans Showed the Power and Dignity of Black Labor," *The Nation* (October 30, 2017), https://www.thenation.com/article/the-houston-texans-showed-the-power-and-dignity-of-black-labor/.

19. Seattle Seahawks (@seahawksPR), (September 24, 2017 at 2:39 p.m.).

20. Cornel West, interviewed on *Democracy Now!* (August 14, 2017).

21. Amitai Etzioni recently defended a thoughtful version of this argument in "Notes for Antifa from a Former 'Terrorist,'" *Boston Review* (November 29, 2017), http://bostonreview.net/forum/etzioni-notes-antifa-former-terrorist (accessed December 13, 2017).

22. Transcript of Trump's August 15, 2017 press conference available at https://www.cnbc.com/2017/08/15/read-the-transcript-of-donald-trumps-jaw-dropping-press-conference.html (accessed December 13, 2017).

23. My articulation of their argument is based on Mark Bray, *Antifa: The Anti-Fascist Handbook* (New York: Melville Books, 2017).

24. Maria Stephan, "Staying True to Yourself in the Age of Trump: A How-To Guide for Federal Employees," *Washington Post* (February 10, 2017), https://www.washingtonpost.com/news/democracy-post/wp/2017/02/10/staying-true-to-yourself-in-the-age-of-trump-a-how-to-guide-for-federal-employees/.

25. Laura Rosenberg, "Career Officials: You Are the Last Line of Defense against Trump," *Foreign Policy* (January 30, 2017), http://foreignpolicy.com/2017/01/30/career-officials-you-are-the-last-line-of-defense-against-trump/.

26. David Luban, "The Case against Serving," *Just Security* (November 14, 2016), https://www.justsecurity.org/34404/case-serving-trump/.

27. Arendt, *Responsibility and Judgment* (New York: Schocken Books 2003), 17–48.

28. Masha Gessen, "Autocracy: Rules for Survival," *The New York Review of Books* (November 10, 2016).

29. New York Times senior editor Carolyn Ryan interview: "The Leakiest White House in Decades," *CNN* (February 5, 2017), http://www.cnn.com/videos/tv/2017/02/05/leaks-already-plaguing-trump-administration.cnn.

30. Kaye, "Anticipating Trump."

31. See "Trump Campaign Had at Least 18 Undisclosed Contacts with Russians," *Reuters* (May 18, 2017), https://www.reuters.com/article/us-usa-trump-russia-contacts/exclusive-trump-campaign-had-at-least-18-undisclosed-contacts-with-russians-sources-idUSKCN18E106 (accessed December 15, 2017).

INDEX

INDEX